Democratic Delusions

For Isaac and Jude – for the hope they bring

Democratic Delusions

How the Media Hollows Out Democracy and What We Can Do About It

Natalie Fenton

polity

Copyright © Natalie Fenton 2025

The right of Natalie Fenton to be identified as Author of this Work has been asserted in accordance with the UK Copyright, Designs and Patents Act 1988.

First published in 2025 by Polity Press

Polity Press
65 Bridge Street
Cambridge CB2 1UR, UK

Polity Press
111 River Street
Hoboken, NJ 07030, USA

All rights reserved. Except for the quotation of short passages for the purpose of criticism and review, no part of this publication may be reproduced, stored in a retrieval system or transmitted, in any form or by any means, electronic, mechanical, photocopying, recording or otherwise, without the prior permission of the publisher.

ISBN-13: 978-1-5095-4847-7
ISBN-13: 978-1-5095-4848-4 (pb)

A catalogue record for this book is available from the British Library.

Library of Congress Control Number: 2024935489

Typeset in 10.5 on 12pt Sabon
by Fakenham Prepress Solutions, Fakenham, Norfolk NR21 8NL
Printed and bound in Great Britain by CPI Group (UK) Ltd, Croydon

The publisher has used its best endeavours to ensure that the URLs for external websites referred to in this book are correct and active at the time of going to press. However, the publisher has no responsibility for the websites and can make no guarantee that a site will remain live or that the content is or will remain appropriate.

Every effort has been made to trace all copyright holders, but if any have been overlooked the publisher will be pleased to include any necessary credits in any subsequent reprint or edition.

For further information on Polity, visit our website:
politybooks.com

CONTENTS

	Acknowledgements	vi
1	Democratic Delusions and the Media	1
2	Power and Powerlessness	21
3	Political Participation and Political Exclusions	45
4	Freedom and Repression	72
5	Equality and Injustice	100
6	Public Good and Private Interest	131
7	Trust and Distrust	162
8	Hope and Hopelessness: Democracy and the Media Reconfigured	190
	Notes	213
	References	216
	Index	245

ACKNOWLEDGEMENTS

This book was written through difficult times and carries the marks of that journey. From the Covid-19 pandemic, to wars and conflict, to political disarray, environmental catastrophe, and institutional breakdown – my writing backdrop has been complex and conflictual. Frankly, it's a small miracle that this book got written at all. The only reason it did is because of the incredible support, intellectual friendship and political solidarity of so many people that deserve far more recognition than I can do justice to here.

Huge thanks go to the entire community of staff in the Department of Media, Communications and Cultural Studies at Goldsmiths, University of London, for the astonishing and enduring collegiality amidst the chaos from a pandemic, two brutal university restructures and a sector-wide crisis resulting in perpetual industrial action as a consequence of poor pay, conditions and contracts that remain unsustainable. Your refusal to be beaten, your determination to see justice done and resolve to stick together has been a constant source of inspiration for the book and sustenance for the soul.

To all my doctoral students and those on the MA Political Communications who unwittingly provided much of the impetus for writing this book – thank you for helping me understand the multiple crises we find ourselves in and bringing fresh perspectives from around the world.

To everyone at the Annenberg School of Communication, University of Pennsylvania for their kind hospitality and intellectual generosity during my semester as a visiting scholar – thank you for giving me space to air the ideas and refine the arguments. Special thanks to Sarah Banet-Weiser for making it all possible and Aswin Punathambekar for giving me a cubicle to work in amidst a

ACKNOWLEDGEMENTS

brilliant and intellectually nourishing group of doctoral students and postdocs. Huge thanks to Alison Hearn, my fellow visiting scholar, for the many 'cubicle conversations' challenging ourselves to think through and beyond capitalism and for the friendship and solidarity of thinking together and sharing ideas.

To the incredible group of friends who gave their precious time to give me critical feedback on drafts, who sat discussing politics with me until the early hours or helped me forget it all in cafés and bars, on the dance floor, on the picket-line, on walks and in water: Veronica Barassi, Lisa Blackman, Clea Bourne, Jack Bratich, Benedetta Brevini, Bart Cammaerts, Kirsten Campbell, Paula Chakravartty, James Curran, Lina Dencik, Omega Douglas, Lee Edwards, Becky Gardiner, Myria Georgiou, Ros Gill, Julian Henriques, Dave Hesmondhalgh, Feyzi Ismail, Sarah Jackson, Helen Kennedy, Tassia Kobylinska, Ben Levitas, Jo Littler, Richard MacDonald, Mirca Madianou, Angela McRobbie, Liz Moor, Rachel Moore, Mariam Motamedi-Fraser, Jacob Mukherjee, Kate Nash, Kaarina Nikunen, Victor Pickard, Liz Poole, Catherine Rottenberg, Todd Wolfson and Barbie Zelizer.

To the fellow activists of the broader Media Reform Coalition network in the UK who share a passion for transforming our media and tech worlds and have been crucial in helping me think through how it might be possible; especially: Sara Badawi, Hani Barghouthi, Thomas Barlow, Steve Barnett, Brian Cathcart, Tom Chivers, Deborah Grayson, Rizwana Hamid, Evan Harris, Jonathan Heawood, Lexie Kirkconnell-Kawana, Shirish Kulkarni, James Lock, Riaz Meer, Tom Mills, Joe Mitchell, Eliz Mizon, Sameer Padania, Julian Petley, Justin Schlosberg, Nathan Sparks, Damian Tambini and Hugh Tomlinson.

Endless gratitude goes to those soulmates who have played a key part in all of the above, who have shared my joy and despair, fed me, swam with me, made me laugh and occasionally cry – thank you Des Freedman, Gholam Khiabany and Milly Williamson for the enduring solidarity and friendship during good and bad times.

And of course, a lifetime of thanks to Justin, Isaac and Jude – who endure my rants and ramblings and make it all count.

1

DEMOCRATIC DELUSIONS AND THE MEDIA

'To be truly radical is to make hope possible rather than despair convincing.'
Raymond Williams, *Resources of Hope*

This book argues that our major media outlets and digital intermediaries are captured by global capitalism to the detriment of democracy. It then poses the crucial question of what we can do about it. What are the actual and potential responses of society when the ability to speak truth to power has been restricted by corporate media and big tech logics? How do we react when the possibility of an independent check on the activities of political and media/tech elites has been limited by their entanglement? What happens when terms like 'freedom' and 'pluralism' are used to undermine those very ideas? How can we reclaim concepts that have traditionally served dissident struggles as part of radical democratic agendas but are now corrupted and used to prop up capital? How can we respond to an abuse of media/tech power that isn't based on breaking the law but on the application of the law itself? How do we tackle a deep-rooted market logic that shifts the contours of public debate towards the normalization of illiberalism and authoritarianism and marginalizes progressive perspectives? How do you build a media and a movement that recognizes social injustices and seeks to repair and redress the damages they have inflicted, a media and a movement based on a wholly different, more democratic and transformational approach to communication?

Our systems of media and communications have long been heralded as vital to this thing called democracy. In particular, a free media is inextricably linked to a healthy democracy, or so we are told. The relationship between the two is repeatedly asserted but rarely interrogated in full. And too often the very concept of democracy falls back on liberal representative framings, freezing the debate in ways that insist on the primacy of Western nations' version of democratic superiority, which has largely failed to deliver what this notion of liberal democracy claims to entail. Where forms of liberal democracy have existed, they are now deemed to be dying (Levitsky and Ziblatt, 2018) or at least to be on the doomed path of a drawn-out demise (Runciman, 2018), a demise that many forms of media have enabled while heralding themselves as democracy's saviour. So as Crouch (2004) decries a condition of post-democracy where politics has morphed into spectacle and decisions are made elsewhere, so our media thrives on sensationalism and feeds off clickbait, channelling our attention to celebrity politicians and affirming sound bite culture. As authoritarian forms of government emerge and hold on to power and far-right parties gain in popularity in many places around the world, so digital media fragment debate, foster extremism and contribute to the catastrophic loss of accountable knowledge. As burgeoning levels of inequality within and between nations distance ever greater numbers of people from the political systems that have overseen their immiseration, so mainstream media narratives extol the unworthiness of the poor and impoverished. As political responses to climate catastrophe fail dismally in their reach and ambition, so our media focus on 'natural' disasters that shock but rarely explain the complexities of Western imperialism, the enduring power of the fossil fuel industry and its command over governmental politics around the world, while techno-solutionism becomes the norm (captured by the very forces of capital accumulation that have caused the problems in the first place).

This book charts many of these debates but it does not claim that it is the media and tech giants alone that have sounded the death knell of democracy. That would be far too easy. Not least because it would suggest that simply changing our media and tech systems would rescue democracy from its free-fall into irrelevance. Unsurprisingly, the story is far more complex and requires a critical evaluation of what this thing called democracy means and what it could become before we can begin to determine how we might get there. It also requires a reimagining of what our media and tech systems could be if they were to become *democratic media*. We cannot do either without situating our political systems and mediated worlds within global capitalism.

The power of governments to enact manifesto pledges endorsed by electorates is subjected to a greater power and domination of global financialized capitalism and unfettered capital accumulation. Since the World Bank's conversion to strict neoliberalism in the 1980s nation states have lost much of their ability to bind economic power into a democratic structure of justification and regulate it because they lack political structures capable of controlling and curbing the global economy. Indeed, Streeck (2014; Schäfer and Streeck, 2015) argues that in Europe the transition from consolidated states to states based on public and private debt (dependent on borrowing from financial markets) represents the victory of capitalism over democracy. Streeck theorizes the financial crisis as a product of the fundamental contradictions of 'post-war democratic capitalism', whereby states have been structurally required to balance the needs of two sovereigns: their people below, and the international markets above. He argues that ever since the financial crash of 2007/8, 'the dialectic of democracy and capitalism has been unfolding at breathtaking speed' (2011, p. 29) with the International Monetary Fund and European Bank insisting on specific state responses and conditions to bailouts in order to restore investor confidence through an extended project of state retraction known as 'austerity', which in turn has generated huge social problems that nation states have no resources left to deal with. Streeck argues that:

> more than ever, economic power seems today to have become political power, while citizens appear to be almost entirely stripped of their democratic defences and their capacity to impress upon the political economy interests and demands that are incommensurable with those of capital owners. (2011, p. 29)

Moreover, Fraser (2022, p. 46) posits that as industry migrates and finance metastasizes, global financial institutions pressure states to collude with investors in the 'cannibalization of wealth from defenseless populations' leading postcolonial states to abandon 'developmentalism in favour of liberalizing policies which transfer wealth to corporate capital and global finance . . . condemning countless generations to expropriation'. And as wages fall and low-waged precarious labour replaces industrial unionized labour, workers are also expropriated. With wages declining, the tax revenues that used to go to the welfare state and public infrastructure are diverted to service debt and enable 'deficit reduction'. In a bid to appease the markets corporate taxes are cut, further depleting the public purse and justifying yet more 'austerity measures'.

We are still living with the consequences of the 2007/8 financial crisis, and austerity politics continues to reverberate through economic discourses and practices. But one major difference since 2008 has been the invasion of the tech giants into all aspects of our lives, leading some to claim that capitalism is over and we now have something far worse that dominates the global economy: technofeudalism (Varoufakis, 2023) – a totalizing power which controls how we shop, do business, listen to music, play games, read the news, access healthcare, are educated, meet people and fall in love. A privatized digital landscape in which gatekeepers don't reinvest profits to expand output or increase labour productivity but rather use sophisticated data extraction from all of our digital lives to extract value, increase shareholder dividends or buy back their own stock and secure their monopoly position. As Durand (2020) (cited in Morozov, 2022, p. 115) argues, '[t]he ascent of the digital feeds a giant economy of rent [because] the control of information and knowledge, that is intellectual monopolization, has become the most powerful means of capturing value.' Even as technofeudalist thinking resonates at one level, it is also true that capitalism is still alive and kicking. Cost-cutting continues to be the norm among tech giants, driving profits ever higher and wages ever lower. Tech companies continue to exploit their workers and also invest billions in research and development (Alphabet invested $27.5bn and Amazon $42.7bn in 2020) to accumulate ever more capital; the vast amounts of data they process requires the property ownership of huge data centres and extensive physical networks, underscoring that they are not only rentiers (Morozov, 2022). Meanwhile, capitalist media and tech industries determine who gains from their forms of production and who will be exploited, how we share information and communicate with each other for the purposes of profit via the datafication of everything, under the guise of enhancing democracy.

The chapters that follow critique how neoliberal democracy has been hegemonized in and through the mainstream media as content producers, power brokers and key players in the establishment of the social order of institutional capitalism. And how, in the process, mainstream media have legitimized anti-democratic responses and mutated political culture, political subjectivity and the law. This hollowing-out of democracy has left many people questioning the value of the (neo)liberal democratic societies they live in: if this is what you call democracy, do we want it? But allowing democracy to be ensnared by and reduced to its neoliberal interpretation brings many dangers. The demise of democratic values, such as power sharing and political equality, have energized anti-democratic political powers in neoliberalized orders. As neoliberal policy fixates on restricting and undoing regulation and redistribution, while extending market freedom and commercial ownership rights, so the concentration of media ownership increases and public service broadcasting weakens (see Chapter 6). So the book asks, when we consider our media and tech worlds and their relationship to capitalism, what happens to democracy both in its existing form and in relation to how it could be otherwise? This entails critically deconstructing democracy rather than defending its current reality, while at the same time, working through the idea of democracy as an unfulfilled promise.

What does it mean to have democratic delusions? Delusions are false and irrational beliefs that are held on to, even when there is evidence that they are not real. Democratic delusions are manifold, but two grandiose delusions are threaded throughout this book. The first one is the belief that media are (in their current forms) one of democracy's vital organs and, without them, democracies (in their current form) will cease to function. This democratic delusion is peddled by the vast majority of media across the world. Yet this book argues that while it is certainly the case that our media systems often support these *neoliberal* democracies, they do not fare so well when we consider the core constituent elements required for a different type of democracy to emerge, one that adheres to the norms and principles of democracy as rule by the people of the people. Rather, seen through this lens, evidence points to chronic organ failure and the desperate need for an organ transplant if anything approximating a democratic polity is to prevail.

Second, and related, is the delusion that the version of (neo)liberal democracy that is clung to has any remnant of democratic character left. Rather, I argue that (neo)liberal democracy has evacuated all meanings of the common good associated with democratic intent to become no more than a racket for the powerful that far too often provides cover for global capitalism's exploitative and expropriating ways. And that even as (neo)liberal democracy portrays the symptoms of chronic disease from the spread of political corruption and parasitic infestation of unelected power mongers in the form of PR gurus and corporate lobbyists, to the festering wounds of massive and increasing inequalities embedded in legal and bureaucratic mechanisms that silence and exclude voices through forms of expulsion and punishment, it is still to liberal democratic norms that many return as their ultimate social and political landing place.

Delusions can, of course, also be paranoid and expressive of profound fear and anxiety along with the loss of the ability to tell what is real from what is not. Sedgwick (2003, p. 131) notes that paranoia is anticipatory, namely: 'no loss is too far in the future to be pre-emptively discounted'. So as critical theorists we can become caught in the paranoia of despair, incapable of realizing a future that may be different from the present. She also points out that paranoia is reflexive and mimetic – a spiralling architecture of escapes and recaptures – where one door opens, another leads us back to where we came from. Undoubtedly, we need critical theoretical enquiry, but we also need to go beyond a reliance on the efficacy of knowledge as being enough to address the issues revealed. This book is an attempt to avoid the paranoia of delusion. It is not only an attempt to rethink how we conceive of media and communications in relation to this thing called democracy and some of its defining characteristics, but it is also an attempt to future think what democracy might or could be in a mediated world to come. One where current structures of dominance and oppression are likely to pertain unless there is a break with the forces that make them what they are. That break cannot be an intermediary pause. Rather, it must be a transformational shift in the way that the world is calibrated. Because it cannot continue its current trajectory without planetary disaster.

This thing called democracy

What is this thing called democracy? The term is often used flippantly with little regard or thought concerning its deeper meaning. On the surface, the meaning of democracy seems simple: rule by the people of the people is wholly different to rule by monarchy, namely by a single person, or aristocracy, rule by the elite, or anarchy: rule by no one (Barnett, 2017). However, rule by the people is very far from a simple affair. The notion that everyone has an equal say; that each person can participate in society and forms of governance freely; that one person has another's interests in mind and that all will be willing to act collectively for the common good is not a straightforward endeavour. But, as Barnett (2017) argues, at the heart of the notion of democracy is an egalitarian imagination that shuns domination and the notion of superiority and seeks justice. Even as this may be true, as Shivji (2020) notes, Western nations have been all too eager to claim democratic superiority over the rest of the world while disregarding their own colonial histories that have, among other violence and destruction, actively destroyed (and continue to destroy) indigenous peoples' rights to have control over their own lives. Indeed, Forst (2019b) refers to the dialectic of democracy that begins with the ideal of the practice of equals but that has been morphed into a majoritarian instrument of oppression and exclusion that has enacted gross injustices and led to all of us losing a grip on the concept of democracy itself.

In a similar vein, Santos and Mendes (2020) argue that those countries who now claim to be democracies are at best low-intensity democracies in societies that are both politically democratic and socially fascistic; all the while these countries cling to some notion of a liberal democratic horizon that has a far from liberal or democratic history. Rather, forms of liberal democracy in imperialist-capitalist countries have been a means of justifying, defending and protecting private property, which has always operated to the detriment of indigenous peoples. As Shivji (2020, p. 68) notes, the 1948 Universal Declaration of Human Rights excluded Africans because they were considered 'natives' not human beings: 'Colonialism was anything but democratic. It was a despotic state meant to control, subjugate and dehumanize the colonized so as to facilitate the exploitation of the natural and human resources of the colonies.'

Thus, the construct of the nation state, so central to ideas of democracy, has itself been built on the dispossession of land and genocide of indigenous peoples. Nowhere is this more prevalent than in the United States and Canada, where dreams of the promised land of democracy are indelibly tied to settler-colonial mythology – which as TallBear (2019) states, are in reality premised on hierarchical violence that refuses indigenous peoples' own will to self-determination. Lipsitz (2019, p. 46) argues that inside this version of liberal democracy: '[a]ggrieved groups are encouraged to seek inclusion and equality rather than justice. Desires for self-determination and dignity become channelled by the power structure into demands for roles inside oppressive systems rather than for changing those systems.' The advancement of these sorts of logics are in the words of Santos and Mendes (2020, p. 2) 'tied to Northern epistemologies in the reproduction of capitalism, colonialism and patriarchy'.

But with the advancement of neoliberal capitalism and the increasing separation of the economy from politics (in the form of governance by nation states), so these logics have also failed to deliver the redistributive promises to those inside liberal democratic states. As Rancière (2007) notes, with the collapse of the Soviet system after the fall of the Berlin Wall in 1989, the values of democratic debate were increasingly aligned with those of the liberal economy, as people were seen to be literally breaking apart the bricks and mortar of a socialist economy and clambering to reach the promised economic freedoms liberalism claimed to offer. The reality, of course, has been rather different, with massive and increasing inequalities between the Global North and the Global South and within nation states themselves (see Chapter 5). So-called consensual democratic states across the Western world are seeing the violent re-establishment of racist, xenophobic and misogynistic movements. Far from being the ability of all to have a say in the decisions that affect their lives, political democracy in its (neo)liberal form has been reduced to the simple power of wealth.

If, as Mentan (2010, p. 271) asks, the idea of democracy, as with the previous ideas of development and Western civilization, is nothing more than a banner for continued recolonization, exploitation and oppression by the West, is there any point in clinging to it as a term? Certainly not if liberal democracy is taken as the be all and end all of democracy. But liberal democracy has become the dominant model of democracy precisely because it has proven to be so compatible with capitalism and poses little threat to coloniality. If we disentangle ourselves from the drift nets of liberal democracy as practice and concept then we can point to emergent forms of democracy across the world that seek to break with capitalism, to decolonize practices and to establish economies of solidarity and care that eschew exploitation and expropriation, thus enabling different understandings of democracy to breathe and surface. Part of the point of this book is to make visible some of these practices through mediated forms that have long been devalued; to foreground the resistance of groups against the capitalist logics of expropriation of land and nature and the exploitation of peoples (most of which align with racial oppression) and to point to practices of governance that can reveal democratic forms aligned with social, political and economic justice.

Towards these ends the book takes seven key concepts associated with democracy and shows how they have been appropriated by capitalism and hollowed out of meaning as well as documenting the role of the media, in all its forms, in these complex and multiple processes. Various conceptual vocabularies are used to develop arguments relating to the term 'democracy'. I have chosen to focus on those most often aligned with debates on our mediated worlds. In doing so, I have left out many others. Each chapter has three main sections: the first section addresses a foundational concept relating to the meta concept of democracy: power (Chapter 2), participation (Chapter 3), freedom (Chapter 4), equality (Chapter 5), public good (Chapter 6), trust (Chapter 7) and hope (Chapter

8), describing and explaining the main contours of each. The second section offers a normative critique of the contemporary manifestation of each concept and the role the media/big tech have played in establishing and sustaining a particular hegemony that runs counter to the conceptual account outlined in the first section, often leading to powerlessness (Chapter 2), exclusions (Chapter 3), repression (Chapter 4), injustices (Chapter 5), private gain (Chapter 6), distrust (Chapter 7) and hopelessness (Chapter 8). While cursing the darkness can be therapeutic, the third section of each chapter seeks to go beyond this to shed light on the hopeful by offering suggestions as to how these practices could be otherwise and what it would take for the conceptual premise associated with democracy in these seven foundational themes to be realized in and through our mediated landscapes. What more power in the hands of more people could be? What freedom could look like? What equality would enable? And the relationship of the media in all of its forms to each of these concepts.

I am therefore approaching democracy as a creed defined by constant struggle and as a permanent construction site. Like influential scholars such as Rosanvallon (2008), I see democracy as an emergent practice whose meaning is not just essentially contested in daily forms of struggle but whose very meaning and value lie in its essential contestability. Unlike Rosanvallon, however, I do not see such struggles as indicative of democracy in action – a marker of misfunctioning democratic regimes in need of repair whose citizens will find ways of ensuring that elected officials stick to their promises through mechanisms of 'counter-democracy'. Such mechanisms ultimately do little more than return to the dominance of electoral democracy and compensate for the worst consequences of global financial capitalism. Rather, I foreground struggles and practices that seek to transform economic power structures and address this thing called democracy by way of the social and political practices of justice – a call to combat oppression, exploitation and injustice such that those who are subjected to systems of domination are able to participate as equals in codetermining the institutionalized social order to which they belong – arguing, along with Forst, that '[t]he demand for democracy is a demand for justice' (Forst, 2019b, p. 380). In this manner I hope the book adds to a critical theory of democracy as the deepening and extension of the egalitarian imagination.

Hence, while the book interrogates the failures of (neo)liberal democracy in relation to the mainstream media and tech giants alongside those theoretical approaches that align with this version of democracy and thus reproduce its systems and values, it also aims to offer alternatives to how democracy could be done differently and, crucially, how systems of media and communications could be part of progressive transformative political visions. So in addition to tracing the many ways in which media and mediated discourses have appropriated democratic concepts, each chapter explores how different relationships of mutuality and forms of doing democracy are emerging in different contexts: cooperative forms of ownership, collaborative partnerships and alliances of workers and communities seeking to meet social need, and create new more democratic forms of existing: from media cooperatives around the world to forms of solidarity journalism; from the rise of organized labour in industries either situated in or reliant on digital media to solidarity economy initiatives and alternative currency networks around the globe. This book, in other words, ventures beyond contemporary democratic delusions in order to consider what a politics of hope might look like and what a democratic media for democracy could be in the twenty-first century.

Democracy is permanently undone – that is its fate and its fortune. And we must recognize this if we are to find the political imagination to make a *transformational democracy* possible.

This thing called the media

When I talk about 'the media' in general I am referring to mediated forms of communication: from television and radio to social media platforms, technology companies and everything in between. In recognition of the confluence of media, entertainment, business and politics I am not constrained by issues relating to news and current affairs within these mediated forms (although these are key to my argument) that too often are (wrongly) seen as the sole domain of the public sphere and democratic concerns. The various chapters draw on all of these to critique the relationship between our mediated worlds, democracy and capitalism. Of course, the different mediated forms of communication all come with their own particular forms of production, content and reception and each are situated in different social, political and economic contexts and many are interrelated with one another in some form or other. Thus, I am also attempting to understand the interlinking factors between political, economic, social and cultural concerns and the complex consequences for democracy that ensue. Issues about political economy – ownership and control, state interference and market distortions, media/tech production and circulation and media/tech labour – are key. But so too are issues pertaining to media/social media content: (mis)representations and constructions of reality, framing, bias, and agenda setting, as well as concerns of differential subject production and political affect in all our mediated experiences. As media scholars, we must attend both to the institutions, policies and economic relations of the media and communications systems we analyse and to the many ways in which subjects and political subjectivities are transformed by certain types of neoliberal reasoning within these systems. After all, capitalism is sustained by particular forms of political rationality. This rationality shapes our institutions of media and communications not simply through marketization and privatization but also the ways in which the subject and citizen are (re)made as consumer and (prod-)user, thereby constraining political sense-making and restricting political visions.

So, while a debate that focuses on the relationship between democracy and capitalism encourages us to take economic factors seriously, this does not mean that the analysis is economically reductive. Far from it. While a consideration of global capitalism is concerned with the corporate capture of institutions of the state and the hijacking of political decision-making power at the transnational level by global finance, it also brings to the fore a politics of inequality and maldistribution of wealth. This politics of inequality, in turn, forces an explanation not just of social class but also of race, gender, sexuality and disability along with other markers of difference that reveal ingrained, historical status hierarchies, injuries of misrecognition and harms of social injustices. These are characteristics not just of a capitalist economy but of a capitalist society (Fraser, 2022). Power and wealth are differentially distributed not only at the level of corporations, states and citizens but also at the level of the social and the cultural and must be understood in these ways too (Zelizer, 2017). As Ellen Meiksins Wood (2005) argues so persuasively, it is capitalism itself that detached what are in essence political issues – the power to control production and appropriation, or the allocation of social labour – from the political arena, displacing them to the economic sphere as a means of disciplining them. An emancipatory critique requires acknowledgement that such a separation is both contrived and ideological.

Through this approach the book offers a critique based on examples from around the world and from a range of social and mainstream, commercial and public service media, largely (but not only) in places where neoliberal capitalism is most entrenched and various calibres of democracy exist. Interrogating a contested concept such as democracy, and operationalizing it through diverse and often conflicting practices, requires situating the discussion in political systems and contexts bounded by mechanisms and principles that have emerged from particular histories. But this is only one small book and although it is concerned with regimes that claim to be democracies, it is *not* a comparative analysis. Rather it is reflective of an awareness of the changing nature of politics in different contexts, and the ways in which this may open up or expose criteria required for democratic enquiry at any one time.

That said, there are some things that appear to be recognizable (albeit with crucial differences) in many places around the globe. There is a widespread sense of disaffection, distrust and dissatisfaction with representative democratic regimes, which, rather than activating new forms of political engagement, are leading to a deep distrust of political elites and 'an increasing disconnect between citizens and government' (Kundnani, 2020, p. 8). While some chart this as democratic demise, others argue that disaffection and apathy are also political affects that act to spur citizens to seek out new routes of engagement and participation outside of the electoral system (Carpentier and Dahlgren, 2013). Similarly, as Chapter 7 discusses, distrust in mainstream media appears pervasive (at least in the Anglophone world), with a 'post-truth' angst emanating from Donald Trump's presidency and politics, combined with an 'info-glut' (Andrejevic, 2013a) of the digital age designating meaning as unhinged and specious. In this regard, media moguls and tech giants are seen as part of a consolidated oligarchy that is making even a sorry pretence at democracy impossible.

In Levitsky and Ziblatt's (2018) book *How Democracies Die*, they argue that American democracy is moribund – a feeling shared by many after Donald Trump's election to president in 2016. Trump's four years in power were marked by an abuse of power and violations of democratic institutions and norms from the free press and the federal judiciary to the electoral process itself, becoming the first US president in history to be impeached twice – the second time for inciting an insurrection at the US Capitol that left five people dead during the certification of the election he lost. As of September 2023, he had been criminally indicted four times relating to a string of election corruption charges, mishandling of classified material, falsifying business records and over efforts to overturn the result of the

2020 presidential election. All of which he denies. He is also a media celebrity. From 2004 to 2015 he hosted the reality TV show *The Apprentice* on NBC and later co-hosted *The Celebrity Apprentice*. He is a two-time Emmy Award-nominated personality and has appeared as versions of himself in many films and TV series and been in television commercials from Pizza Hut to Pepsi. He also had his own daily radio programme *Trumped!* As president he sent more than 26,000 tweets providing a real-time and unfiltered account of his immediate responses on a range of issues that ultimately proved so provocative that he was banned from Twitter (Brown, 2020) only to be reinstated by Elon Musk in 2022 when he took over the platform.

Another common pattern is the rise of the far-right. In the US, white-supremacist and far-right violence is on the increase (Leichnitz, 2023). Europe has also been experiencing a rise in popularity of far-right politics and politicians since the early 2010s in Hungary, Austria, France, Italy, Spain, Germany, Greece, Slovakia, Poland, the Netherlands, Denmark, Sweden, Switzerland, Romania and Bulgaria. Each case is different, but many of the politicians place the scapegoating of immigrants for the diminishing of living standards for the working class at the heart of their politics. Commentators and theorists (e.g. Inglehart and Norris, 2016) have suggested that this rise of populism has been triggered by a populace that feels they are losing power to elites. Trappel and Tomaz (2022) point out that there are more countries becoming authoritarian regimes than adopting liberal democracy. They note that Larry Diamond (2015) coined the phrase 'democratic recession' to describe what he sees as a halt in the expansion of freedom and democracy in the world since the mid-2000s.

Around the world, the Covid-19 pandemic also laid bare the devastating consequences of years of austerity-based economic policy in many neoliberal democracies – with crumbling systems of health and social care – as well as the deathly consequences of social and economic inequalities (see Chapter 7) firmly demarcated by what Du Bois (1903) called 'the color line'. Political systems were exposed as mechanisms of capital as a state of crisis was used to feather the nests of corporate opportunists quick to exploit their connections and networks and secure huge government contracts for the production of (sometimes faulty) personal protective equipment (PPE). Billionaire wealth soared. The poor, marked by race and gender, lost jobs, housing and health. Vaccine apartheid was brutally enforced while budget cuts continued to decimate public health services, exposing once again how global capitalism propped up by (neo)liberal democracy will never serve the interests of the majority. The pandemic also highlighted deep problems with political institutions and the complete incompetence of many politicians. Will Davies (2020) notes how over the last decade this political democratic demise occurred amidst the proliferation of political referendums and binary choices accompanied by the rise of social media platforms, and the centrality of the 'like' function. He argues that clicking 'like' or 'dislike' is about as much critical activity as we are permitted, creating a society of perpetual referendums. When fundamental questions of national sovereignty, colonial histories and how to respond to a pandemic become reduced to binary choice, it simplifies political deliberation to good versus bad and like versus dislike, generating bitter divisions: you are either with us or you are against us. This reduction of complex matters to simple and extreme binary choices allows dominant narratives around democratic change to become binary dualisms wherein the only alternatives to capitalism are claimed to be Stalinist Soviet Union or contemporary North Korea.

One way to counter the simplistic (and dangerous) politics of binary dualisms is to try to think through how politics could become more meaningful to more people – how we could democratize so-called democracies. How we might conceive of an alternative politics that can advance freedom, equality, collectivism and ecological sustainability while avoiding, or ending entirely, corporate, financial and market domination. In a similar vein, Latour (2004) argues that a hermeneutics of suspicion has become the preferred weapon of conservative thinkers and conspiracy theorists. Tactics forged by the left – scepticism about what counts as 'facts', interrogation of the motives of scientists and the legal professions – now drive the arguments of the right, as evident in climate change denial. It is time, he suggests, to adopt new tools, to move from a spirit of debunking to one of assembling, or from critique to composition. While I certainly do not want to forego the critical analysis that emanates from a spirit of debunking, there is no doubt that in attempting to explain the failures of neoliberal democracy and global capitalism we also need to think beyond them. And in showing that things could be different there is also the imperative to change predominant understandings of what is of value in and about this thing called democracy. Dominant hegemonic understandings of (liberal) democracy have been encultured and cultivated over time. We need to interrogate these processes and practices, but we also need to consider what a counter-hegemonic approach to *democratic media and communications systems that work for democracy* might be. This book hopes to contribute to these debates.

Imagining new democratic possibilities for media and society

As a response to the expansiveness of the concept of democracy and the effusiveness of media and communications this book offers an unapologetically big-picture analysis regarding the relations of both to political life, also conceived of in its broadest terms. These are, after all, the key structures, forms and technologies that enable meaning-making, legitimate decision-making, sustain consent and occasionally give cause for uprisings. In concentrating on the big picture, it inevitably misses detail and specificity that are crucial, and I have tried throughout to indicate where these substantive analyses can be found elsewhere. But I have long felt that if we don't have the hard edges of our analysis the middle never quite coheres and we are too frequently left with granular descriptions of particular sites with no road map of how we got there, what those sites sit in relation to, or how we might take our leave of them. So, while we need a more expansive view of capitalism than a classic Marxist reading might provide, in order to address the issues this book raises, capitalism nonetheless provides the hard edges of the analysis.

In *Democracy Against Capitalism*, Wood (1995) scrutinized the conflict between capitalism and democracy, arguing that by legally relegating issues of property, ownership and work to the private sector, capitalism confines public power to electoral politics. Consequently, it empties democracy of its original meaning as the power of the common people, leaving workers precariously exposed to market forces. In order to counter this, she argued that we must reimagine democracy as comprising freedom from the dictates of the market. This would require democratic control over the conditions of wealth's production and distribution by those who produce it. Many of the examples drawn on in this book speak to this necessity but they also relate to the importance of meeting peoples' informational and communicational needs as construed by those people in all their diversity.

No one would deny that capitalism has brought with it massive technological advances. But we can no longer deny that it has also caused immense suffering and death of great multitudes of people from the massive inequality (Chapter 5), dispossession and catastrophic climate destruction that it has engendered. Wood (2017) argues that capitalism is incapable of engendering sustainable development because its purpose is the creation of exchange value, not use value, profit not people, producing both massive waste and inadequate provision of basic necessities (see Chapter 8). Translated to the world of media and communications, what we are faced with is the glut of overabundant information alongside the lack of public media infrastructure and the increasing commodification of public knowledge that render capitalism as a way of life:

> As capitalism spreads more widely and penetrates more deeply into every aspect of social life and the natural environment, its contradictions are increasingly escaping all our efforts to control them. The hope of achieving a humane, truly democratic, and ecologically sustainable capitalism is becoming transparently unrealistic. (Wood, 2017, p. 198)

If democracy and capitalism are fundamentally incompatible, what might this mean for our systems of media and communications? As most of our media are capitalist by nature or have supported and justified (implicitly and explicitly) various shades of capitalist enterprise, they cannot serve democracy well. In an article on digital socialism Morozov (2020) maintains that over the past few decades the social democratic project has been forced into defending what was left of its institutions rather than innovating for social change:

> the result has been to limit the capacity of social democratic and socialist forces to think about technological change and the kinds of institutional innovation necessary in order to place the economic dynamics involved on a path that is not only more egalitarian but also more efficient and productive.

He argues that the neoliberal project has prevented forms of social coordination based on values that have nothing to do with the market and competition from occupying the kind of spaces that public institutions like libraries (or indeed schools) currently do in society. Of course, libraries and schools have not escaped years of neoliberalism unscathed. In the UK almost 800 public libraries have closed since 2010 due to cuts to public spending (Walton, 2021). And many countries have forms of public media funded (at least in part) by the public purse often stemming from more liberal times. But when institutions of public media are seen as a threat to capital accumulation they come under attack and often find they must dilute their public mission to suit capital interests in order to survive (see Chapter 6 for a discussion of the BBC).

When it comes to tech giants, the debate has become firmly entrenched in neoliberal hegemony, enabling big tech to largely evade paying appropriate taxes and avoid anti-trust reform. The possibilities for alternative configurations of social forces and systems of communication – whether through different ways of organizing labour and the workforce, providing for media citizenship with cooperatives or trade unions, or varied ways of ensuring data sovereignty through municipalities or public ownership at a national level – are rarely considered. Rather we are stuck in the mode of trying to promulgate good behaviour of these giants who devour us through legal reform that at best will leave us with a form of benevolent digital dictatorship.

Given the difficulty of arguing against the centrality of technology to our social and political life-worlds, we surely need to think through what it would mean to conceive of our systems of media and communications in terms of public value rather than private gain; to imagine how our media and communications infrastructures could become something similar to that experienced in established systems of welfare that serve public health and social care, however tentative and fuzzy these imaginings may be; and to conceive of new relationships of ownership and control for newly imagined digital infrastructures. For, as Williams (1989, p. 118) says in the epigraph that begins this chapter, '[t]o be truly radical is to make hope possible rather than despair convincing'. This book has tried to do this difficult task and sketch out some of the parameters of what this sort of *media commons* might entail. How a more egalitarian and solidaristic imagination might recast participation and reconceive of the public good producing collaborative forms of mediated public knowledge infrastructures for *communicative justice*.

The notion of a media commons elaborated on in this book reaches well beyond notions of nationalization and public service media. These have been proven in many instances to deliver media services far preferable to commercial models but also stand accused of replacing private oligarchs with distant cumbersome bureaucratic institutions that are largely removed from the publics they serve, being populated by elites and of lacking in workplace democracy (see Chapter 6). It also extends outside of the media and tech organizations themselves to include the people and places such organizations are speaking to and about and extracting data from. Public service media does not translate into *democratic media for democracy* unless people also have the power to influence decisions and have a say in how the public good is defined.

Democracy is both value and practice – it refers to collective and relational modes of being in the world and situates the importance of media and communications for our collective and relational well-being engaging in 'the production and reproduction of ourselves as a common subject' (Ticktin, 2020). Any theory of communication is, as Williams (Williams, 1963) noted, a theory of community. And the act of communing involves multiple inequalities that must be taken into account. A media commons speaks to the sharing of resources and services stewarded for the public good rather than for private gain in a manner that is necessarily different from commercial media and offers an alternative value system to capitalism. A commons does not common alone. It sees publicness as a site of resistance and collective struggle and a place of democratic imaginaries (Della Ratta, 2020). A media commons is a wholly different way of conceiving of our media and communications systems, and one that would promote an array of alternative media/tech ownership models at different levels: from the hyperlocal to the international. A media commons is thus engaged in media and communicative justice that requires the understanding, exposing and challenging of historical and systemic (media and tech) injustices that ideologically, institutionally and operationally reproduce the harms of capitalism, heteropatriarchy and settler colonialism. Rather, media commoning sees publicness and its creation as a process (Kavada and Poell, 2021) that can enhance collective lives among heterogenous publics.

Conclusion: Democratic media for democracy

I began this chapter by arguing that media and communications are vitally important but also insisting that they are never the whole story. So too, I hope that imagining alternatives to our dominant systems of media and communications that have failed democracy will also help us to conceive of how democracy itself could be otherwise. In thinking about how we may decentralize media and communications practices and (infra)structures I am also thinking about how we decentralize economic and political power more generally for transformative ends. As Santos and Mendes (2020, p. 234) write when arguing for the need for imagining new democratic possibilities:

> Alongside the dominant conception . . . there are other conceptions and democratic practices that are instituting dignity and equality. These alternative democratic conceptions and practices constitute tools for

decolonizing, decommodifying and depatriarchalizing social relations, transforming society into places of democratization that traverse all the structural spaces of contemporary societies.

The implication is that new forms of participation and deliberation through transformed (infra)structures of media and communications will sooner or later lead to new, more demanding forms of representation and accountability to more people. Bringing into clear view a small slice of the democratic experiences arising in mediated forms in different parts of the world may help us to conceive of how we can democratize democracy. It is an act of possibility-disclosure (Kompridis, 2005), bringing into view alternative ways of thinking and acting and offering up potential for new configurations of democratic government, representation, participation, freedom and hope. While deeply uneven, violent and exploitative structures have sustained capitalism and liberal democracy over many years capitalism is also prone to constant crisis. It is not a stable social and economic system. Constant crisis is now conjoined with a sense of pending chaos and the doom of climate catastrophe. So other models, out of necessity and latent desire, are always emergent, both filling the cracks and shining a light through them – offering up different ways of doing media and communications emanating from more control by more people. These emergent models work towards the production and validation of knowledges anchored in the experiences of resistance among all social groups which have systematically suffered the injustice, oppression and destruction caused by capitalism, colonialism and heteropatriarchy. Models that seek to transform society 'into fields of democratisation that permeate the structural spaces of society' (Santos and Mendes, 2020, p. 23).

Fraser (2022) insists that safeguarding the planet requires building a counterhegemony and creating a new commonsense that will address the full extent of our general crisis through a common project. And the thing that all crises share in common is capitalism as the sociohistorical driver of social injustices, of climate catastrophe, of financialization, of de-democratization. Capitalism is deeply and constitutively undemocratic because it creates and feeds off social inequality. In the capitalist workplace, it is capital that has the last say, not forms of worker self-governance. Our capitalist systems of media and communications not only sustain a capitalist economy but also nourish a capitalist society and hegemony – they decide for us what our media and communications should be, how they should be run and for whose benefit. To build a counterhegemony requires decision making that is inclusive, where all those affected are entitled to participate on equal terms to decide what media and communications systems are needed in any one place at any one time. And if it is to be genuinely democratic it must also be just and address injustices. In other words, it must be transformative. A democratic media for democracy must then confront capitalist power. It is to the question of power that the next chapter turns.

2

POWER AND POWERLESSNESS

Liberal democracy depends on the idea of popular sovereignty – the notion that the people are the ultimate authority who confer legitimacy on the authority of government who exercise political power on their behalf. But wrapped up in this deceptively simple idea is a complex and fraught relationship between the practice of democracy and the exercise of power that also draws our attention to democracy and powerlessness. Is democracy about rule and order or rather, is it defined by dissent and struggle? Is power something to be resisted from below or as a force of rule exercised from above? Ideal notions of democracy are concerned with the power of the people and the capacity of people to act collectively to bring about change. It is worth remembering that the idea of democracy cast in this way has not always been well received. Rather, those with power, in the upper echelons of society, have shunned the 'power of the people' as the unruly and downright dangerous power of the masses (Macpherson, 2006). Seen from this perspective the masses require controlling rather than seeking their inclusion in any notion of shared power attached to democratic ideals. Others, such as Rancière (2004), have sought to firmly locate democracy within a more defiant meaning, attaching it to the inclusion of those who have been traditionally excluded from any say over public affairs (amounting to those without wealth or entitlement by birth). In other words, different conceptions of democracy understand power (and hence powerlessness) in different ways and point to different approaches to social and political change. In practice, it is power relations that define both the nature of democracy and the position of all social actors within its realms.

Interpretations of the meaning of democracy generally fall into two main camps. On the one hand, there are those who foreground the necessity for accountability, legitimacy and representation in systems of rule and point to things like mechanisms of voting representatives into government and referendums that offer intermittent checks on executive power as a means of establishing forms of governance that reflect the desires of the people. In this manner, democracy is used as a normative principle for conferring political legitimacy. This is usually where we find liberal deliberative theories of democracy. But elections in themselves do not fulfil the requirement of modern democracies. The people must also monitor and influence officials' behaviour while in office – and this has proven problematic in a context where the views and opinions of certain institutions or elite actors have taken precedence over others. Popular sovereignty has been difficult (and some would say impossible) to maintain in the age of global capitalism where corporations, banking and financial agencies, who show patent disregard for the will of the people within nation states, continue to be a dominant influence on the nature and practice of political economic decision-making (Schäfer and Streeck, 2015). This is one reason why the role of the media in holding power to account is seen as paramount in functioning democracies. As overseers of government, the people must have alternative sources of information. No single source, especially an official government source, is sufficient. Freedom of the press is therefore considered to be an essential aspect of democratic governance (see Chapter 4). Furthermore, mainstream media and commercial media institutions in particular have in many cases revealed themselves to be part of the system of global capitalism that they are supposed to be monitoring and deeply entangled with political power brokers in governments, throwing the idea of popular sovereignty into question.

On the other hand, there are those who consider a key characteristic of democracy to be autonomy and collective self-rule – the rule of everyone by everyone – that inscribes equal political status (and power) to all and refuses domination by any one person or class. This approach often refers back to power from below and relates to practices and organizations external to mainstream political institutions such as those found in civil society. Here, democracy is used as a precondition for justice with the claim that equal political participation is necessary for fair and just collective decision-making. This sort of conceptual splitting of power into two factions, positions social and political change within radical democratic theory as a form of extraordinary disruption of a routinized institutional order. It is in these acts of insurgence where it is claimed that democracy takes place. This is where agonistic theories of democracy tend to reside (Mouffe, 2009). Between deliberative and agonistic democratic theory we can see the distinction between the articulation of power as the force of a centralized, hierarchical command, and power as the force of collective constitution. As Saar (2010, p. 11) notes:

> One the one hand there is a concept of power as domination, whereas on the other hand there is the concept of power as constitution. The former is concerned with realisation and subjugation of wills, whereas the latter with the unleashing and channelling of multifarious forces.

In these formulations, power is understood as either 'power over' or 'power to' – where the former is wielded by some people over others (relating to thinking such as Weber (1994) and the Frankfurt School); and the latter tracing back to Spinoza (1996) in the seventeenth century, where power is a constitutive feature of social life and is not so much wielded as embodied in social relations and collectives (Barnett, 2017). Although these differing approaches have often been deemed incompatible, both these traditions of thought are relevant and useful to an understanding of media, power and democracy. Concentrated media ownership exerts a level of domination over symbolic power and it can also exert political power and influence (see Chapter 6). Politicians fearful of what news organizations will print or broadcast about them are more likely to seek their favour through forms of media deregulation and tax privileges or subsidies. Of course, this doesn't always work and does not preclude the constitutive power of subjects as free agents able to resist and counter domination both through rejecting dominant media discourses and indeed establishing their own media forms and outputs, as we will return to at the end of this chapter.

Media power, people power and democracy

In recent times there has been no shortage of instances where media institutions and communication practices have become both concrete sites and compelling symbols of systemic political crisis and democratic struggle. The movement for media reform in the UK precipitated by phone hacking and ever-increasing concentration of media ownership has sought to make the media accountable for its illegal and unethical practices and to increase media plurality. We have also seen opposition to oligarchic media concentration in Italy, Hungary, Australia and Argentina, to mention but a few key sites. Or we can point to intensive conflicts involving state actors with deterritorialized networks of informational activism – from the ongoing cases of WikiLeaks and Julian Assange to Edward Snowden, Glenn Greenwald and the National Security Agency (NSA) (Scahill, 2013). These struggles for the right to communicate and hold power to account have ensured that public debate on whether or not – and in what forms and ways – the media enhance or frustrate the practice of democracy endures. But they are usually situated within the conceptual framework of liberal democracy and the role of the media therein – hence the battle is conceived as one where the media are (or should be) enablers of democracy to the extent that they provide people with a full range of views so that they can better vote for political representatives who will then make decisions on their behalf.

As media scholars we tend to focus on and problematize the media side of this debate. Media, as Dahlgren writes, 'are a prerequisite – though by no means a guarantee – for shaping the democratic character of society' (2009, p. 2). By examining such issues as media ownership and pluralism, freedom of the press and the emergent digital possibilities for citizens to claim increased communicative autonomy, media studies scholarship has long sought to specify the institutional arrangements, public processes, civic practices and political-economic conditions that give substance to media's role as a democratic prerequisite. However, less attention has been paid to what the democratic character of society should be. And scant attention has been given to the implications of the significant shifts in the distribution of power within existing representative democracies for established ways of considering media's democratic functions, particularly in light of the global dominance of tech giants such as Google and Meta. Those concepts that position 'media as democratic prerequisite' need to account for how the democratic character of societies is not only 'not guaranteed' under conditions where the agency of representative democratic institutions has been diminished (Crouch, 2004, 2011) but where, under conditions of neoliberal capture, democracies, as Jeremy Gilbert argues, are riven by a 'fundamental democratic crisis . . . a crisis in the capacity for collective decisions to be taken and upheld' (2014, p. viii). Broken party political manifesto pledges, political lies and corruption, misinformation and illegality have always been part of the dark underbelly of political life, but in the era of Donald Trump and Boris Johnson (as the most obvious examples of political leaders of so-called liberal democratic states) they have become an explicit part of political strategy (see Chapter 7). In such circumstances, liberal democracy may have very little by way of democratic character left.

There is now an extensive literature (e.g. Crouch, 2011) that points to a crisis of representative democratic systems in the Western world, long regarded as weakened by the competitive imperatives of economic globalization and the declining counter-power of organized labour (Crouch, 2004). Scholars have pointed to the shrinking range and register of party political action and conceivable, alternative political projects and policy interventions in postmodern societies (Gilbert, 2013); to the retraction of the state from the provision of public goods and infrastructure (Seymour, 2014); the increased power of corporations and transnational financial agencies over public priorities (Crouch, 2011); as well as the elite choreography of 'adversarial' politics in democracies that speak without listening (Dean, 2009). Crouch has famously termed our current democratic decay as a continuing process of dissolution towards 'post-democracy', a state where the forms of democracy remain fully in place, yet 'politics and government are increasingly slipping back into the control of privileged elites in the manner characteristic of pre-democratic times' (2004, p. 6).

The cumulative evidence of fissures and failures in the project of liberal representative democracy has consequences for the theoretical constitution of liberal democracy in media studies, a dominant constitutive framework that all too frequently organizes discussions of democracy through concepts such as the public sphere, pluralism, and communicative freedom (albeit not only through these concepts). Indeed, we are told that free media are the lifeblood of democracy; that mediated information runs through the very veins of the body politic of democratic states. When media are placed at the heart of all systems, as the pulse of democracy, then it is all too easy to claim that enhancing this thing called democracy simply requires a media solution – more plurality, less concentration, better representation. Of course, all of these concerns are of vital importance. And yet, they tend to distract our attention away from the broader context of which they are but a part. In other words, we need to interrogate the political context that has, more often than not, prevented meaningful media reform from taking place and prioritized corporate desires for profit over public interest requirements to feed democratic intent.

One recent example is in Australia, where the former prime minister Kevin Rudd called for a Royal Commission into the power of the Murdoch media. Australia's print media is overwhelmingly controlled by News Corporation, founded by Rupert Murdoch with more than 140 newspapers and around two-thirds of daily newspaper readership as well as owning the Australian Sky News

TV channel, the pay-TV company Foxtel and a raft of magazines and radio stations. A Senate inquiry into media diversity noted that Australia has one of the most concentrated media markets in the world with a regulatory regime that is not fit for purpose. It stated that large media organizations have become so powerful and unchecked that they have developed corporate cultures that consider themselves beyond the existing accountability framework (Senate Environments and Communications References Committee, 2021). The Murdoch media empire was found guilty of climate-denialism, gendered, partisan attacks, providing a platform for racism and publishing Covid disinformation.

The Senate inquiry backed the call for a full judicial inquiry into media ownership and existing media regulation as well as for guaranteed long-term funding for public service broadcasters ABC and SBS and Australia's only independent newswire, the non-profit news agency Australian Associated Press (AAP). They also argued for keeping the National Broadband Network (NBN – a national government-owned open-access data network) as a public asset; and called for the establishment of a public trust fund for emerging news outlets, especially in regional areas. But it is highly unlikely that the incumbent conservative government of the day, who benefit from support from the Murdoch Press, will ever act on the Senate recommendations. Meanwhile, Australia has struck a 'News Media Bargaining Code' with Meta and Google that was supposed to increase media plurality by payments from the tech giants to other news outlets in compensation for advertising revenue lost to them. However, the power of concentrated media in Australia is such that News Corporation gained more than A$100 million a year while smaller news outlets lost out (Brevini, 2023). And as the initial three-year contracts with news organizations began to expire, Meta announced that it would not enter into new deals with Australian media companies. So, even in instances where the power of concentrated media ownership is recognized and challenged, the relationship of interdependence between media elites and political elites means that media fixes to liberal democracy's shortcomings are few and far between. And more often than not dominant forms of media power and political power reinforce each other.

The issue for media studies paradigms then becomes why they have held fast to a normative and often somewhat teleological relationship to particular – ideal – liberal democratic forms, even as these forms mutate and fail, and power appears to become ever more concentrated in ever fewer hands? In Wendy Brown's essay 'Neoliberalism and the End of Liberal Democracy' (Brown, 2005), focused on the US, she invites political philosophy to 'mourn' a liberal democracy that has been eviscerated through the intensification of neoliberal governmentality while eroding political citizenship and helping to produce a system of control without responsibility. For Brown, neoliberal governmentality amounts to a new political formation that diminishes the relative autonomy of democratic and state institutions from the market and entails the 'erosion of oppositional political, moral, or subjective claims located *outside* capitalist rationality yet inside liberal democratic society, that is, the erosion of institutions, venues and values organized by nonmarket rationalities in democracies' (2005, p. 45). Liberal democracy, over and above established critiques, has provided a modest ethical and pragmatic buffer between citizens and the 'free hand' of the market, thus 'while liberal democracy encodes, reflects and legitimates capitalist social relations, it simultaneously resists counters and tempers them' (2005, p. 46). The steady progress of neoliberal interventionism and hegemonic construction of neoliberal formations has resulted in a process of capture, where, Brown contends, 'liberal democracy' no longer signifies a set of independent institutions, civic practices and the principle of popular sovereignty but rather 'indicates only a state and subjects organized by market rationality'. What we are left with under neoliberalism are no more than the 'residues of old-fashioned democracy inside the legitimation project of neoliberalism' (Brown, 2005, p. 56).

It is part of this transition, Brown argues, that poses a problem for critics attuned to representative democracy's shortcomings, but compelled to defend principles that are being eroded. So, for example, we see in debates over the 'freedom of the press' in the UK and in Australia a noble ideal based on an independent journalism of integrity that has been reappropriated by the libertarian right and used to fight against the establishment of a fair and effective system of press accountability. In the process, 'freedom' has been transmuted into the freedom of powerful media corporations to say and do whatever they like in pursuit of profit. In such jurisdictions, the press have an awful lot of freedom but not of the sort that necessarily defends or deepens democracy (see Chapter 4).

These forms of neoliberal governmentality void liberal democracy of substance but take shape in and act through democratic discourses of freedom, participation, choice, empowerment and pluralism. The question, for Brown, is how to engage with a democratic vocabulary that also acts as neoliberalism's cloak. The need to evade terms and discourses saturated in market rationality compels Brown to invite political philosophy and activists to 'mourn' liberal democracy and to develop counter-rationalities for human flourishing and alternative visions of a good political life. Brown's argument about the profound rearticulation of democratic discourses is of consequence for media studies paradigms that, while fully capable of identifying the gaps between democratic principles and practices, too often end up accepting and prioritizing democracy in a certain form – a form that frequently masquerades as liberal democracy through donning some of its easily recognizable accoutrements – the insignia of 'freedom' on the shiny veneer of 'pluralism' – that hide grossly unequal power relations and a body politic beneath that has morphed in to something rather different – *neo*liberal democracy (Fenton and Titley, 2015). In other words, unless we interrogate liberal democracy as a set of power relations and address its failures as a political project and a political system, alongside the role of media therein, we collude with the neoliberal capture of democracy and of its increasing demise and hand power over to media and political elites in the process.

Part of the problem may well be that the normative framework of liberal democracy has become so entrenched and so well-serving for modern Western states and their mechanisms of soft power that academic discourse has fallen prey to the seduction too. Democracy has come to mean liberal democracy, which today, in practice, is neoliberal democracy enclosed in the constitutional shell of the Western neo-colonial state. In media and communication studies, all too frequently any discussion of media and democracy hinges on Habermas (1989) and his concept of the public sphere that is also captured by a liberal democratic framing and horizon. This is understandable, as it is one of the few prominent theoretical frameworks that link the media and its practices directly to the exercise of democracy. But when we are faced with an abundance of evidence that liberal democracy has failed it is surely time to let it go (Fenton, 2018). We need, more than ever, new theoretical insights capable of addressing the complexities of power in the digital age of global capitalism if we are to reinvent our democratic futures and search out what democracy could become. One way of opening up the interrogation of the critique of democracy is to insist on a concurrent evaluation and critique of power and powerlessness. In 2013 the Indignados movement in Spain was inspired by banners that stated 'our democracy is kidnapped by the Parliament' and 'democracy is in the street not in Parliament' (Johnson and Suliman, 2020). The intention was to bring to the fore the powerlessness felt by people on the street – not to fix representative democracy but rather to find a wholly other, better way, of doing democracy.

It is in this spirit that the debates in this book take their leave as an attempt to share power and deal with powerlessness and to combine debates over power as domination with power as constitution. Creating a conceptual dualism of *power over* and *power to* leaves us with an all-or-nothing approach that is bound to disappoint from either side. So how can we take account of both in the formulation of democratic futures? The theorist Enrique Dussel (2008) tries to synthesize the top-down ascendency view of power and the bottom-up agency/action-oriented view of power. Dussel is interested in how collectively generated power can be wielded in the interests of social justice through delegation to political institutions to exercise what he calls 'obediential power' – governing while obeying – a term he took from the Zapatistas in Mexico. In this process he sends a clear warning that power is a risky undertaking highly susceptible to corruption and fetishization, which in turn can cause injustice and harm to the oppressed: workers, the exploited, indigenous peoples, women, etc. This is not a conceptual battle but rather a struggle based on differing interpretations of vulnerability and harm in our understandings of democratic politics. Hence foregrounding powerlessness is as important as understanding powerfulness. The key point for Dussel is to overcome the opposition between reform and revolution in left political thinking and to move towards 'transformation' based on the harms exerted upon and via the actions of the oppressed or the excluded through new ways of exercising delegated powers – democracy reimagined. By contrast, the end point for liberal democrats is limiting the abuse of power and the intimidation of the powerless that constitutive power can fall prey to via new laws and mechanisms of accountability.

Anarchism also turns on a deep suspicion of the harms that can be done by the concerted exercise of power via authority and rule, reminding us that the exercise of democratic power is not without risk or problem. Graeber (2014) claims that anarchism recognizes the immanent presence of communism in social life and is expressive of the real meaning of democracy. When we engage in cooperative activity with one another, we are all communists. Although anarchist thought is useful in order to highlight the harms that power can bring, it is also rather simplistic as it hinges on an analysis of top-down power (verticality) always involving forcible commands and imposition that comprise domination and oppression and are therefore bad, whereas bottom-up power is conceived as non-coercive, self-organized, collective acts of resistance (horizontality) and is therefore good. It is also overly simplistic in its distinction between consent and consensus. In anarchist thought when we consent to being governed (by voting in elections, for example) then democracy becomes a system of authority, whereas consensus is a form of self-government via collective agreement and a more authentic expression of democracy. Yet institutionalized authority is not necessarily all bad – take an institutionalized system of healthcare or transport, forms of authority that many of us would grant some positive qualities – and similarly, many of us have been part of collectives where the rosy view of human togetherness doesn't always ring true.

John Dunn (2000) addresses this issue by arguing that all politics are fundamentally concerned with rule, and democracy is one form of being ruled. The fundamental issue is rather how rule is to be shared. For Graeber, believing in the fundamental goodness of humankind, this would be by consensus. For Dunn, equality requires more intervention (and the exercise of dominant power). How one interprets this debate, as Barnett (2017, p. 36) notes, 'might well depend on one's willingness to accept that demands for democratization arise from feelings of powerlessness that can have multiple sources'. Foregrounding an analysis of powerlessness forces us to acknowledge that a liberal democratic approach based primarily on limiting or legitimizing dominant power will never be enough for democracy to flourish. It also encourages us to recognize that, in order to address powerlessness, democracy requires a facilitation of constitutive power: the ability of everyone to be makers of rules that apply to them. This has direct consequences for how we view the relationship between media and communications and democracy. If we view our media and communications systems purely from the perspective of 'power over' then we may decide that addressing too much power simply requires a regulatory response that will limit the concentration of media ownership. However, if we view media and communications systems from the position of 'power to' and the need to address powerlessness, our response will be quite different.

This chapter now turns to two examples where the sources of power and powerlessness have been revealed through the practices of media and communications: the Cambridge Analytica scandal and the mainstream media coverage of the financial crash in 2008 and the decade of austerity policies that followed.

Cambridge Analytica

The Facebook–Cambridge Analytica data breach was claimed to have influenced the outcome of the European referendum with a dramatic impact on the political future of the UK (Cadwalladr and Graham-Harrison, 2018). Cambridge Analytica were accused of distorting democratic processes through illegally scraping people's data from the likes of Facebook (now Meta), psychologically profiling their digital identities and then bombarding the 'persuadables' with unattributable memes and messages aimed at shifting their voting behaviour in the direction of their clients' political will and ambition. The Cambridge Analytica scandal put data-driven political campaigning in the spotlight. This sort of digital political campaigning is possible due to the vast global archive of personal data created from what are in essence, global, monopolistic advertising platforms built on the principle of ensuring that advertising (of any sort) sells better than it ever has before. Tambini (Moore and Tambini, 2018) shows how Facebook advertising was crucial to the UK 2016 Referendum on Europe and the UK 2017 General Election – the platform became a one-stop shop for fundraising, recruitment, profiling, segmentation, message targeting and delivery. But there remains no publicly available data on what parties' money was spent on, what the actual content was, or who digital campaigning was targeted at. The scale and dominance of the tech giants enables highly targeted, relatively invisible and totally unaccountable political campaigning.

Cambridge Analytica was driven ultimately by a commercial imperative and the immense possibilities of harnessing the financial worth of billions of people's data to better target their insecurities and fear and channel their voting responses (a politics of capital accumulation). They have been accused of hacking democracy and directly impacting on the election of Donald Trump and the European Referendum in the UK. Yet, Mark Zuckerberg, founder and CEO of Meta, persistently refused requests to appear before a Parliamentary Committee in the UK in relation to the Facebook–Cambridge Analytica data breach. Although the extent of the impact on the electoral process is impossible to determine and hotly contested, what is clear is that this is an example of wholly unaccountable corporate power that has the potential for adverse political consequences. The data tech firms harness gives them immense power over the perceptions, beliefs and behaviours as well as the outcomes and political configurations that people inhabit. Meanwhile, the data providers (people using social media) have little power to determine how their data is used or information that enables them to adequately assess the material they are targeted with as a consequence of their data being harvested.

In the UK, both the Electoral Commission (2018) and the Information Commissioner's Office (2018) issued reports about digital campaigning trends, raising concerns about whether political parties and other campaigning organizations and companies are complying with electoral and data protection law. Both made recommendations for greater transparency in political campaigning, reflecting a growing consensus that the regulation of online campaigning needs to change. They noted that the move to targeted messaging, and the inability of all citizens to view and adjudicate between information in a targeted online campaigning environment, raises questions about equality of information, open debate and transparency. But it remains unclear whether proposed changes (that have not been enacted) deal with the problem, or how they could be enforced and who would be responsible for their regulation. In other words, once again, the institutions of liberal democracy are able to recognize the problem but are unprepared or unable to counter powerful forces to make change happen. And even if they could, none of the recommendations challenge the underlying premise of the current commercial, advertising-first, data-driven system. While they may be concerned with addressing issues of transparency, accountability and privacy, they do this in relation to already existing systems that exploit personal data for the purposes of personalized targeting for ad sales. Consequently, they all fall short of providing a long-term solution that can be fully trusted to support democracy (even if they were enforced). In this example we see how commercial systems of data capture are intricately entangled with state power and the institutionalized order of capitalism to the detriment of democracy.

Meanwhile, Meta is fast becoming the dominant digital platform for news. Google has some 86 per cent of global desktop search (Statista, 2023), and in 2022 Google and Meta together accounted for around half of all digital advertising in the US (McGee, 2022). And in 2022 Alphabet, Meta and Amazon soaked up over 70 per cent of the world's digital ad spend (Otto, 2023). These companies are the most concentrated forms of media and communications ownership we have ever seen: the powers they possess are vast and immunize them from scrutiny while also opening them up to government capture for covert surveillance (in return for weak privacy regulation). They control entire markets, setting the rules for the way people communicate (controlling the means for different communities to interact) and the way businesses trade (Amazon and Alibaba link retailers and shoppers, Facebook links advertisers and social media users). The way tech giants act as intermediaries alongside their monopolization strategies allows them to collect rent from users in the form of fees or data enabling them to reap vast profits and accumulate huge financial assets that make possible their expansion into a wide range of sectors including education, health, food distribution and finance (through the fintech industry): they are key to the contemporary condition of advanced capitalism.

Reporting the global financial crash

While the subterfuge involved in the techniques of propaganda and persuasion in the digital age are crucial to understand and take account of, we should not forget or sideline the persistent power of legacy media in legitimating capitalism. One key example is the reporting that led up to and followed on from the global financial crash that comprehensively failed to interrogate the wrongdoings of the financial sector, ignored the experts, let the banks off the hook and legitimized austerity economic policy. In his analysis of media reporting of the economic crisis in 2009, Wren-Lewis (2018) notes how the media's misrepresentation of economic ideas led to the legitimation of austerity policies with dire consequences for people's lives. He points to how less than 20 per cent of academic economists surveyed by the *Financial Times* thought that the recovery of 2013 vindicated austerity, yet the paper's editorial line was that it had. The problem, he says, is not only that large sections of the UK's print media have their own political agenda but also that their reporters tend to turn to City economists who have a set of views and interests that do not reflect the profession as a whole but are geared towards keeping their firm's clients happy and hence reflect the economic arguments of those on the right: regulation is bad, keep taxes low, the state is too large and budget deficits require immediate redress.

Austerity policies that were rolled out in the UK between 2010 and 2020 (and are still ongoing) have left vicious social scars, many of which will never heal. Toynbee and Walker (2020) chart how during this period the gap between rich and poor widened; the young became worse off than their parents at their age; and home ownership declined steeply – with families stuck in lifelong and precarious private renting. In the same period the public realm shrank: for every £100 spent on public services in 2010, only £86 in real terms was spent in 2020. Rebuilding schools and hospitals simply stopped. A quarter of local government jobs vanished, local government grants were slashed. Criminal justice was hard hit: courts closed; prisons overflowed with violence, and drug abuse was rife; legal aid was pared to nothing. Grants to arts organizations fell by a third, funding for national galleries and museums by a half. Years of frozen welfare benefits left families thousands of pounds short. State spending per child fell from £11,300 to £10,000. Early intervention for families was so scarce that the numbers of children in care rose rapidly. In 2018, 130 libraries shut and 760 youth clubs closed. Child poverty soared to its highest level since before the Second World War. Infant mortality rose for the first time in two generations. More than 2,000 food banks opened, four times more in districts where a form of welfare benefit called universal credit was rolled out. In 2022 the UK had more foodbanks (2,500) than McDonald's restaurants (1,350) (FactCheckNI, 2022).

The pro-austerity argument was rolled out again by the media in response to the consequences of the Covid-19 pandemic, promoting the view that the government had reached the limit of public borrowing and simply run out of money. Yet, the consensus among economists was that government should be focusing not on reducing the deficit but on delivering the spending necessary to enable a recovery from the pandemic, with modelling suggesting public debt as a proportion of GDP could actually fall were the government to embark on a major investment package boosting jobs and growth. Yet austerity policies continued as the cost of living rocketed, exacerbated by the fallout from leaving the European Union and the energy crisis resulting from the war in Ukraine.

Wren-Lewis argues that the misreporting of austerity is a result of 'neo-liberal overreach': attempts to pursue neoliberal goals that are no longer popular by deceiving the public – for example, by lying about the need to eliminate the deficit. Similarly Berry (2019), in a comprehensive and devastating analysis of media coverage of the financial crash, notes how all of the mainstream UK media, to varying degrees, constructed a narrative that the economic deficit constituted a major threat to the economy that required quick and significant cuts to the welfare state. Austerity was presented as largely inevitable. Berry (2016) also shows how public attitudes were influenced by media coverage leading to a widespread acceptance of austerity that has devasted large swathes of the country and played a key role in the 2010 and 2015 elections, as well as the 2016 Brexit vote.

Orienting those institutions that should be holding power to account towards performing the duties of capitalism exposes the contradictions of (neo)liberal democracy. Our news media may say one thing – the only way out of a financial crisis is to slash public spending and get rid of the financial deficit – but on the ground this is experienced as another: diminished public services leading to greater impoverishment and less economic growth. These contradictions are complex because the media are neither all-powerful nor ever entirely powerless. As is well documented in the field of media and communication studies, and as Berry's study (2019) brings to the fore, the media not only set the agenda for what people think about, they also build the agenda over time for what is seen as important and what an appropriate policy response may be. Mainstream news media viewed austerity not only as legitimate but often presented it as the only response available. But if this policy response fails consistently, its credibility will eventually wane, even with the mainstream media behind it. This then results in a dwindling legitimacy of political power. If those who have political power are not constantly called upon to be accountable for their actions and to reveal the ways in which they are using their power responsibly, then a culture of distrust and disdain for power holders (and those whose are supposed to hold them to account) ensues (see Chapter 7). And so paradoxically, while the neoliberal state (supported by neoliberal media) promotes free-market capitalism, it simultaneously sows the seeds of its own possible demise. As people begin to reject elite political power, and as public trust in governments and media fall, alternative means of sharing power involving forms of democratic media begin to emerge.

What can we do about it? Recognizing powerlessness and redistributing power

We see from the discussion above that the sharing of power that democracy entails requires active (re)cultivation, renewal and institutional support. It is an intrinsically political project. We also see that limiting the sharing of power (in order to accumulate more wealth or further legitimate the accumulation of wealth by others) requires delegitimation and containment of democratic claims that can bolster economization and privatization of government activities. This sort of ideological congruence between media and political elites results in increased powerlessness among citizens, particularly those who find themselves at the sharp end of neoliberal justificatory narratives, such as migrants and welfare claimants. It also removes power from journalists themselves, who, in order to retain their post in an increasingly precarious working environment and gain organizational recognition, resort to reproducing ideological congruence instead of challenging it. So what might it mean to think of our media landscape in terms of sharing power and addressing powerlessness?

Dealing with the multiple crises that we face – economic, geopolitical, environmental, social – necessitates having a media system oriented towards the common good rather than towards the vested interests of politicians, wealthy owners or powerful businesses. Media and tech ownership matters but dismantling and limiting concentration of media and tech ownership takes us only so far. It may relax the stranglehold of power that certain media and tech corporations exert but it does not necessarily alter the neoliberal nature of the system they operate within. This is where an understanding of powerlessness becomes crucial. If we take account of the need not only to limit power over, but also to grow power to, then it becomes crucial to enable, support and sustain forms of media and tech ownership that are *not for profit*, are fully independent of commercial pressures and government preferences, are organized cooperatively and democratically and are responsive to the needs of the communities they serve rather than at the behest of the market. This means creating and cultivating systems which are able to harness the huge potential of digital technologies and data for the common good, rather than seeing them captured for private benefit and distorting democratic practice. Structural change must not only confront and dismantle forms of monopolistic and oligopolistic power but must also include both large-scale forms of democratic governance and localized forms of production and collective management.

If we see all forms of media as part of a shared public information and communications resource necessary for a healthy functioning democracy – a form of public utility (see Chapter 3) – then we have to shift from viewing media and communication systems as primarily commodities for corporate entities to seeing them as shared resources for democratic well-being, resources that can be not only co-owned but also co-governed by the users and workers according to their own rules and norms. Just as democracy speaks to the capacity of people to act collectively and bring about change, so, too, it requires a reckoning with power. A media system that is explicitly designed to work for democracy and the common good would necessarily require media organizations that are themselves democratically constituted such that users and workers have power and control over how these organizations operate, what they produce and for whom. The struggle for a democratic media is also a fight to devolve power more generally and to give communities more control over their lives. An organization designed to operate democratically must recognize the ways in which the media industry in all its various guises has held certain people back, thereby contributing to powerlessness – Black people and other marginalized communities, old(er) people, disabled people, working-class people – and seek to counter those forms of injustice by taking special measures to compensate for the social and economic inequalities of unjust social structures. This recognizes that power is relational – and that most of these problems did not originate with the media and thus cannot be solved simply by changing how our media works.

One attempt to embed democratic practice within media organizations is via media cooperatives. A cooperative is an autonomous association of people who have come together voluntarily to meet their common economic, social and cultural needs and aspirations through a jointly owned and democratically controlled enterprise. The cooperative movement can be traced back to 1844 and a group of twenty-eight artisans – called the Rochdale Pioneers – working in the cotton mills in the north of England who established the Rochdale Society of Equitable Pioneers. The weavers, who were working in poor conditions on low wages and couldn't afford basic necessities, pooled their scarce resources so that they could access basic goods at lower prices and retain their economic autonomy. The Pioneers believed that shoppers should be able to share in the profits they created and should have a say in the business so that every customer became a member. By the 1930s the Rochdale method was growing with institutions like the Central Cooperative Wholesale in the US developing entire regional economies based upon it. In 1937 the International Cooperative Alliance officially endorsed the Rochdale derived principles, which remain in use by co-ops around the world. These are: voluntary and open membership; democratic member control; member economic participation; autonomy and independence; education, training and information; cooperation among cooperatives; and concern for community.

According to the International Cooperative Alliance (ICA) there are now more than 3 million cooperatives operating around the world, all of which are based on the values of self-responsibility, democracy, equality, equity and solidarity. Media co-ops are on the rise. The Global Newsletter for the International Organisation of Industrial and

Service Cooperatives (CICOPA) reported that in 2017 there had been a 27 per cent increase in co-ops in the field of information and communications around the world, with many emerging in response to the need to preserve pluralism, escape commercial and state pressures and ensure independent journalism. Most of these are worker cooperatives with democratic governance at their core. Part of the growth is due to the emergence of platform cooperatives where users and/or workers ultimately own and control the platforms or mobile app (Scholz and Schneider, 2017) to trade, connect people and pool resources or data.

While these developments are interesting, it is not always clear how meaningful the democratic ownership and governance of co-ops is in practice. There are many different types of co-ops offering different forms of democratic governance. Multi-stakeholder co-ops have a broader membership and can include workers, service users, volunteers, local authorities, etc., and hence provide the most inclusive form of democratic governance involving the communities within which they are embedded. Worker co-ops are owned and run by the people who work in them who have an equal say in what the organization does and how it develops as well as an equitable share of the wealth created. Worker co-ops are not without criticism and have been variously described as being too small-scale to make any difference, too weak to counteract capital (Hahnel, 2005) and even as a means of revitalizing capitalism by improving employee morale (Reeves, 2007).

In the UK, *The Bristol Cable* is changing the face of local journalism as a grassroots community-led media cooperative. It prints a free quarterly magazine with a circulation of approximately 30,000 copies and publishes investigative and community-led journalism regularly online. It prioritizes holding power to account through investigations, raising up marginalized voices and community engagement. It also delivers free media training, equipping local people with the skills to report on issues that are important to them. It is funded by over 2,500 members, each paying a small monthly fee (who all have a say and own an equal share in the co-op), by foundation support and crowd funding. Income is also generated from advertising in the print edition regulated by an ethical advertising charter determined collectively by its members. Each year its members vote on the annual budget, the overall focus for content and on the makeup of the board of directors. They also have a collectively decided ethical advertising charter. They rely on a strong online presence alongside face-to-face engagement and monthly community meetings and have also developed a membership platform that allows them to store member data securely without the risk of it being sold to advertisers. The team is paid a real living wage, and freelancers get competitive rates, but they are also aware that they need to do more to diversify the range of people involved. They insist on democratic decision-making throughout the organization. They believe that having members isn't just a good way to fund journalism but improves what gets produced. By giving members a say in how stories are selected and framed, journalism is able to meet the needs of those communities.

The impact of this kind of reporting became clear during protests against the controversial Police, Crime, Sentencing and Courts Bill in its final legislative stages of enactment. The Bill (now an Act) adds to already increased restrictions on the right to protest and call strike action. In early 2021 in Bristol (as in many other cities around the UK) people took to the streets to oppose the Bill's additional restrictions to the right to protest and the expansive policing and sentencing powers it included, ones that would further entrench racial disparity in the criminal justice system. Today, the Act enables the police to impose a start and finish time to static protests, set noise limits and apply these rules to a demonstration of just one person. It has made it an offence to 'intentionally or recklessly cause public nuisance', a move designed to stop people occupying public spaces, blocking roads or employing other noisy and 'annoying' tactics to get their voice heard. During protests against the Bill mainstream media generally reproduced police press releases that misrepresented the number of police injuries, until reporters from the *Bristol Cable*, who were present on the ground, were able to provide more accurate coverage.

The *Bristol Cable* most closely fits the description of a multi-stakeholder cooperative (MSC) whose membership includes both the workers and readers. The first multi-stakeholder cooperatives emerged in Italy in the 1990s and are often referred to as social co-ops set up to provide a range of social services such as care, prison services and mental health provision. Their memberships can include workers, service users, volunteers, local authorities, etc., and they provide the most inclusive form of democratic governance involving the communities they are embedded within. MSCs also offer a means of financial sustainability through membership payments. *The New Internationalist*, a magazine on human rights, politics and social justice, describes itself as one of the largest media cooperatives in the world. Founded in 1973, it became a workers' co-op in 1992 and then an MSC in 2017; by 2024 it had more than 4,600 co-owners who have a say in how the magazine develops and enabling them to do more investigative and long-form journalism.

Worker co-ops are owned and run by the people who work in them, who have an equal say in what the organization does, how it develops and an equitable share of the wealth created. In Cairo the online news site *Mada* was born out of the crisis in 2013 and formed by a group of journalists who had lost their jobs and were worried about the future of independent journalism in Egypt. They describe their journalism as the kind that constantly challenges, raises questions and proposes different possibilities. They operate an open and ongoing editorial conversation on the ethics of their journalism, especially with regard to protecting the rights of the oppressed and the vulnerable and preserving the privacy of sources. The workers own and run the business themselves, collectively. In Uruguay, the daily newspaper *La Diaria* was formed in 2010 as a worker cooperative focusing on independent journalism that is critical of the establishment and seeking social transformation. It has become the country's second most read daily news publication (CICOPA, 2019). In 2023 it had 20,000 subscribers.

Media coops like those referred to above are trying to figure out what workplace democracy could be in the media industry – from who gets to do what jobs to who makes decisions on content and resource distribution. A substantive commitment to democracy inside media organizations would enable the broadening of a range of voices involved in decision-making that, in turn, would help to ensure that our media systems meet a wider range of needs and serve a more diverse set of interests. To guard against this evaporating into the 'diversity washing' of liberal pluralism (whereby employing a few more women or people of colour is seen to do the job), it must be based on ownership models premised on genuine democratic collectivism. This links the traditions of labour struggle and unions traditionally associated with issues of work and wealth, class and poverty, to a broader politics of status and (mis) recognition associated with race and patriarchal heteronormativity. Media co-ops are collectively owned and controlled. There is no employer and employee but a membership of worker-owners. The media worker is no longer solely answerable to capital; rather, capital serves the cooperative, which is democratically organized and governed. Linking this to theories of the commons, de Peuter and Dyer-Witherford (2010, p. 45) talk of the worker co-ops where the 'workplace is an *organizational commons*, the labour performed is a *commoning practice*, and the surplus generated, a *commonwealth*' to build what Gibson-Graham (2006, p. 125) calls a 'generative commons'. Power is shared and powerlessness addressed.

Other examples can be drawn from digital platforms. The Platform Cooperativism Consortium (2019) website suggests that platform co-ops reject an online economy based on short-term profits for the few in favour of a digital economy for all based on cooperative principles 'such as democratic ownership and governance . . . economic fairness, training and democratic participation'. Platform co-ops are a response to the gig economy and the Uber-ization of everything. Characterized by insecure, temporary and freelance contracts, the gig economy has increased the number of jobs and kept unemployment low but has also further eroded basic workers' rights (Armstrong, 2018) as well as contributing to consumer concerns over safety and accountability. Zero-hours and short-hours contracts, the norm of the gig economy, have disrupted dominant markets and have both exploited and contributed to a low-wage workforce, with Uber growing dominant in personal transportation services and take-away food services like Deliveroo gaining popularity. Often such workers are forced into 'self-employment' by employers keen to reduce their tax liability, avoid paying the minimum wage and deny workers' rights. In the UK, the TUC (2018) noted that of 4 million adults over twenty-five classified as self-employed, 49 per cent (1.96 million) are earning less than the minimum wage. Platform co-ops offer a potential route to a fairer, more inclusive digital economy with tangible benefits for workers and users but they also struggle to raise the money needed to start and scale up (Borkin, 2019).

Muldoon (2022) argues persuasively that most people now agree that tech companies control the digital infrastructure of twenty-first-century social life but disagree about what to do about it. Should we encourage digital literacy and learn how to protect ourselves? Should we increase privacy rights? Or, should we use digital hacks to stop us spending excessive amounts of time on screen? All of these potential solutions, Muldoon suggests, offer individualized responses that miss accounting for the structural requirements of the industry based on a capitalist model of private ownership of digital assets and the pursuit of shareholder profit from the data we provide them. An anti-trust agenda that seeks to limit monopolies and break up big tech may well restore competition and bring increased plurality to the tech sector, limiting the dominance of these companies and their ability to act as gatekeepers to the marketplace. But, while this may improve consumer services, it does not ultimately shift the focus to tech working for people and for the common good. Consequently, we need to think beyond competition and beyond the market and turn our attention to non-commodified versions of a digital economy based on social ownership of digital assets and democratic control over digital infrastructure and systems.

Similarly, we need to acknowledge that while cooperativism may seek to address powerlessness and augment 'power to', it will never be enough. Indeed, cooperativism has been around for a long time without making any noticeable dent in the past two centuries of capitalism. One of the reasons for this is that it does not seek to address dominant forms of 'power over'. Muldoon (2022) deals with this by bringing ownership and democratic governance to the fore for all tech industries, but this framework could also be applied to media organizations more generally. Drawing on the history of the workers' movement and the theorists G. D. H. Cole (based on socialist pluralism) and Otto Neurath (based on democratic planning and resource allocation), Muldoon (2022, p. 5) points to six main goals:

> freedom as collective self-determination through participatory governance;
> social ownership over assets;
> community control over (digital) services;
> equal distribution of social value produced from tech (or media);
> combatting of power inequalities based on social hierarchies;
> culture of solidarity collaboration and hope.

Lawrence and Laybourn-Langton (2019) agree with Muldoon, arguing that if we want to change the way platform companies behave and ensure that the mass of data we now have is used to help us solve planetary and social problems: 'we will have to reshape the governance and ownership of digitally generated data and the underlying infrastructure. In short, we must overthrow the data oligarchs and build a digital commons' (Lawrence, 2019).

Democratizing platforms and media organizations means radical reform of media ownership – from the few to the many. This might mean worker ownership, municipal ownership or hybrid models that include users, producers and consumers. Larger platforms with big infrastructure could be owned by larger associations at the regional or state level. It also means radical reform of media industry governance based on inclusivity of all those who are impacted by operations of the platform, including workers.

Conclusion: A democratic media for a transformative democracy

Locating a discussion of democracy in the concepts of power and powerlessness brings to the fore the need to attend to the balances of power between people, state institutions and markets with care. A discussion of the meaning of democracy as an ideal and as a practice requires a questioning of not only what we mean by power and powerlessness but how these are distributed across society and with what consequences. Dussel's (2008) notion of political power argues that democracy's main concern is not with whether or not power should be exercised but rather the manner in which it is exercised – this follows from Arendt's (1970, p. 39) rejection of the anarchist view that power is always a 'form of mitigated violence'. Rather, she conceptualizes power democratically as a means of cultivating freedom – the power to realize your capacity to participate in the shaping of social life. Hence power is relational, and our critique of it should be directed to the ways in which people's capacities are limited or constrained and whose interests are being served by the exercise of power in different situations.

In other words, when we critique democracy, media and power we must also address powerlessness. When we do so, the pursuit of democratic media also becomes the pursuit of social justice through the rectification of power imbalances and extends beyond the liberal normative principle of journalism 'holding power to account'. In this manner social theory tackles democracy seriously as a problem to be solved rather than merely a utopian ideal. Power and democracy are not mutually exclusive but *inter*dependent on each other. How this interdependence is manifest and managed will have consequences for how powerless people are in our mediated worlds. It is in this understanding of the interdependency of media power and democracy that we are able to reimagine what a democratic media might become.

The sort of critical analysis applied in this book recognizes that the balance between *power over* and the *power to* shifts over time, space and in particular political conjunctures. In many Western states, the delusion of liberal deliberative democracy that insists we have more choice, more creative control and that the public sphere is expanded in the digital age has become enmeshed within a neoliberal hegemony that conveniently avoids acknowledging that both 'states and subjects are [still] organized by market rationality' (Brown, 2005, p. 48) in ways that limit (but do not cancel out) our ideological imaginations.

How, then, can media and cultural studies offer substance to the democratic project? This chapter has introduced the necessity of the reinvention of *a democratic media that works for democracy* by recognizing powerlessness and redistributing power accordingly. Democracy that speaks to the capacity of people to act collectively and bring about change requires a reckoning with power.

Further, for a renewed transformative democracy to work, its institutional translation must not end in institutional power for itself; rather it must create the means whereby the potential for everyone to share in power is realized. Democracy cannot work for some and not for others. The next chapter on participation and exclusion deals with this theme.

3

POLITICAL PARTICIPATION AND POLITICAL EXCLUSIONS

A (neo)liberal democracy depends on citizen participation in systems of representation. At a basic level, citizens participate by voting for elected politicians, who are then supposed to represent the interests of their constituencies. Prospective parliamentarians must try to convince voters that they have the right agenda that can best meet their concerns. They are then enabled to rule over the electorate who have given legitimacy (albeit fleeting and momentary) to their chosen government. And yet, such aspirations and norms have been challenged as political elites remodel themselves as a professional class and distance themselves further from the electorate; as non-democratic agencies and practices proliferate and influence political processes; and as inequality increases, excluding ever more people from activities of citizenship (Davis et al., 2020). The 'disconnect' (Kundnani, 2020) between citizens and political elites is becoming a chasm. In this sense, as Badiou notes, electoral democracy 'is not representative except to the extent that it is the consensual representation of capitalism' (cited in Agamben et al., 2011, p. 22). And it is not participatory except to the extent that it confers legitimacy to political elites.

But, as noted in the previous chapter, democracy seen differently, as something that refers to the rule of the people by the people, infers a very different type of participation, one that involves building something together in a constant process of reflection and renewal and that involves cooperation among equals who may have deep disagreements about what constitutes the common good. It has an egalitarian principle at heart that seeks to permanently challenge and transgress its instituted forms (Agamben et al., 2011), unsettle universalism through constant recognition of difference and permanently struggle for routes to equality and citizenship. Seen in this way, a democratic society functions through a sense of justice that is endlessly renewed through broad participation in public forms of deliberation and political engagement that cannot be confined to electoral cycles. Both conceptions of democracy depend on adequate information and understanding of what is at stake in the decisions being made for the various forms of participation to be democratically meaningful. This is where the role of our systems of media and communications come in. Of course, what constitutes *adequate* information and *how* we gain understanding are hotly contested topics that in recent times have led to what has been called 'the culture wars' (discussed in Chapter 4).

Questions of participation in relation to media and communications relate both to media content and the means of communication and invariably centre their attention on technology. Every time a new form of technology emerges, our hopes are raised by eager optimists who herald its participatory and hence liberatory potential. From radio, to community television, to hand-held video cameras to YouTube – the more participatory possibilities technologies offer, the more democratic they are assumed to be because their content is considered to be more wide-ranging and their production processes more diverse (Curran, Fenton and Freedman, 2012). In the age of the internet and social media we are encouraged to think about how technology-enabled processes and practices enhance (or restrain) citizen participation and civic agency; how technical affordances of particular platforms lend themselves to citizen engagement (or not); how algorithms govern and automate decision-making to the detriment of democratic principles (or facilitate choice). These concerns became ever more urgent during the global pandemic (see Chapter 7), when so many had to rely so heavily on digital communications for education, work, social life and healthcare. With the experience of home-working, quarantine and self-isolation, we experienced, ever more keenly, the importance of our digital connections for participation (of any kind) in so many of the activities of daily life as well as the global, national and local inequalities that the lack of digital connection exposes. This has further revealed the paucity of, and problems with, the sorts of participatory engagement digital lives so often bring.

Unequal access to political participation inevitably produces political silences and exclusions that are as relevant in the world of media and communications as they are in any industry. But as our lives are ever more digitally mediated, exclusions from participation in media and communications increasingly influence all aspects of life. Just as patterns of economic inequality are replicated in relation to access to health care and educational attainment, so too, they map onto access to technology (Pew Research Center, 2021b) and the ability to navigate the information and communication privileges it brings. The more digitally entrenched our lives become, the more digital inequalities are enmeshed with and heighten patterns of inequality in all aspects of our lives. So the digital divide becomes an ever more glaring reality (Graham and Dittus, 2022) with one-third of the world's population unconnected to the internet in 2022 (ITU, 2023). The ITU 2023 report notes that although internet use in increasing, regular internet users are still, in general, younger, more highly educated and richer than non-users, and are more likely to be men than women as well as to live in cities.

This chapter charts some of these exclusions and discusses how they impact on citizen participation. It documents how these exclusions impoverish and hollow out notions and practices of participation, noting how these mistakes are endlessly replicated in responses to the lack of political engagement through processes like e-politics that promise technological fixes for much broader social and political issues. We then turn to areas where the harms of exclusionary practices have been recognized and attempts at participatory practices have taken root and suggest ways in which these could be adapted and implemented in our media worlds in order to render participation transformational. But first we turn to how participation has been conceptualized and what we can learn from these debates.

What do we mean by participation?

Participation has been theorized in many different ways and disciplines (Carpentier and Dahlgren, 2013). Here, I am interested in political participation linked to notions of democracy and its practice, and the role of the media therein. As such, I am not focusing on participation in culture and civil society more broadly, a focus that may concern itself with a wider and more nebulous notion of participation, for example, as engagement with the arts and with sport. Participation in culture can be as wide-ranging as watching films, listening to music and visiting museums; undoubtedly, these play an important part in how we approach our political lives on a daily basis. Chapter 5 addresses concerns of inequality and discrimination in relation to the broader issues that cultural democracy brings into play. But here

I am considering political participation as our interactions with and influence on the *institutionalized exercise of power*. This may include the ways in which governing authorities have made access to information and voting easier through digital platforms, or how political parties have tried to address issues of participation among their own members, or how social movements attempt to influence power.

There are clearly qualitatively different levels of political participation. Pateman's (1970) influential book *Participation and Democratic Theory* sets out how power is at the heart of defining whether political participation is partial or full. According to Pateman, partial participation ultimately relinquishes power to one person or group over another, where 'two or more parties influence each other in the making of decisions but the final power to decide rests with one party only' (p. 70). Full participation, by contrast, is 'a process where each individual member of a decision-making body has equal power to determine the outcome of decisions' (p. 71). Such a notion of full participation has been embraced by many social movements seeking to adopt a more horizontalist form of democracy (see Fenton, 2016). There are clearly many degrees of participation between partial and full, but we can safely say that voting for governments in general elections once every five years on manifesto pledges that may never be realized and in which the electorate will likely play no further part is at the minimal end of the spectrum and entrusts the majority of people with little power. Indeed, for many political leaders, this may be precisely what they want. Representative democracies have long been criticized for offering the illusion of participation without conferring any actual power on citizens to change anything (e.g. Williams, 1963).

Sherry Arnstein's (1969) influential ladder of citizen participation describes how public institutions and officials deny power to citizens and how levels of citizen agency can be increased by equating citizen participation with citizen power. Arnstein opens her article with a key question: '*What* is citizen participation and what is its relationship to the social imperatives of our time?' She goes on to argue that citizen participation is equated to citizen power where the have-nots who are excluded from political and economic processes are deliberately included in the future for the purposes of 'determining how information is shared, goals and policies are set, tax resources are allocated, programs are operated, and benefits like contracts and patronage are parceled out', stating that 'participation without redistribution of power is an empty and frustrating process for the powerless' (p. 216). Arnstein's typology of citizen participation is presented as a metaphorical 'ladder', with each ascending rung representing increasing levels of citizen agency, control and power. She includes a descriptive continuum of participatory power that moves from *nonparticipation* (no power) at the bottom of the ladder, which includes therapy and manipulation; to *degrees of tokenism* (pseudo power), which includes, informing, consultation and placation; to *degrees of citizen participation* (actual power) at the top of the ladder, which includes partnership, delegated power and citizen control.

So power, as discussed in the previous chapter, is central to our analysis of political participation. Considered in relation to something like public service broadcasting (PSB), at the top of the ladder 'the public' would be involved in governance, programming, commissioning and scheduling; they would be in charge of policy and direction, and would be able to negotiate the conditions under which those outside the public service broadcaster might change these policies and direction through processes of accountability. In citizen-control situations, for example, public funding (distributed in a participatory and democratic way) would flow directly to a community radio station or a local newspaper, and that organization (and its publics) would have full control over how that funding is spent. At the bottom of the ladder lies 'illusory' forms of participation. Here we find *manipulation* when public institutions, officials or administrators mislead citizens into believing that they are being given power in a process that has been intentionally manufactured to deny them power in the name of citizen participation. So people are put on advisory committees or boards to engineer their support when in reality these are no more than rubber-stamp committees such that 'the bottom rung of the ladder signifies the distortion of participation into a public relations vehicle by powerholders' (Arnstein, 1969, p. 218).

However, while power is seen as a central concept in theories of participation, it is rarely adequately theorized and does not address the depths, complexities and origins of power and powerlessness (as discussed in Chapter 2). Arnstein notes that the ladder does not include an analysis of the 'roadblocks' to authentic citizen participation and empowerment on both the side of the power-holders such as 'racism, paternalism and resistance to power redistribution; as well as on the side of the have-nots' such as 'inadequacies of the poor community's political socioeconomic infrastructure and knowledge-base, plus difficulties of organizing a representative and accountable citizens' group in the face of futility, alienation and distrust' (Arnstein, 1969, p. 217). While *citizen control* appears at the apex of the ladder, and it offers many advantages as a model of citizen participation, Arnstein points out several potential disadvantages, including supporting separatism, creating balkanization of public services, being more costly and less efficient and enabling 'minority group "hustlers" to be just as opportunistic and disdainful of the have-nots as their white predecessors' (Arnstein, 1969, p. 224).

Arnstein's critique alerts us to the fact that before we get to the *how* of participation, we must first consider the *who* of participation (not only who in the human race but also non-humans and future generations). When considering the who, we need to take account of who *is* able and who *should* be able to participate. It is helpful here to draw on Robert Dahl's (1970, p. 49) discussion of 'affected interests'. The principle of affected interests follows the ideas embedded in the simple claim of 'no taxation without representation' – in other words, anyone who is affected by the decisions of a government (or organization) should have the right to participate in that government (or organization). This is enticingly simple but fraught with problems – not least in a globalized economy where citizens may be affected by the activities of a global corporation (from Shell to Apple and Walmart to Amazon) but have no means of holding them to account. Dahl addresses three further problems: the principle implies that the set of people affected differs from one decision to another; it fails to recognize that people affected by a decision may not be affected equally; and ignores that what affects your interest may rely upon highly subjective factors (such as forms of media representation, etc.). In other words, political participation is generally much messier than these sorts of definitions or typologies suggest (Carpentier, 2016).

What does this mean for political participation?

Accounts relating to political participation point to two apparently contrary contemporary developments: the decline of voter participation and engagement with formal representative political systems, and the increase in social movements and protest politics. In a study that looked at elections in 116 democratic countries around the world, Kostelka and Blais (2021) note that in the late 1960s, more than 77 per cent of citizens typically voted in national legislative and presidential elections. After 2010, however, the global average voting rate fell to 67 per cent, with the poorest least likely to vote. Low and unequal turnout then leads to ever more excluded communities, since politicians tend to engage with the groups they perceive to be their active supporters, cultivating fertile ground for clientelism and patronage. So perhaps it should come as no surprise that a decline in participation in formal institutionalized politics points to a decline of trust in party-based political systems and a turn to 'life-politics' outside of the political establishment. A survey based on twenty-two OECD countries in 2020 notes that only 51 per cent of citizens trusted their national government (OECD, 2021). In the UK, research has noted that in 1944 one in three British people (35 per cent) saw politicians as 'merely out for themselves'; by 2014 this had risen to 48 per cent and by 2021 to 63 per cent (Quilter-Pinner et al., 2021). The authors warn that declining political trust is associated with rises in disengagement from the political system, populism and the polarization of society.

This increasing bifurcation of political life also speaks to the common problem of how to theorize the relationship between the participation and influence of social movements and the institutionalized exercise of power in governments. This reflects the debate in the preceding chapter regarding whether or not democracy refers to forms of governance or forces of democratization that reach beyond state forms in social movements and counter public spheres. The former may seek a widening (albeit controlled and limited) level of participation in order to effect the *exercise of power* in a certain direction but the latter actively seek extended levels of deliberative participation to reap enhanced *influence of power*.

Political participation has also been heralded as being enhanced via new technologies that have enabled e-government and opened up access to government business in unprecedented ways. They were central to the Obama's administration concept of 'open government' that became the open government initiative joined by many countries seeking to increase citizen participation and fight government corruption. In 2011, Iceland produced the first crowdsourced constitutional proposal in the world. In Spain, Podemos used digital platforms to increase citizen participation in policymaking and prioritization (Gerbaudo, 2017). Taiwan has been leading experiments with digital democracy since 2014, when activists involved with the Sunflower Movement were invited to collaborate with government. Using a platform called vTaiwan established by a civil society movement called g0v, citizens have been able to inform and guide government policy on a range of issues, such as whether Uber should be allowed to operate in the country. It does this by creating several stages, including an initial 'objective' stage for crowdsourcing facts and evidence, and a 'reflective' stage using the mass deliberation tool Pol.is, which encourages the formation of 'rough consensus'. Finally, key stakeholders are invited to a livestreamed, face-to-face meeting to draw up specific recommendations.

Outside of official institutions of power, participation in and through social movements also attaches hope to the emancipatory possibilities of new technology. Once more, this is not without substance. Greater connectivity has enabled activists the world over to reach across space at great speed and share content to mobilize people in huge numbers – the Arab Spring (Aouragh, 2011), the Umbrella movement in Hong Kong (Lee and Chan, 2018), the MeToo movement (Boyle, 2019) as well as climate action groups in the US and Europe (Fisher and Nasrin, 2021), to name but a few, have all put social media to good effect. In the United States, hundreds of thousands of people in more than 2,000 localities across the country protested the killing of Black Americans such as George Floyd and Breonna Taylor by police officers. The wave of public grief and fury marked a level of protest exceeding that of previous US protests against police brutality and were enabled by social media that facilitated protests to reverberate beyond US borders (Jackson et al., 2020). At least sixteen countries – ranging from the UK and France to Australia, Brazil, Japan, Kenya and South Africa – saw major demonstrations over police violence against Black or minoritized populations and related issues, such as systemic racism and the mass incarceration of marginalized communities.

However, these participatory advantages come at a high cost: as the profusion of content swamps the internet and floods our platforms, the public sphere has been both fractured and negated. As the architecture of social media platforms seeks to broaden its capture of and deepen its hold on our attention to sell to advertisers, so it builds filter bubbles and echo chambers where we 'like' those who 'like' us back. Social media platforms shape what we get to see and do online. Fractures can lead easily to splintering of opinions and sometimes violent polarization of political viewpoints. The more vicious the disagreement the more traction the posting will garner, the more data is captured, the more advertising revenue flows in. Chun (Chun and Barnett, 2021, p. 6) notes how ProPublica's 2017 investigation into Facebook revealed that Facebook '"helpfully" suggested that their reporters add "How to burn Jews" and "Second Amendment" to "Jew hater" in order to boost their ad's target audience size'. In the world of social media, outrage has become profitable. The so-called public sphere – the space where we are all supposed to be able to evaluate a wide range of information and opinion through rational deliberation

– is dissipated. Others point to the weaponization of social media to subvert elections and undermine democratic processes as discussed in Chapter 2 (Sloss, 2022). Whom should we believe? Whom can we trust? Misinformation (honest mistakes), disinformation (intentional deception) and fake news (wholly fabricated information) become impossible to tell apart (see Chapter 7). State-sponsored propaganda merges into mainstream media narratives.

And statecraft is big business in the digital age. The pandemic, the war in Ukraine and the Israel–Gaza conflict have ushered in ever more covert operations on social media. In the UK, psyops (military-grade psychological operations) are the purpose of the British army's 77th Brigade, which is based at Denison Barracks in Berkshire, southern England. In a 2018 speech, the chief of the General Staff, General Nicholas Carter, dubbed it an 'information warfare' initiative, affording the military 'the capability to compete in the war of narratives at the tactical level . . . Twitter troops . . . shaping behaviours through the use of dynamic narratives' (Carter, 2018). While citizens experience tidal waves of unverifiable information, participation often feels like a being sucked into a whirlpool of information chaos that disorients you and drags you deeper into the digital maelstrom in a never-ending spiral of doom scrolling that knows no end and likely leaves you none the wiser.

Inequality and participatory exclusion

Participation is closely connected to socio-economic inequalities. As noted above, the poorer you are, the less likely you are to vote. But the participatory exclusions extend far beyond elections. Numerous studies have evidenced how inequality makes certain political subjects less visible and excludes others altogether. Wilkinson and Pickett's (2009) ground-breaking study shows how economic inequality damages our societies, our economies and our democratic systems. Inequality is a form of political evacuation – it pushes people out of the possibilities of political participation. In the UK, several reports (e.g. IPPR, 2018) identify deep alienation among many people when it comes to politics, alienation that is exacerbated by poverty and is profoundly damaging for democracy. They reveal people in communities who are isolated (Pyle and Evans, 2018) and lonely (HM Government, 2018) and document how public life is increasingly hollowed out of meaningful participation (Commission on the Future of Localism, 2018). Prominent reports in the UK have observed, '[t]he need for change; the need to seek the voice of marginalized and disadvantaged people in decision-making processes is of undeniable and acute local, national and global relevance' (RSA, 2016).

Civil society groups are often where the work to address these democratic deficits takes place. Yet research into civil society activity has shown that if you are poor and preoccupied with putting food on the table then you are less likely to be involved in civil society activities (Mohan and Breeze, 2016). Further research has shown that the ability of British civil society to play an active role in democratic processes has been significantly reduced over the past decade. The reports produced by the Panel on the Independence of the Voluntary Sector from 2013 to 2016 found that its independence of voice had declined each year that they reported (Panel on the Independence of the Voluntary Sector, 2016). The UN special rapporteur described 'the closing space for civil society' in the UK (Kiai, 2017, p. 18) mirroring growing attacks on freedom of assembly and expression across the globe (CAF, 2017). This highlights the need to look at civil society from both an empirical perspective – what is happening to, and in, civil society today, and where this trajectory might be leading – as well as from a normative one, linking it to questions of power and social justice, and what civil society needs to do to in order to help create futures that address these deficits.

However, if we want to answer the question of how we can better intervene in society and who has the power to bring about social change, we first have to answer the question of why certain citizens and forms of civil society have been largely excluded from political participation.

Civil society and participation

If people feel that their political participation in society is at best minimal then the role of civil society organisations (CSOs) in highlighting and ameliorating social inequalities and political injustices (Civil Society Futures, 2018) is ever more important. Notions of civil society, its purpose and how we conceptualize it, change over time and speak not just to traditional ideas of associational life – that part of society that sits between the state and the market, most commonly referred to as the 'voluntary', 'third', 'NGO' or 'non-profit' sector, where people come together for uncoerced human association, but also to a whole host of other activities: from running the local football team to welcome groups for refugees. My own research also indicates a sense of civil society as something that runs counter to particular ideologies derived from competitive individualism and me-first approaches to life deemed dominant for too long. This is a conception of civil society driven more by a values-based understanding of what makes the 'good society'. It is not necessarily connected to philanthropic impulses – the desire to do good – but rather it is concerned with practices and the promotion of social norms of tolerance, non-discrimination, cooperation and trust. The notion of civil society as the 'good society' can also be indicative of a perception that a profound lack of trust, tolerance and cooperation is pervasive in a deeply unequal society, coupled with a strong desire for a different way of living based on kindness, compassion and understanding alongside the need for systemic change (Civil Society Futures, 2018).

Bound up with each of these interpretations is the clear sense of civil society as public sphere – the space where people come together to gain understanding, learn about difference and engage with systems of power. It is in these spaces where civil society as the good society meets new forms of politics, economics and public policy that hold the possibility of translating into better forms of democracy. Such ideas form the basis for the current resurgence of interest in new forms of civic agency, participatory democracy, cooperative practices and renewed forms of self-determination. The common denominator across all these initiatives is more power in the hands of more people to shape the decisions that affect their lives, thus creating new publics in the process. 'In this sense civil society – as a set of capacities – and politics – as a set of processes – become united in the public sphere, providing an essential antidote to the depoliticisation and fatalism that are so marked in contemporary societies' (Edwards, 2014, p. 63). Yet CSOs' own activities are subject to instability, inequality and segregation in the digital age, leaving them often ill-placed to respond adequately to social and political need.

Depoliticization of civil society

When we look closely at political agency in civil society in the UK, there is clear evidence that British civil society has become *less* able to play an active role in democratic processes over the past decade as digital tools have multiplied. Rather, civil society has seen a deliberate hollowing-out of its ability to 'be political' (Kiai,

2017). This has included legislation such as the Lobbying Act, which has had a 'chilling effect' on civil society campaigning (Sheila McKechnie Foundation, 2018); New Grants Standards, which have restricted recipients of public money if they engage in 'advocacy' (Slocock, 2017); the extension of the Preventing Violent Extremism agenda, which has disproportionately been used to target Muslim organizations (IHRC, 2019); and increasing restrictions on the right to protest (see below). Registered charities have faced particular hostility from government ministers for being 'too political' (Panel on the Independence of the Voluntary Sector, 2016). The Charity Commission has increasingly scrutinized charitable campaigning and issued guidance for the Brexit referendum and the 2019 General Election that implied a more restrictive interpretation of charity law than previously, actively discouraging registered charities from campaigning around issues that matter to them during an election period. Challenging powerful institutions in the UK is increasingly seen as outside the boundaries of legitimate civil society, which are being ever more tightly drawn in favour of those that pose little or no threat to established structures of power.

The depoliticization of civil society has come within the context of austerity policies and over ten years of economic stagnation that have increased demands upon civil society while reducing its capacity to meet these demands, including the ability to campaign for change. These pressures were exacerbated by Covid-19, which extended concerns of financial sustainability for the charity sector (Murray, 2020), while centring digital solutions as the answer to restrictions on physical contact.

My own research as part of the Civil Society Futures inquiry (Civil Society Futures, 2018)[1] found that CSOs were often struggling to cope with restrictions on funding, the loss of public spaces, the impacts of public spending cuts and increased difficulties in finding volunteers, given ever-more precarious work conditions. In addition, it found that there was a widespread sense that it was illegitimate for these organizations to undertake activities that could be considered 'political', stating that government policy was an inhibiting factor in their work. This was found to be a major block on their ability to effectively achieve their aims, such as protecting the natural world or addressing social inequalities. The research captured the more diffuse impacts of these changes on the political activity of smaller CSOs and identified the multiple levels of silencing experienced by these groups, where the pressure to stop or avoid political activities was accompanied by additional injunctions – often implicit – to not speak publicly about how their work was being affected. These dynamics often undermined their ability to act in ways that would most effectively generate social change.

Within this broader context of limited political voice and agency, the research showed the crucial but ambiguous role that digital communications play for these small CSOs. In their digital presence civil society groups reported forms of *algorithmic silencing*, where several CSOs experienced a marked reduction in their online reach as a result of algorithmic changes within Facebook. One organization had their relevancy score downgraded so the content was only being shown to 1–2 per cent of their page's followers, with the only option for improving their 'relevance' being to pay to boost their content so it would be seen and shared by more people, a payment they could not afford. Overall, a common theme was that contrary to oft-held assumptions regarding the expansion of voice in the digital age, on the ground *both* political agency *and* digital voice have shrunk in recent years for many civil society groups and organizations. This shrinkage is a consequence of government policies that deter and constrain civil society activity directed at actual social change (because they are 'too political') and a communications system that rewards only those with large and established followings (because they are more attractive to advertisers).

Legislative frameworks of constraint and repression

Attempts to repress the political activity of civil society has been accompanied by more aggressive policing and the criminalization of protest. In many parts of the world, the freedom to protest has come under threat. In the UK, new powers for the police over protests and new sentences for associated crimes were introduced in the controversial Police, Crime, Sentencing and Courts Act 2022, as noted in Chapter 2. Meanwhile, a new Elections Act 2022 (House of Commons, 2022) infringes on the right to vote by introducing the requirement to show voter ID, in a bid to tackle the nearly non-existent problem of voter fraud. The result is that disproportionately minoritized and working-class Britons without photo identification are being deprived of the most basic of democratic rights. Each of these legal frameworks amounts to an extension of the scaffolding of political constraint and repression introduced to deal with the problems that a neoliberal politics of austerity have engendered. These frameworks of constraint and repression are heavily racialized and discriminatory. For example, figures for 2019–20 in England and Wales show that Black people are nine times more likely to be stopped and searched by the police than white people over suspicion of possessing drugs (Home Office, 2020) and far more likely to be sent to prison for drug offences than white offenders (Sentencing Council, 2020). The government's increasing powers during the pandemic have been applied through the same racist prism. Even as crime levels fell during the first lockdown, stop and search more than doubled, with Black people in London up to eleven times more likely to be targeted (Harris et al., 2021).

Attempts to police people's participation are also deeply enmeshed with our digital activities. Research points to how software analyses of large sets of historical crime data are used for predictive policing to forecast where crime is likely to occur, perpetuating a vicious cycle of excessive surveillance and scrutiny in minoritized and poorer neighbourhoods (O'Neil, 2016) that is often strikingly unreliable and reinforces discriminatory policing practices (Angwin et al., 2016). Thus, as should be clear from the above discussion, when we talk about political participation and political exclusions we are not only talking about access to resources, we are also talking about social and communicative justice.

Communicative oppression and communicative justice

Many theories on conceptions of social justice focus on the socio-structural dimensions of exclusion that pivot on distribution of economic resources. However, Iris Marion Young is an exception. She argues that 'justice should refer not only to distribution, but also to the institutional conditions necessary for the development and exercise of individual capacities and collective communication and cooperation' (Young, 2022, p. 3). Young understands justice to consist of the social and institutional conditions necessary for achieving both non-domination and non-oppression, where the latter means the achievement of human flourishing, for all members of society. She displaces the distributive paradigm for analysing justice, which concentrates on allocations of material goods, to focus instead on the contributions made to the pursuit of justice by decision-making processes, divisions of labour, and culture – of which digital communication systems clearly play a major part. She pays close attention to oppression, which she divides into five aspects (exploitation, marginalization, powerlessness, cultural imperialism and violence), and uses this analysis of oppression to identify as political a range of phenomena that had conventionally been seen by political philosophers as 'merely social'.

Young argues that inclusive forms of communication are a vital means to alleviate marginalization and exclusion that come as a result of entrenched systems of oppression enabling the marginalized to be seen and known. She speaks of barriers to access of communication that are material, geographic and informational. While Young's focus is face-to-face communication, this can easily pertain to media and digital exclusions: material exclusion relates to the cost of computer or mobile hardware; geographic exclusion could refer to the lack of broadband or absence of newspapers in certain areas; and informational exclusion to not knowing how to search effectively for information in a context of online abundance. Both the material and the geographic have traditionally been conceived of as part of the 'digital divide' that often points to the multiple ways in which economic inequality maps onto information and technology inequalities (Trappel, 2019). In many parts of the world the basic cost of connectivity excludes people from participation. Graham and Dittus (2022) note that almost all of the countries with an internet usage rate of above 75 per cent are found in Europe or North America, and more than half of all African countries only have an internet penetration usage rate of under 25 per cent. In certain regions of the world such as parts of Africa and the broader Global South the cost of fixed broadband is more than the average monthly wage and deemed unaffordable in 56 per cent of world economies (ITU, 2020).

Taking this into account, Graham and Dittus (2022) analyse Wikipedia. The online encyclopaedia of the world, written by citizens for citizens, in which the community collectively governs its use, Wikipedia is often heralded as an exemplary participatory and democratic platform. They note, however, that for many places around the world digital exclusion means that digital representations of people and the places they live are often written by outsiders from the perspectives of other cultures that can amplify and create social injustices that can be inherently disempowering: 'Digital representations don't just convey information and fact, they also deliberately constitute and rearticulate propositions about a desirable social order . . . And by having a politics they can give rise to epistemic and material injustices' (Graham and Dittus, 2022, p. 146).

And even in the Western world digital exclusions still apply. Ofcom[2] research (2022c) shows that 6 per cent of the UK population (over 4 million people) still do not have access to the internet at home. This rises to 14 per cent (over 3.6 million people) of those in lower socio-economic households (semi-skilled/unskilled manual occupations, unemployed and lowest-grade occupations). In the US, 24 per cent of the poorest households (with an income under $30,000 a year) don't own a smartphone, in contrast with the 4 per cent of the wealthiest households (over $75,000 a year of income) (Pew Research Center, 2021a). Despite having less access to technology, the poorest households spend far less in absolute terms but proportionately more of their disposable income on communications services, leading to what Golding terms a 'citizen detriment' (Golding, 2017, p. 4313), a form of harm caused by economic inequality and the resulting lower levels of disposable income that prevent poorer communities from securing access to a healthy diet of information services. Digital exclusion extends to all aspects of life – access to work, quality of education, availability of healthcare, costs of goods and services and the ability to connect with loved ones as well as voice, information and political participation. All of these exclusions also correlate to the intersectional issues of race, social class, gender and disability.

In relation to geographic barriers to access, research has established a relationship between access to local news and political participation. In a range of studies in mostly Western liberal democracies, political participation has been shown to increase in cities and regions with strong local news outlets. Kubler and Goodman (2019) found that the bigger the share of newspaper readers in a municipality in Switzerland, the higher the rate of electoral participation. Local news outlets not only increase people's knowledge of local candidates and forms of accountability for public institutions and private corporations, they also nurture social cohesion and grassroots activism. Yet, across the Western world, the decline in local newspapers is commonplace.

In the US in the past fifteen years nearly one in five newspapers has disappeared. In a continuing study, Abernathy (2016) documents the loss of papers and readers, the consolidation of the news industry and the social, political and economic consequences for thousands of communities across the US. Their research shows a net loss of almost 1,800 local newspapers since 2004. The pace of closures accelerated during the pandemic. With those that remain, they describe a significant diminishment in staffing and resources with direct implications for the news they are able to provide. They also indicate how new media barons (hedge and pension funds, private and publicly traded equity groups) have swooped in to take advantage of the situation and have purchased hundreds of newspapers with a focus entirely on profitability to the detriment of news itself.

A similar picture can be seen in the UK, where the Media Reform Coalition (MRC) has been researching the crisis in local news and campaigning for solutions for many years. They note how two decades of consolidations and cost-cutting measures by the largest commercial local news providers has led to the loss of many titles and hundreds of journalist jobs (Media Reform Coalition, 2021) with the closure of 245 newspapers between 2005 and 2019 (Cairncross, 2019). While many new independent local news outlets have sprung up, these are often run on tiny budgets and struggle to sustain themselves. Research has documented the growing news deserts resulting from these trends. In 2017, MRC showed that 45 per cent of Local Authority Districts (LADs) in the UK – in which 57.9 per cent of the population live – had no daily local newspaper (Media Reform Coalition, 2017). More recent research in 2021 found that 4.6 per cent of postcodes had no local print newspapers at all, and 30.7 per cent had only one title – usually a weekly newspaper. The average reach of these newspapers was 23 per cent of the local adult population monthly, and this reach was lower when fewer newspapers were available (Gulyas, 2020). Gulyas (ibid.) shows that in England the most deprived communities tend to have most restricted access to local news. In 2023 the Public Interest New Foundation (PINF) identified thirty-eight news deserts in the UK covering 4.1 million people, noting a strong correlation between deprivation and local news coverage – the more deprived the area, the fewer the number of news outlets (PINF, 2023).

In the absence of universal affordable broadband, the fact that local news outlets are increasingly digital-only also exacerbates digital exclusion. The collapse of the local reporting infrastructure has affected the national news agenda, since traditionally the regional press has been an important source of stories for the national media, and, in its absence, many parts of the UK now go routinely ignored or forgotten in national news coverage (Watkins, 2021). Local and regional newspapers also offered a route into journalism for those without an elite education, and their disappearance contributes to journalism being one of the most elite professions in the UK (The Sutton Trust, 2019) (see also Chapter 5).

The notion of informational exclusion also speaks to more recent debates related to forms of news consumption. Research has shown time and again that higher-educated, higher-paid and politically interested people consume more news and are more likely to search out 'quality' rather than 'popular' news providers than lower socioeconomic, less formally educated groups (Thorson, Xu and Edgerly, 2018; Bergström, Strömbäck and Arkhede, 2019; Chan and Goldthorpe, 2007; Ksiazek, Malthouse and Webster, 2010; Ohlsson, Lindell and Arkhede, 2017). These inequalities in news consumption have been linked to exclusions in political participation and a weakening of democracy. Moreover, increased news consumption is seen by certain social groups as a form of cultural capital that may be lacking in those lower down the social hierarchy, reinforcing a sense of entitlement and self-righteousness that further demarcates and maintains social exclusions (Lindell, 2020) while enhancing audience segmentation.

In addition to external exclusions, Young (2022) points out that exclusions can also be internal to discursive communities – even when you are part of a group (e.g. an online community) you can still be excluded within it (through things like trolling and hate speech). This is what Gangadharan refers to as internal exclusions of predation and lack of privacy (2013, 2017). Young states that for an inclusive and just communicative society both forms of exclusion – external and internal – must be solved. Giving free broadband to all will not necessarily mean that everyone will have equal access when the terms of engagement are often unfamiliar or impenetrable to certain groups. Digital illiteracy is not just about how to use a computer or the latest mobile phone but also relates to what extent a user understands the complexity of targeting and tracking online and how skilled they are in protecting their privacy. Furthermore, being privacy literate often requires paying for services to encrypt access and protect data, leading to further exclusions.

Young's approach reminds us that democracy and political participation function on multiple levels. Communicative democracy requires attention to both the structural political and economic order of capitalism, which creates inequalities and marginalized groups, as well as to the institutional and organizational dynamics of discursive practices that silence certain people and elevate others. And so, access and connectivity alone are not sufficient to foster political participation – educational levels that include media and digital literacy also play a part.

However, Young has been criticized for putting the onus of change in the hands of the powerful – namely, those who maintain the norms of communicative practice need to ensure they are non-exclusionary. Fraser (1990) notes that this is inadequate and unlikely to be realized. Marginalized groups themselves should be recognized as having political will to transform social conditions. Gangadharan sets out a similar argument describing five forms of digital exclusion that inhibit the ability of marginalized peoples to collectively self-determine:

> [U]navailability of digital technologies, inability to meaningfully use digital technologies due to digital illiteracy, inability to meaningfully use technologies due to low or nonexistent digital privacy, forced or coerced use of surveillant digital technologies, and inequalities between privileged tech elites and members of marginalized groups. (Gangadharan in Bernholz, Landemore and Reich, 2020, p. 45)

She argues that those most vulnerable to technologies' exclusionary powers must be part of deciding what technologies make possible or impossible in their lives – it cannot be left to benevolent designers or policy-makers. Similarly, Kidd's research (Kidd, 2019) with indigenous communities in Canada reminds us that data collection and control (in the form of land surveys and mapping) have always been key to the European imperialist project of resource extraction and colonization, and has always engendered resistance to these processes. She shows how 'counter-mapping' has become part of larger projects of redistributive, transformative and restorative justice that fight against practices of surveillance that seek to further exclude marginalized citizens from participation and control of land and resources.

This extended discussion indicates that if we, as diverse peoples, are interested in the possibilities of participating in decision-making processes in order to facilitate social change, we first have to confront a political-economic context that has created less participation and enhanced exclusionary practices where dissenting voices are disciplined within a repressive regulatory framework that is structured to favour the status quo. The conditions of actually existing democracy reveal a structural inability of people to acquire, process and analyse independent information and to make their own decisions regarding the scope and direction of their democratic participation. Participation, then, is about fundamental questions of concentration and consolidation of power and control driven by a mediated (data) capitalism.

This reality requires a critique that can account for key structural and infrastructural concerns that circumscribe what people can and can't do and is guided by the question of 'who does what to whom for whose benefit' (Geuss, 2008, p. 23). This is not just a question of who is able to exercise individual autonomy in the digital age but extends to the very possibility for agentic social change: the forms of deliberation available to us, mutual recognition of personhood and the social fabric of trust, the actual conditions for a democratic politics to function.

What we can do about it

When we consider issues of political participation and forms of exclusion we are discussing both issues of political agency and the legitimate exercise of institutionalized power. One of the recurring problems is how to theorize the relationship between the 'influence' generated by social movements in the public sphere and the institutionalized 'exercise of power'. Cohen and Fung (in Bernholz, Landemore and Reich, 2020, pp. 23–61) refine the tension between exercising and influencing power referred to above by identifying a fundamental difference between two approaches to radical democracy: one that emphasizes the goal of broadening participation but with an implicit acknowledgement of attenuated effects on the exercise of power; and one that focuses on improving the quality of deliberative participation and enhanced impact. They focus their conception of democracy around three interrelated areas: (1) a democratic *society* whose members are understood in the political culture to be free and equal persons but with different interests, identities, capacities, social positions and resources in complex relations of cultural, social and political power; (2) a democratic *political regime* with regular elections, rights of participation and the associative and expressive liberties necessary to making participation informed and effective; and (3) a *deliberative democracy* that appeals to rationales of justice, fairness and the common good and is suited to cooperation among free and equal persons with deep disagreements. By taking account of all three areas, their aim is to strengthen the communicative conditions for a deeper democracy. In this manner, democratic politics and political engagement are broadened beyond the formal realm of voting or lobbying to include the informal, open-ended and dispersed mediated communication that can influence civic activism as well as formal political power.

These types of democratic rhetoric are easily uttered, but realizing the intentions of such claims is very much harder. Equal standing in political culture requires favourable social conditions and the diminishment of socio-economic inequalities. Making participation informed and effective means removing concentrated private ownership of communicative spaces and opportunities. Ensuring deliberative spaces that are conducive to cooperation among free and equal persons while airing deep disagreements requires a shared understanding of the common good and of justice as well as monitoring and regulation for harms and privacy, alongside mechanisms of accountability. While taking into account social, political and deliberative concerns all together may feel like an impossible challenge, thinking about participatory mechanisms through this lens enables us to begin the process of broadening our thinking beyond piecemeal reforms or regulatory quick-fixes that function within the dominant system, to thinking about what sort of democratic society we may want to develop.

To do this means breaking out of 'elite capture' (Taiwo, 2022) by powerful interests. The concept of elite capture was first applied to the study of developing countries to reveal how privileged elites gained control over foreign aid meant for the socially and economically disadvantaged. The concept has since been applied more broadly to illustrate 'how public resources such as knowledge, attention and values become distorted and distributed by power structures' (Taiwo, 2022, p. 10). We can include in the knowledge economy systems of information and communication oriented to serve particular vested interests even when regulation is purported to serve public interests. We can also include the very idea of liberal representative democracy that holds the illusion of giving more power to more people when in practice societies are increasingly unequal and exclusionary and function to the benefit of finance, capital and thus the very wealthy.

One example of this in the UK is the so-called 'Online Safety Bill'. The bill promises to introduce new protections for the public from hate, abuse and other harmful content online. But in doing so, it has bowed down to the press lobby and made newspaper comment sections exempt. So the racism, conspiracy theories and other harmful information on these platforms are exempt as well. Press comment sections in the UK are rife with disinformation, abuse and the most extreme forms of racism. Moderation is often minimal, and the comments that are deliberately inflammatory are often prioritized to generate the most clicks. The proposals may clamp down on the fringe extremists of X (formerly Twitter) and rightly so, but exclude the professionalized, organized and well-funded extremism of forums that spread racism, hate and other harms. What we are left with is a policy approach to data justice that is anything but just. Rather, it's an easy, market-friendly fix that explicitly avoids the very idea that structural injustices exist.

Returning to the argument in Chapter 2, if our conception of democracy is grounded in cultivating freedom and the power to realize the individual and collective capacity to participate in the shaping of social life, then the reinvention of a democratic media that works for democracy will consciously function to address issues of powerlessness and enable publics to participate collectively and fairly, including those who are socially, economically, politically or technologically disadvantaged. What follows are examples of how we can begin to conceive of this through different forms of democracy and participation in the three inter-related areas that Cohen and Fung (ibid.) refer to.

A democratic society: starting with a democratic society allows us to consider what kind of society would be able to respond to the challenges noted above and what our media and tech systems would be for. This would mean a society that is far more devolved in terms of political power, and more bottom-up and participatory in terms of decision-making. Such a society would be one in which people would expect (and be expected) to be involved in democratic and economic decisions, which are made as locally as possible, through public institutions and cooperative companies/organizations. It would be one where everyone is supported by a social guarantee of a living income and basic universal services (Coote and Percy, 2020); where nobody is dependent on precarious work, and working less than five days a week is the norm, giving people time to participate in community and democratic activities. In a brave attempt to think beyond current (often impoverished) systems of welfare, that focus predominantly on health and education, Coote and Percy (2020) show how expanding the principle of collective *universal service provision* to everyday essentials like housing, transport and childcare is the best, most efficient, practical and affordable way to tackle problems such as inequality, poverty and sustainability facing our contemporary world.

Coote and Percy (ibid.) extend the need for universal basic services to access to the internet but they say very little about it. In line with many debates on the digital divide, access via universal connectivity is prioritized over all else. But having connectivity is of little use if you are poor and still have to pay for it. Rather, the minimum starting point should be access to universal free broadband as a public utility. Under public ownership the digital technologies we use day-to-day would be not-for-profit, accountable and under democratic control. Data about how they are being used would be transparent so that people can tell if they are causing harm, and they would be designed to facilitate people's offline lives rather than designed to be as addictive as possible to enable profiteering.

A democratic political regime: if there is free universal broadband as part of universal basic services, then digital democratic participation starts to look more meaningful and hold more democratic potential. The City of Barcelona's Digital City Plan also sees high-speed internet connectivity as necessary for economic development and social mobility. It has built the Decidem platform, which aims to give all citizens a voice, so that they can decide on the future of their own surroundings, and the Open Data Portal, so that people can retain data sovereignty and information self-determination. It is a digital space put together using open-source software and open code, one that forms part of a participatory process involving online and offline debate around a set of proposals suggested by participants. It treats data as a social (not commercial) asset to be used for public good rather than private gain. It has been used to support policy-making and participatory budgeting in Barcelona while guaranteeing data sovereignty and privacy. The Barcelona Digital City approach is based on addressing social challenges and promoting sustainability through 'circular economy' principles (of sharing, reusing, repairing, recycling) while empowering alternative ownership models like platform cooperatives. It shows us that one of the first steps in a digital democratic political regime is having a policy on data ownership anchored in the collective good, solidarity and citizen participation.

Barcelona City Council is one of the most prominent examples of the new municipalist movement that emerged out of the local 15M (15 May) protest movement in 2011 and the anti-eviction movements across Spain. The 15M movement gave rise to the construction of the new political party Podemos and a broad coalition of transformative leftist movements and parties such as Barcelona en Comú. In 2015 housing rights activist Ada Colau was elected mayor of Barcelona, winning re-election in 2019 on a manifesto pledging to tackle corruption and radicalize democracy (Scharenberg, 2020). En Comú refers to 'the commons' and seeks to work with civil society actors and existing political parties to create new platforms that foster greater participation in governance and greater control over one's own forms of production (including the data we produce).

In 2019 Barcelona en Comú published the book *Fearless Cities – A Guide to the Global Municipalist Movement*, which outlines fifty examples of cities in nineteen countries across all continents involved in transformative local practices as part of an internationalist municipalist movement. From fighting municipal debt and poverty in Valparaíso, Chile, to tackling poor air quality and waste management in Beirut, Lebanon; from developing new institutional processes for public partnerships and experimental forms of governance to allow citizens and others to co-design processes for the city of Bologna, to the city of Naples enabling citizen-based claims on public spaces: there are multiple attempts to reinvent democratic practices from the ground up, bringing activists, citizens and politicians together for a transformative politics that enables co-ownership, co-production and co-determination. Democracy is conceptualized and practised in these cases as the sharing of rule and the constant re-creation of new publics. Structures of exclusion and how to address these are seen as key to unlocking political participation.

A deliberative democracy: if we are aiming for a democratic society and a democratic political regime (as a newly democratic political economy) the means of democratic deliberation becomes imperative. Too often debates around deliberative democracy focus on legal enforcement of 'good' behaviour of individuals online. The solution to trolling and abusive behaviour online, which are seen to cause 'harms' and thereby to be anti-democratic, is to fine either tech companies for inadequate content moderation or individuals for harmful actions. While an approach that focuses on the symptoms rather than the systems may momentarily alleviate the harms incurred, they will not address the underlying issue that controversial content online is more likely to go viral and is therefore more profitable. Neither will it address the unchecked use of data to influence voters directly and surreptitiously in things like the Cambridge Analytica scandal discussed in Chapter 2 or the complexities of the free speech debate dealt with in Chapter 4. Just as the UK Data Protection Act passed in the wake of that scandal failed to address this issue, so it looks like the UK Online Safety Bill will do the same. These regulatory constructs may offer some fleeting solace, but they do not come anywhere near offering long-term solutions.

Understanding the consequences of content circulation, curation and commodification is then key to generating a more deliberative democracy. The problem lies not with individual pieces of content but with how, by whom and for what purposes that content is managed and made available. As noted in the previous chapter, the answer to the 'by whom' question is relatively easy: only a very few global oligopolies are involved in making decisions over questions of production and distribution. Participation in this realm is restricted to those with large amounts of capital to the exclusion of everyone else. Because the ultimate aim is profit maximization, this capitalist model of production makes it harder for us to find information that will help us to better understand the world and enhance forms of deliberation. What Jodi Dean (2009) has termed 'communicative capitalism' insists on the imperative of participation through compulsive refresh-and-rescroll, post-and-share technologies, generating a constant data stream with the illusion of deliberation, but where no considered response ever comes.

A deliberative democracy requires an entirely different order of participation. Once we move away from a focus solely on content, we can begin to understand deliberative democracy as extending far beyond words in a tweet to be more about participation in socio-political systems. Take the BBC as an example (discussed further in Chapter 6), often referred to as a paragon of public service broadcasting (PSB). It has been argued that a decade of funding cuts, increasing government interference and commercial pressures have made the BBC much less able to fulfil its public mission (Chalk, 2020). So, although the BBC is often held up as the model of PSB, over the last three decades its independence is said to have been steadily eroded and its programme-making increasingly commercialized (Puttnam, 2016). PSB is all too easily reduced to the content provided by the BBC. But public service refers to a wider media ecology and set of regulations that foreground the public interest ahead of economic or partisan political interests. Its underlying principles confirm commitments to universality and citizenship, independence, transparency, redistribution and diversity (ibid.). Public service media environments have demonstrable political and cultural benefits. Research (Curran et al., 2009) shows that where independent and viable public service broadcasting exists, citizens are better informed about public issues – all of which are vital to democratic deliberation. However, the independence and viability of PSB needs to be constantly renewed if it is to positively shape a broader media ecology in the digital age.

Proposals from the Media Reform Coalition (MRC) (Media Reform Coalition, 2021) to make a People's BBC more democratic are premised first and foremost on it being significantly more decentralized than today, with programme-making, editorial functions and budgeting largely sitting with the devolved nations and English regions. A more devolved structure would be better placed to make programmes that more comprehensively represent the concerns and experiences of the whole country, while also creating new avenues for citizens to participate and bringing to the fore the sorts of producers and content that are currently excluded from its purview:

be it community radio, podcasts, festivals or local independent newspapers. MRC suggest that participation by the wider public in a People's BBC could be coordinated through a network of citizen media assemblies overseeing a range of forms of participation such as elections for regional boards, selecting citizens' juries to monitor coverage of controversial issues and auditing commissioning to ensure that people from minoritized groups are represented. Greater democracy would also be facilitated among the workforce, with a strong voice for media unions and worker representation on internal BBC boards.

Extending the PSB institutional infrastructure for the digital age would mean creating new public media organizations, to provide a public alternative to privately owned digital platforms that is freely available to all, equally serves all citizens and is adequately funded to meet this challenge. In other words, democratic deliberation seen as not only a concern of content disseminated or platform design but rather as public alternatives that are democratically organized and run with the possibility of generating pioneering digital content and innovative technological solutions to advance democracy and harness data for the common good.

Conclusion: Social ownership and collective control

In his essay 'The Uses of Democracy', Rancière (1995) notes that participation in what we normally refer to as democratic regimes is usually reduced to a question of filling up the spaces left empty by power. Genuine participation, he argues, is something different and inclusive of forms of counter power that are not dependent on the dominant order. Forms of participation that reduce individuals to little more than cogs in a media or digital machine over which they have no control and whose direction is set by politicians or corporate owners with little genuine accountability is at best pseudo-participation. At worst, it is participation that is seduced by capitalism through small individualized gains that appeal to personal rights and freedoms rather than the common good to the extent that we can no longer imagine what democracy might mean beyond it. As Muldoon notes 'private control over digital infrastructure enables companies to shape the structural conditions of our politics' (Muldoon, 2022, p. 63) and it is this that we must change.

When we consider the concept of participation alongside the concept of power in the previous chapter then we can appreciate that a transformative and just democracy does not translate into participation in a system (whether that system is a social system, political system or media system) that exists to maintain unequal power relations and operates only to the benefit of a few. It cannot mean participation in a system that is governed and regulated by someone else – where the privileged get to set the agenda, organize the space and direct the conversation. If the goal is not merely inclusion but transformation, then participation in a democracy must be borne of the people and constituted by them as a form of social ownership and collective control.

4

FREEDOM AND REPRESSION

Democracy requires that everyone is free to participate in the political community's self-government. Political freedom lies at the heart of the concept of democracy. Political freedom is interrelated with other freedoms commonly referred to as: freedom of the press, freedom of expression and freedom of association.

Freedom of the press and freedom of expression are strongly associated with a *healthy* news media that is often claimed to be the life-blood of democracy. This is because news provides, or should provide, the vital resources for processes of information-gathering, deliberation and analysis that enable citizens to participate in political life and democracy to function better. For this to happen we need news media to represent a wide range of issues from a variety of perspectives and with a diversity of voices. It requires a journalism that operates freely and without interference from state institutions, corporate pressures and fear of intimidation and persecution. In an ideal world this would mean that news media would survey the socio-political environment, relentlessly hold the powerful to account, provide a platform for intelligible and illuminating debate and encourage dialogue across a range of views. However, this is an ideal relationship hinged on a conception of *independent journalism in the public interest* – journalism as a 'fourth estate', linked to notions of public knowledge, political participation, citizenship and democratic renewal. The reality is often quite different. Identifying the gap between the admirable aspiration of a fully functioning public sphere and the actual conditions of practice and production of news media, and then understanding why this gap exists, is critical to discussing how journalism should be defined in a democracy and how the discourses of all types of 'media freedom' but in particular 'press freedom' have been (re)formulated in neoliberal times. This chapter begins by charting these waters.

The chapter then goes on to link the debates on freedom of the press to those of freedom of expression. Narratives of freedom abound in much of the mainstream media. Yet these narratives of freedom ultimately embolden and legitimate the far right and enable the positioning of the liberal left as tyrannical social justice warriors responsible for society's demise by encouraging unworthy recipients of welfare, enabling immigrants to pass through unsecured borders and thus overwhelming our health services, and as guilty of disintegrating norms of gender and sexuality by advocating for trans rights. In this formulation of freedom, the social is demonized and becomes yet another way for the powerful to trample on the freedoms of the weak. Market freedom is heralded as the be all and end all of human need, and a democratic version of political life that requires addressing inequalities and insisting on state-administered social (and media) policy, planning and justice is repelled.

This chapter argues that freedom divorced from the social leads to disregard and un-care for society as a whole and 'renders invisible the social norms and inequalities generated by legacies of slavery, colonialism and patriarchy' (Brown, 2019, p. 42) as well as by capitalism. It leads to a form of liberal privatism and reduces freedom to naked assertions of power and entitlement – a wholly unsocial liberty. Using the rhetoric of freedom as a means to curtail political power (particularly of the most disenfranchised) has justified the repealing of the regulatory state that has, in turn, limited the voice of the people. Here, the first example used will be the failed attempt to introduce an effective form of press regulation in the UK to hold the press to account for their own wrongdoings. Drawing on the author's personal experience as a researcher activist at the heart of the campaign for an accountable press following the phone-hacking scandal in the UK, this chapter argues that much of the commercial press fell in line with the neoliberal argument advanced by the likes of Friedman et al. (1962), namely that capitalism promotes (all kinds of) freedom by limiting and restraining government. By falling in line with neoliberal framings of freedom, capitalism wins out rather than democracy, and the relationship between democracy and the media is severed with long-lasting consequences. Commercial media industries function as big capital and seek to instrumentalize the state in their favour (as the tech giants have done since). Curtailing the reach of political power in the name of freedom (for capital) then justifies repealing the regulatory state.

A further example focuses on the notion of freedom of expression in mainstream and social media and how it too has been distorted in capital's favour. Social media flourishes on controversy and invites abusive behaviour – it intimates that you have unqualified freedom to say anything about anyone anywhere. In these instances, social media builds communities of hate and dissolves social bonds rather than builds them. Far right tweets, trolling and public misconduct come to stand in for freedom of expression. In England, one example is the issue of trans rights. The Gender Recognition Act reforms in the UK (due to be enacted in 2020 but then dropped) would have streamlined the process of changing one's legal gender. Instead, they fuelled a toxic debate on social media about the basic human rights of trans people. Social media thrives off toxicity because toxicity travels far and fast, generating ever more clicks that sustain the advertising model upon which social media platforms are premised. Mainstream media feed into and off this frenzy, and politicians are quick to join the bait ball. Meanwhile, freedom of association – claimed as open, inclusive and liberatory on social media – is revealed as algorithmically curated to support a business model that prospers from hate, as anti-discrimination laws are undermined by assertions of normative heteropatriarchy. Free speech becomes entangled with discourses of deregulated markets and, perversely, equality becomes its enemy.

The logical conclusion of this argument is that we must remove the business model on which both news media and social media function. The answer is not asserting the rights of the sovereign consumer for more and better-regulated consumption but rather to focus on the rights of citizens and their knowledge needs in a democracy. Media and communications systems have been engulfed by commercialism and in this form will never be able to serve democracy well. Regulatory mechanisms can keep some types of excessive malpractice in check but they will never manage effectively to tame a beast that hungers constantly for the fresh meat of exploitation.

What is freedom of the press?

The freedom of the press debate is irrevocably yoked to the notion of liberal democracy. We are frequently told that one leads to the other. A healthy news media provides the very sustenance for democracy to function well. And a healthy news media is a 'free' media. But if we think about this for a moment, we uncover a whole set of complex relations that defy such a simplistic correlation. If news media are to provide the vital resources to ensure everyone experiences a wide range of cultural and informational content so that we can all participate fully in social and political life and enable democracy to function better, then it must do so without fear or favour and without misrepresentation or distortion. It would require our news media to represent a wide range of issues from a variety of perspectives and with a diversity of voices. As soon as we question who is saying what to whom; what types of issues are favoured or given legitimacy; what subjects of news are disfavoured, or marked as illegitimate; what types of people are able to be agents and actors as news sources; what types of people are able to be journalists/news professionals in what roles and in what areas of media; then it becomes clear that the relationship between news media and democracy is not a given, is frequently skewed to serve powerful interests and commercial purposes and therefore requires checks and balances within a legal and/or constitutional structure to become established and maintained.

To secure the privileges of being a 'free media at the heart of democratic life', social value for all rather than political or capital gain for the few must be at the core of news media practice. This will certainly require a journalism that operates freely and without interference from vested interests that include state institutions and politicians, corporate pressures and fear of intimidation and persecution. But the routes to achieving such high ideals are riven with multiple impediments.

Suffice to say that the relationship between media and democracy is far from guaranteed. Rather, it depends on the *existing* state of the media and the market and on the state of *actually existing* democracy in each individual context – where context is likely to be state-led because of the prevailing dominance of state legislatures but not state-bound due to globalization. Thus, this relationship also depends on a range of other factors, from political culture, media policy and the nature of the economy and the market to media and communication technologies and formats as well as social and cultural issues such as literacy, poverty, religious differences and daily rituals. This combination of factors impinges, sometimes directly, on the relationship between news media and democracy, as each have an effect on media circulation and on media consumption and influence how and to what extent freedom of the press functions in a generative relationship with democratic practice. Yet, these factors are all too frequently sidestepped by media scholars, leaving us analytically moribund.

Benson (2010) addresses this analytical lack by adopting a structural field theory perspective on journalism, arguing that news content is shaped primarily by its positioning in relation to other powerful fields, namely, in the first instance, the political and economic fields, and second by factors internal to the journalistic field itself, such as the cultural logics of practice and social class differentiation. Each field overlaps to an extent but can also be usefully distinguished for analytic purposes. The political field exerts structural influence when the state powerfully 'constrains (or enables) the diversity of voices and views in the press, as well as the amount and types of criticism and critical reporting, through its power to regulate or subsidize the media, provide official information to the press and shape the system of parties and elections' (2010, p. 616). The economic field refers to commercial constraints that encompass a range of elements, such as concentration of ownership (Baker, 2006) and profit pressures relating to types of ownership (Cranberg, Bezanson and Soloski, 2001); types of funding such as advertising or paying audiences (Baker, 1994); and the level and intensity of market competition. While the political and economic fields establish the foundations for news and journalism, the cultural logics of journalism practice from one country to the next are also important. These include assumptions about what constitutes 'news' and the purpose of journalism as well as the practices of news-gathering and sourcing; norms of objectivity and impartiality – the ethics and practice of journalism that contribute to the news ecology in any one place at any one moment in time. Cultural logics are also influenced by class stratification and organizational formations (referred to in Chapter 5) that will impact upon the amount and types of news and journalism and the economic and professional relationships between news organizations.

The classic free market argument present in historical accounts of the emergence of the free press in Western democracies emphasizes the political constraints on news media. Here we find debates that highlight how authoritarian states control the media through a mixture of funding, law, taxation, sponsorship, appointments, etc. The argument is that there needs to be alternative forms of media to challenge state information and that this can only come about through a media that exists in the private sector. In other words, the logic underpinning this argument is that commercial media funded through sales and advertising do not risk losing their income each time they are critical of the state. Within this paradigm, commercialization brings decentralized media, new spaces of expression, operational autonomy and freedom of expression. This model has long been celebrated by the US and UK liberal models that were reacting against state-sponsored journalism of authoritarian regimes. However, in the process, advocates of this model have disregarded anything in between and frequently offered an overly simplistic analysis.

A critique of this neoliberal argument often adopts a largely economic perspective in pointing out the problems of free-market media under a Western model. Corporate conglomerates have been shown to exert pressure on news organizations that impact upon their structures and content through advertising, sponsorship and board-level pressures to produce ever more profit (Baker, 1994, 2006). Corporate media are largely profit-led and not guided by public good considerations. Consequently, they are not obliged to fund unprofitable news production or cater to all groups and interests in society. They are prone to draw ratings and offer entertainment or tabloid/infotainment forms of news. Media corporations can also grow so big that they are difficult to challenge. So, we can see how the political and the economic fields impact on each other. Regulation or deregulation relating to media concentration may emanate from the political field but it clearly has ramifications for the economic field. Some of the key features of these constraints are outlined in more detail below.

Regulation/deregulation for media freedom

Government regulation can set out the limits of legally acceptable journalistic practice. For example, restrictive laws may at times be seen to constrain journalism through definitions of defamation and libel that prevent full and frank discussion of government officials. Constraints can also be placed on journalistic practice through an increase in police or state surveillance over journalistic investigations that can endanger journalists' sources and put news-gathering activities under legal jeopardy. Certainly, in the UK there has been much debate about the Regulatory and Investigatory Powers Act (RIPA), which enables state surveillance of citizens, journalists (and their sources) and is justified under an 'anti-terror/national security' banner but can seriously impinge on the news media's ability to operate in the public interest (Sambrook, 2014).

On the other hand, laws can provide journalists with access to confidential government or other public sector information and hold such powers to account. Regulations regarding press freedom,

freedom of information and public interest defences are often important protectors of the journalistic endeavour. Regulation can also protect the public's right to privacy from a hungry news media desperate for a scoop. So regulation can help temper the worst excesses of corporate news media and try to ensure, at the very least, that journalism as a commercial practice does not impair democracy.

Government regulation can also limit or increase the range and nature of concentration of media ownership. Concentration of media ownership creates conditions in which wealthy individuals can amass great social, cultural and political power. Media owners have been shown to influence the sorts of news their organizations publish and so have some bearing on public debate and political opinion. Sometimes this is evident through *direct* intervention, as with Rupert Murdoch, who was happy to state that he had 'editorial control on major issues such as who to vote for in a General Election and [policy on] Europe' (House of Lords Select Committee on Communications, 2008). Editors of national newspapers have often stated, usually when they have left the newspaper itself, that Murdoch made it clear what he expected of them and the news they produced. But owner influence also flows through *indirect* means, such as the appointment of like-minded editors, emphasizing certain business practices, or by influencing the journalistic ethos of a news organization, which then impacts on the processes of news production (Barnett, 2012).

When concentration of news ownership increases, news proprietors accumulate excessive power and influence and news corporations often begin flexing their political muscles. The available literature underscores that the larger and more concentrated media empires become, the more concerned politicians are to maintain good relations with owners, senior executives and editors to try to keep them on-side and maximize their chances of electoral success (e.g. Davis, 2002). Maintaining good relations can mean limiting press regulation – particularly in areas relating to the accumulation of wealth and power such as the consolidation of media ownership. In the UK, four successive prime ministers who gave evidence to the Leveson Inquiry into the Press (set up as a consequence of illegal phone hacking by news organizations) admitted that they were 'too close' to the big media players because the political stakes were so very high. In such circumstances, political parties, the police and other institutions were revealed to be reluctant to investigate wrongdoing in the news media, hinder the expansion of large media conglomerates or introduce new regulations for news organizations and journalistic practice. Such patterns and relations have resulted in certain public policy areas being avoided for fear of either hostile reporting or media owner conflict (Dean, 2013). And, for the same reasons, politicians are also more likely to discuss populist policies.

The same practices continue today. Analysis by the campaign group Hacked Off (2024) showed that from September 2022 to September 2023 there were 218 recorded meetings between Murdoch representatives and the government, with Rupert Murdoch himself meeting government representatives twelve times during this period and on six occasions meeting the prime minister. There were three private calls between the secretary of state for digital, culture, media and sport and newspaper editors on the date a draft Media Bill was published that included plans to repeal the final crucial element of the Leveson framework for independent self-regulation of the press. These levels of influence are the result of a thoroughly marketized and deregulated newspaper industry in the UK, leading to unchecked media concentration over several decades, allowing some media groups to accumulate vast amounts of revenue along with social and political influence that has had adverse consequences for ethical journalism and democracy.

Market dominance of news media also affects journalists, who are increasingly on insecure employment contracts. Job insecurity breeds vulnerability to intimidation. Journalists become more reluctant to stand up to a bullying culture where market-oriented managers place commercial priorities above journalistic responsibility and integrity. Yet, it is not only journalists whose freedom is circumscribed by corporate compliance. After all, as ordinary members of the public our ability to exercise our own democratic freedom is premised on the basic fact that governments are not distorted by private interest of multi-media conglomerates (Fenton and Freedman, 2014). When governments as well as journalists are beholden to concentrated corporate power then freedom is hard to come by for all but the most powerful. This leads Tambini (2021, p. 24) to argue that there should be an inverse relationship to media power and media freedom – 'the more powerful the media institution, the less free it should be'.

Level and intensity of market competition

Across the globe, media and technological change has impacted on the news environment. A huge growth in the number of news outlets, from the advent of and rapid increase in free news and the emergence of twenty-four-hour television news to the popularization of online and mobile platforms, has meant that more news must be produced and distributed at a faster rate than ever before. The level and intensity of global market competition combined with technological change and business models that have struggled to adapt has also meant that in a corporate news world it is now difficult to maintain the sorts of profit margins and shareholder returns that the industry had grown used to, that is, unless you employ fewer journalists (Fenton, 2010). But fewer journalists with more space to fill means doing more work in less time, which often leads to a greater use of unattributed rewrites of press agencies or public relations material and the cut-and-paste practice now commonly known as churnalism (Davies, 2008). Consequently, original and investigative newsgathering has suffered.

In a bid to maintain a competitive edge, journalists now spend a large amount of time monitoring other media online, the news wires and social media. Rewriting stories gained through this constant monitoring has arguably become the main task of many journalists. As such, the same news often circulates in slightly adapted forms for different brand outlets. The great treasure trove of information online has done little to minimize these negative consequences. Research that has analysed the content of mainstream online news has revealed that much of today's abundant news online is the same: news organizations often cover stories from the same angles and different news organizations repeatedly present the same information in their stories (Redden and Witschge, 2010). Furthermore, because journalists are under so much time pressure, ready-made fodder from tried-and-tested sources takes precedence over the attempt to tackle the enormity of user-generated content or the overload of online information (Fenton, 2010). Add to this the latest innovations in artificial intelligence, such as ChatGPT, which can assemble a story in seconds based on a few keywords from a vast swathe of information and data online, with no trace of where it originated or whether it has been verified, and the concerns over the early days of churnalism via reproduction of press releases start to feel ridiculously quaint.

Churnalism (whether super-charged through AI or not) feeds a clickbait culture because more clicks equal more advertising revenue. In 2019 the News Corp tabloid newspaper the *Herald Sun* started offering journalists a financial bonus for driving digital subscriptions and traffic through their own stories (Meade, 2019). In 2022 the *Daily Telegraph* newspaper in the UK announced that it was going to pay journalists per click in a blatant drive to encourage content that can reap higher commercial reward. This plan caused an outcry from the journalist community and was never implemented but laid bare the value system to which the newspaper operates. Ample research provides evidence that a news environment driven by the principles of commercialism where news organizations foreground rationalization (by cutting back on journalists) and marketization (through the increasing commodification of news) at the expense of ideal democratic objectives has led to the homogenization of content useful for clickbait but detrimental to expanding plurality and thus democratic enhancement, which was one of the promises of the digital age.

Theories of democratic political participation have long since recognized the roles the media play in activating political citizenship and participation. Media coverage plays a significant role in creating awareness and engagement. At a fundamental societal level, news matters. But a simple abundance of news, one that just assumes that the more news we have the more democratic our societies are, speaks to a naive pluralism that has been shown to be blatantly false. If the nature of news content serves the interests of a commercial news industry over and above people's information needs, then more news does not necessarily help democracy, even if consumption is high. In such cases, contemporary coverage can actually lead to a mood of anti-politics, thwart political participation in the public sphere and diminish democracy (Coleman, 2012). In these circumstances how can news organizations be encouraged to act responsibly and be held to account when they do not?

Media freedom and accountability

The balance between media freedom and public responsibility as regards journalistic practice is both complex and a crucial facet of the news media's relationship to democracy. Freedom of the press has always been associated with the ability of news journalists to do their job free from interference from government (Muhlmann, 2010). But, as noted above, media legislation can be used to uphold media freedoms. Many countries have legislative frameworks that repress the practice of journalism such as libel laws, contempt of court, privacy laws and laws relating to 'official secrets'. These laws may operate alongside others that seek to guarantee press freedom (as in the First Amendment of the US Constitution) and freedom of expression (as in the European Convention of Human Rights). Such 'rights' do not override the law of the land and exist in association with other rights such as privacy for individuals. It is often precisely in the conflict between the rights of press freedom and those of privacy where difficulties arise. Insisting that democratic purposes are at the heart of journalistic practice is one way of evaluating such conflicts. This is where 'public interest' defences come in, but these are also fraught with contention.

It has been argued that a clearly defined 'public interest' defence in law can help deal with the central contradiction of journalism – the fact that ethical journalists require defence for rule-breaking if they are to do their job, whereas unethical journalists attempt to use 'public interest defences' to protect themselves against criticism (Barnett, 2012). The 'public interest' is a concept that is recognized by both the public and journalists. The European Human Rights Act already inscribes this concept as a reasonable defence for intrusion. The word 'public' in this instance embodies the notion of a whole society. For something to be in the 'public interest' it must affect the way in which we live together as a social group (Phillips, Couldry and Freedman 2010). It should be information that will help us to live better together, or that will prevent us from being harmed. With a clear public interest defence in place, it should be possible to ensure that codes of ethical conduct are upheld and that those who wilfully ignore them will face some form of legal censure. However, public interest legislation is often fraught with difficulties revolving around who gets to define and decide what is in the public interest, particularly when it comes to issues relating to 'national security' and government secrecy.

Evidently, the practices of media regulation vary greatly, and critiquing how various degrees of regulation or non-regulation support democratic practice is far from straightforward. Those nation states that have adopted a largely free-market position in relation to the news (as outlined above) frequently rely on the cultures of journalism to support ethical practice through self-regulation rather than legislative mechanisms. Self-regulation via professional codes of conduct is often the form of journalistic accountability associated with the freedom of the press because it excludes governments from playing any role in how journalism should be practised. However, to function well, self-regulation requires a strong ethical framework. Ethics refer to a shared sense of equity and justice, rooted in something deeper than obedience, that enables a group or community to set standards which its members freely agree to abide by. To this extent, ethical frameworks are also dependent on the social order of the day and can only be enacted fully if market pressures or owner preferences are absent. News organizations have differing interests, and various ways of operating and do not necessarily have a shared ethical sense to which they can all refer. Journalism is on a spectrum that runs from those editors and journalists who have the freedom of action and conscience to operate ethically to those who operate within a highly structured and competitive environment in which they are under heavy pressure to deliver stories by any means possible and often without the protection of a trade union. The influence and power of a corporate culture can wreak its own havoc and set its own agenda far more blatantly than any democratic government would ever dare.

Ethical journalism requires protection from pressures that might prevent investigations into abuses of power. Journalism that is under pressure due to its commercial environment (and desperate to grab market share) requires firmer rules to prevent the abuse of journalists' power to traduce innocent people as victims of press abuse. Those individuals working for highly competitive news organizations also need protection from their editors and managers if they feel they are being asked to do something unethical. In a high-profile case in the UK, a senior political journalist resigned from the *Daily Telegraph* because of alleged non-reporting of the encouragement of tax evasion schemes by the bank HSBC, which also happened to be a prominent advertiser in the paper. The journalist Peter Oborne felt that the only option available to him was to give up his job. If you are relatively powerless (e.g. a journalist in relation to an editor), then self-regulation can be meaningless, especially when the person in power does not share your views. These power imbalances are also felt in employment practices. When there was a threat of compulsory redundancies at the *Independent* newspaper, Michelle Stanistreet, general secretary of the UK's National Union of Journalists, commented that a precarious workforce that is paid 'bargain basement salaries . . . is fearful and compliant' (*Press Gazette*, 2 August 2013). Hardly the form of press freedom that underpins and buttresses democracy.

Of course, journalists also bring their own personal ethics, which have developed through upbringing, religious belief (or lack of), political affiliations and social, economic and cultural contexts, to their professional roles. Class, race and gender divides have long troubled journalism (Chambers and Steiner, 2010). White, middle-class men are more likely to have the freedom to practise a certain type of journalism they deem appropriate, as opposed to others who may struggle to gain positions of relative power or authority within news organizations (Douglas, 2019). Thus, understanding the socio-demographics of the people employed as journalists is also important when interrogating what this thing called media freedom is and how it impacts on news and democracy.

The above issues point to the fact that journalism is part of the institutionalized social order it exists within and is structured by neoliberalism. These structural factors must be taken into account in any discussion about what media freedom is and what it could become. Understanding the role of the news as an industry and news organizations as corporate entities is crucial to our understanding of how 'freedom' can be more easily claimed by some to the detriment of others. 'Freedom of the press' as an ethical practice does not somehow magically transcend the market it is part of. Rather, it is embroiled in the particular political-economic system it exists within. For example, in certain neo-liberal democracies such as the UK, regulation of the press is seen by some (mostly within the industry) as tantamount to authoritarian rule, an act of deliberate interference with and inhibition of the freedom of the press and as profoundly anti-democratic. Yet this approach, which has existed in the UK for over sixty years, has done nothing to protect the public interest in the provision of news and its contribution to democratic life, and everything to encourage commercial press malpractice that contributed to the phone-hacking scandal (Fenton, 2018).

Partly because the relationship between democracy and media is so complex and contingent, it is also never fixed and is constantly open to contestation. The media, like democracies, are not homogeneous, static entities. Both are ever-changing, both contain power and shape the space where power is competed for, albeit in different ways. As a consequence, both also contain difference and division and are subject to social forces and social movements that may challenge established and vested interests (Fenton and Freedman, 2014). This most often happens at the point of crisis – whether due to the failings of democratic systems or the dismal behaviour of some parts of the media. These points of crisis provide crucial opportunities for rethinking the relationship between media and democracy. Unfortunately, too often these moments become ones in which the complex notion of media freedom is successfully operationalized as a form of common sense to serve powerful interests rather than to support democracy.

The hacking scandal in the UK is one such case where a commonsense understanding of 'freedom of the press' was used to avoid a new system of fair and effective regulation of the press. It is a case worthy of a closer look.

The scandal of press freedom

Much of the news media thrives on scandal. But when the scandal is about news organizations themselves, they must work much harder to defend the freedom they claim as imperative to journalistic practice. In the summer of 2012 the *News of the World*, owned by Rupert Murdoch, was accused of illegal, unethical behaviour through the systematic phone-hacking of politicians, members of the royal family, celebrities, murder victims and their families. Murdoch subsequently closed down the *News of the World*, and several ex-editors and journalists found themselves under criminal investigation. The then prime minister, David Cameron, was publicly embarrassed by the employment of Andy Coulson (a former editor of *News of the World*, 2003–7) as his director of communications, since Coulson was arrested by the Metropolitan Police Service in July 2011 on allegations of corruption and phone-hacking. Cameron subsequently called for an inquiry chaired by Lord Justice Leveson to investigate the issue.

The reasons phone-hacking took place are complex. They involved the increasing entanglement of political and media elites as news coverage has taken on an ever-more important role in policy-making and elections; the failure of the Press Complaints Commission (the newspaper industry watchdog) to uphold ethical standards and enable adequate self-regulation of journalists; alongside decreasing profitability with plummeting circulation and readership figures and the migration of classified advertising to online sites such as Gumtree and eBay (Fenton, 2010). But one thing remains clear: the illegal practice of phone-hacking was not motivated by the fourth estate's desire to hold power to account. Rather, in a thoroughly marketized and deregulated newspaper industry the mission was to gain competitive advantage and increase newspaper sales through salacious and sensationalist stories.

The practice of phone-hacking was widely condemned. However, a common response from the news industry itself was to direct responsibility for phone-hacking towards the law and inadequate policing. The solution must lie therefore with the police and the enactment of the law and not through further regulation of the profession or industry, which should remain 'free' to do effectively as it pleases. The language of press freedom became the main tactic of deflection of scandal by the press lobby. Cries of the 'end of 300 years of press freedom' littered the pages of newspapers. This prompted the prime minister, David Cameron, who had initially said he would implement the Leveson recommendations unless they were 'bonkers', to state that even statutory underpinning – a law to enact the costs and incentives of a new system of press regulation with no interference whatsoever in the actual running of, or decision-making, of the new independent regulatory body – would be 'crossing the Rubicon'. In other words, the sacrosanct position of a free press in a free society would be irreparably undermined, and there would be no going back.

'Freedom' in this sense became a narrative device to sidestep the deeper, systemic problems of the newspaper industry of which these ethical misdemeanours were but one symptom. Freedom of the press came to stand in for *all* activities of the press regardless of whether they have democratic intent or not. This kind of short-cut libertarian defence that aligns freedom with established and vested power interests' ability to do whatever they like within the law means that any form of regulation that may encourage news organizations to behave in particular ways is assumed to be detrimental to democracy, while state involvement in the media in any form whatsoever becomes nothing more than state censorship. Such arguments reveal a particular ideological premise that the 'marketplace of ideas', dominated by publishers who promote a very particular definition of public problems, will deliver this thing called press freedom that will then enable a healthier democracy.

The mythology of naive liberal pluralism of the marketplace assumes that journalists already operate with full independence and in the interests of democracy and that news organizations have democratic intent at their core. But much (although by no means all) tabloid journalism runs counter to the public interest and has little democratic intent. As Trevor Kavannagh, associate editor of the *Sun*, noted in his own evidence to the Leveson Inquiry, 'news is as saleable a commodity as any other. Newspapers are commercial, competitive businesses, not a public service' (Kavanagh, 2011). News in these formulations is primarily for profit – this is a marketplace that operates on market principles. But of course, news is no ordinary commodity – it offers the possibility of directing the public conversation and hence is of relevance to politicians keen to convince voters of the benefits of their particular policy formulations. This puts news proprietors in a particular position of power. The owner of the London *Evening Standard* and *Independent*, Russian billionaire Evgeny Lebedev, tweeted after his appearance at Leveson: 'Forgot to tell Leveson that it's unreasonable to expect individuals to spend £millions on newspapers and not have access to politicians.' Lebedev has since been given a peerage by a UK Conservative government and now sits in the House of Lords. In the UK, it would seem, there is a relationship of sorts between news and democracy but a largely dysfunctional one whose breaking points pivot on issues relating to the commercialism and marketization of news as well as concentration of ownership and deregulation. The notion that somehow truth will emerge victorious in this so-called marketplace of ideas is clearly misconstrued. Indeed, we would do well to remember that just as journalism can be democratizing, so it can also be de-democratizing (Fenton, 2012).

Hackgate laid bare a system based on the corruption of power and neoliberal practice. Rupert Murdoch and the news culture he helped to promote was part of this process in the UK, one that can be traced back to the defeat of the print unions at Wapping and continued with the lobby for extensive liberalization of media ownership regulation to enable an unprecedented global media empire to emerge. Hackgate enabled the naming and shaming of what many had believed to be the case for years. It exposed systematic invasions of privacy that wrecked lives on a daily basis (Cathcart, 2012). It revealed the lies and deceit of senior newspaper figures and the wily entanglement and extensive associations of media and political elites – during the Leveson Inquiry it was revealed that a member of the Cabinet had met executives from Rupert Murdoch's empire once every three days on average since the Coalition was formed.[3] And we got a glimpse of a highly politicized and corrupt police force – Rebekah Brooks, chief executive officer of News International 2009–11 and former editor of *News of the World* and *The Sun*, admitted to paying police for information in a House of Commons Select Committee in 2003 but denied it in 2011 (*BBC News UK*, 15 April 2011), while more than a quarter of the police public affairs department were found to be previous employers of the *News of the World* (Warrell, 2011). This could be construed as a media freedom of sorts, but certainly not one that was defending democracy even in its most populist formulations.

The phone-hacking scandal exposed much of the UK press industry as being part of a system rather than the watchdog of that system. A system that claims that productivity is increased and innovation unleashed if the state stays out of the picture and lets businesses get on with it. Productivity in the market and hence news as a commodity take precedence over the social and political concerns of news as a mechanism of democratic process. In other words, the less 'interference' in the form of regulation and the more liberalized the market, the better the outcome (Jessop, 2002). In neoliberal democracies the power of the market is just as significant as the power of government. In the UK, there is certainly no rush to regulate for a healthy relationship between news media and democracy, yet there is plenty of urgency about the need to deregulate media for the benefit of the market. When the press lobby urge deregulation of their industry, the conceptualization of press freedom becomes a form of market justice disassociated from social justice. Freedom of the press expressed purely as the need to get the state to butt out and give commercial practice free reign is about nothing more than enabling market dominance to take priority over all other concerns. Freedom of the press expressed in this way is not a precondition or even a consequence of democracy so much as a substitute for it, because such freedom disregards concerns of social justice. Rather than watchdogs at the grand gates of democracy, these were the rats of the gutter press using their own power to distort democratic practice, all the while bringing misery and pain to the powerless through the hacking of a murdered teenager's mobile phone messages.

What this example shows is that freedom requires accountability, otherwise those with the most power will be free to do as they please while the powerless are, at best, ignored. The journalistic ethics on offer in this rhetoric is not the coming-together of journalists for the general promotion of journalism for the public good and in the public interest. Rather, it is a post-state capitalist logic based on an elevated sense of market justice (Boltanski, 2011) that has become normative. In the context of the hacking debate the phrase 'freedom of the press' became a term emptied of any social meaning of justice by becoming what Hardt and Negri call 'false universals that characterise dominant modern rationality' (Hardt and Negri, 2009, p. 120), whereby freedom is available to powerful media conglomerates but justice is denied to victims of press abuse. The abiding lesson of the hacking scandal is the enduring power of the press to control scandal, direct the national conversation and set the agenda in their own interests and not in the direction of more justice or democracy. Indeed, the hacking scandal revealed the power of certain news corporations to defy the public interest whenever it suits them. It further revealed their role as part of an elite power complex where commercial priorities reign supreme. This post-state capitalist logic infuses the so-called 'free' market with economic value to the forfeit of social value. In the end, we are left with a form of liberal privatism that reduces freedom to naked assertions of power and entitlement – a thoroughly unsocial liberty that unravels any social contract implied in the press as beneficial for society as a whole and embeds a form of aggressive market competition.

Unsocial liberty on social media: Freedom of expression and trans rights

The above discussion makes the obvious point that freedom of any kind always exists in an intricate relationship to power. Where state power is concerned, this can facilitate the sharing of power or it can restrict powers to certain organizations, groups or individuals. The key question, however, is in whose interest these constraints or freedoms operate and for what ends. Those whose interests, needs and values take precedence in any given situation are often a marker of the social order of the day and reflect prevailing relations of exploitation and oppression. Freedom and agency are always relationally constituted. This is one of the reasons why it is helpful to consider the concept of freedom in relation to the concept of justice (and hence, that of *in*justice) when considering freedom's relationship to democratic theory.

Fraser (1995) argues that there are two key dimensions of injustice – the economic and the cultural – to which a critical theory of democracy must respond. She argues that the economic relates to a 'politics of redistribution' and is analytically distinct from a 'politics of recognition' that relates to cultural dimensions of injustice arising from forms of misrecognition or non-recognition. Each respectively relates to class hierarchies and social orders of status. In her later writing, Fraser added a 'politics of representation' that is implicated in the politics of both redistribution and recognition. This refers to processes of framing – the grammar of politics that determines what is considered a matter of justice, who are its subjects and which actors are able to be agents of redress.

Iris Marion Young's work is also central to the prioritizing of injustice in critical theories of democracy. In particular Young emphasizes structural injustices as forms of harm that subjects may be vulnerable to; as well as how subjects are able to react in response to those harms, bringing to the fore issues of power, privilege, interest and capacity for action and the interrelations between each. In this account, democratic freedom is interrelated with the distribution of capacities to act and with securing the requisite institutional conditions of agency. Honneth (Fraser and Honneth, 2003) adds to this injustice-centred theory of democracy based on the concept of recognition and rooted in structural concerns. His theory of recognition and disrespect relies on an understanding of capitalism as a process that generates systematic social pathologies that impair conditions of self-realization, distorting the capacity for human reason and undermining the social conditions of identity formation. So, for example, the following chapter on inequality argues that one such social pathology is the designation of the 'underserving poor', who are misrepresented as welfare scroungers and work-shy shirkers, supporting a neoliberal emphasis on competitive individualism and meritocracy over structural concerns. Honneth's argument underlines Fraser's insistence that we must take into account problems of both distribution and recognition as constitutive of the quality of democratic politics; and they must be considered together if we are to conceive of a politics of transformation. Freedom does not come easily and cannot be assigned outside of existing structures of socio-economic relations. To illustrate this further we can turn again to Dussel (2008) who argues that a critical approach to democracy must do justice to the perspective of victims of injustice and this will involve having to recognize and negotiate the multiple ways in which people might be subjected to systems of domination. This highlights the importance of the forms and terms of communicative engagement of participants in the determination of interests, needs and values and underscores that people are positioned differentially in relation to structures of injustice that puts them in a differential relationship to democracy and to freedom. Freedom is always socially inscribed.

This debate can be illustrated through the struggle over transgender rights in the UK, which has been played out in national and social media. One such instance was the stoking of a transphobic furore over gender recognition certification processes by the reactionary right. In order to ensure that their correct gender is inscribed on their birth certificate, trans people first require a Gender Recognition Certificate (GRC). Having a GRC can make life easier when it comes to getting married or having your death recorded in the way you would like. The process of getting a GRC is controlled by the Gender Recognition Act (GRA) 2004.[4] The GRA requires trans people to get a medical diagnosis of 'gender dysphoria'. Often this will be from a gender identity clinic, where waiting times can vary between one and five years. Trans people also have to demonstrate that they have lived in their 'acquired gender' for a minimum of two years, requiring evidence such as letters addressed to them and photos of themselves at events in order to convince a panel of people whom they will never meet that they are, indeed, trans. In England and Wales, if they are married, the individual also needs the consent of their spouse, which can leave trans people trapped in abusive or controlling relationships. In 2019 the government ran a public consultation on reforming the GRA, which attracted over 100,000 responses. The vast majority (70 per cent) of respondents supported a demedicalized process so that trans people would not need a psychiatrist to diagnose them with gender dysphoria (King, Paechter and Ridgway, 2020). But the process remains medicalized and dehumanizing for trans people, who are still required to prove that they are who they say they are.

When the GRA consultation was announced in 2018 it was taken up and weaponized by the reactionary right as part of an 'anti-woke' transphobic tirade resulting in increasingly hostile media coverage in many outlets and platforms. The controversy that is stoked around trans people's rights feeds off a history of anti-trans media representations. In their submission to the Leveson Inquiry the NGO Trans Media Watch noted how the mainstream media create and sustain a climate of ridicule and humiliation; single out individual transgender people and their families for sustained personal intrusion; routinely use their previous names, 'before' photos, demeaning and ridiculing language for comic effect; regularly misgender and monster individuals and invade their privacy with no redress from the Press Complaints Commission; and sometimes leave people unable to find employment or accommodation (Trans Media Watch, 2011). The right have built on this transphobic invective in a desperate attempt to use identity politics as a means of increasing support and deflecting attention away from growing economic inequalities.

Research undertaken by the charitable trust Hope Not Hate (2022) suggests that as society has become more diverse and more educated over time, so a new 'politics of identity' has emerged that is more socially open and tolerant on a range of issues from gay marriage to immigration. But as society has become more socially liberal so it has also become more economically unequal. As the politics of distribution (embedded in issues of social class) continue to entrench divisions, economic disadvantages vie with a politics of recognition (relating to identity politics) in a complex and often reactionary manner. In disavowing a politics of distribution, we can see the right-wing swerve towards identity politics as a means to funnel the anger of the economically disadvantaged in the direction of other marginalized and minoritized people (and consequently away from structural concerns) in an attempt to undermine an equalities agenda.

The 2022 Hope Not Hate survey noted that economic inequality continues to offer the far right their best hope to expand as they seek to capitalize on the anger and despair created by economic disadvantage. In the survey, those who felt strongly about being disadvantaged in society were more likely to agree that feminism has gone too far and that British men are not as masculine as they used to be. The same survey in 2023 (of 20,000 people in the UK) notes that 67 per cent believe that the political system is broken. It also charts how anti-trans rhetoric has become increasingly vocal and aggressive among the far right while there is increasing symmetry between the far right and the mainstream right, with both talking about the same issues, often using similar language. Enter the 'culture wars'.

The notion of the 'culture wars' originated in the US and broadly refers to cultural conflicts over values, beliefs and practices in society. In the UK the 'culture wars' have given rise to what has been termed 'cancel culture' and 'wokeism'. A study from The Policy Institute (2021) found that articles on the existence of 'culture wars' in the UK increased by more than twenty-five times between 2015 and 2020, influencing political debates and driving negative perceptions of progressive issues. In the UK transgender rights and recognition have been at the centre of the culture war debate, with frequent calls of free speech suppression and cancel culture by gender-critical feminists.[5] The term 'woke' originates in Black radical politics in the US and refers broadly to an awareness of racial injustices. Research in 2021 (YouGov, 2021) showed that most Britons (59 per cent) didn't know what 'woke' meant. This is hardly surprising when its meaning has become increasingly distorted in the UK context where 'wokeness' and 'cancel culture' have become frequent tropes of right-wing social commentators seeking to undermine progressive values and politics (King, Paechter and Ridgway, 2020).

The so called 'war on woke' builds on a long history of the right's attempts to whip up moral panic (Cohen, 2011) about left-wing 'identity politics' by presenting it as a threat to the British way of life rather than as promoting equal rights; framing the issue(s) as part of the 'looney left' or 'political correctness gone too far' (Curran, Gaber and Petley, 2019) rather than the interrogation of systemic inequalities. The 'war on woke' is an attempt to create an ideological enemy through processes of othering (Pickering, 2001), polarizing issues and feeding off the long-term stigmatization of particular social groups (Krzyżanowski, 2020). It is a political battle designed to garner support for and embolden the right and fragment and repress the left.

One tactic of the American right in these culture wars that helps to explain the success of such polarizing rhetoric is 'owning the libs' – a term from the world of gaming used by hackers to describe their conquered opponents. 'Owning the libs' in political spheres does not require conquering so much as infuriating and distressing liberals with uncompromising anti-liberal right-wing responses guaranteed to promulgate a social media frenzy. A good example of this is when Representative Marjorie Taylor Greene installed a sign outside her congressional office in Washington stating, 'There are TWO genders: MALE & FEMALE. Trust The Science!' opposite the office of Representative Marie Newman, who has a transgender daughter. The ensuing Twitter exchange quickly went viral. 'Owning the libs' is now a common conservative political response in the US and the UK. In many ways this is simply a form of shock jock politics of old translated into the digital era. Legitimacy is declared by insisting on anti-woke sentiments being simply about free speech as a form of abstracted liberal democratic entitlement. In doing so, such tactics also give permission to people to harass, degrade or abuse marginalized others through harmful speech, an anti-democratic form of freedom that denies justices of recognition, redistribution and representation to the most powerless and oppressed.

Anti-trans attacks and hate crimes have jumped exponentially in recent years. In the UK, from 2015 to 2018, there was a 92 per cent increase in the number of reported anti-trans hate crime incidents. The NGO Gendered Intelligence (2020) believe that this rise is partly due to the immense and sudden amount of antagonistic attention the media has given to trans issues in recent years. The GRA consultation was followed by increasingly hostile media coverage and commentary, especially on platforms such as Twitter. As this material exists indefinitely online, it also leaves individuals open to constant persecution, hate attacks and further prejudice. Gendered Intelligence believe that this maps directly onto the real-life incidents trans people are increasingly victim to. In the year ending March 2023 a record number of hate crimes were committed against transgender people in England and Wales – a rise of 11 per cent from the previous year (Goodier, 2023).

In 2022 Mermaids – a trans young people's charity in the UK – reported the media-influenced wave of abuse directed at their workers after an inaccurate and transphobic article in the *Daily Telegraph* went viral. They had to close their helpline and were investigated by the Charity Commission, leading to pauses in their funding. Online abuse and harassment travel fast and are notoriously difficult to get rid of. As the economic model of social media thrives on controversy, so 'cultural' conflicts have become louder and more antagonistic – the more controversial they are the more likely they are to grab attention and the more advertising revenue they reap for the platforms. Elon Musk's purchase of Twitter for $44bn in 2022 led to the sacking of more than half of its 7,500 workforce, including the entire trust and safety teams in some offices, in pursuit of cheaper methods to monitor tweets. Musk calls himself a 'free speech absolutist' (Martin, 2022). His takeover was celebrated by the right and followed by the return of many far right extremists who had previously been removed (including Donald Trump), leading to a rise in hateful and sexist language on the platform. Just as profits for news corporations motivated the hacking scandal, so profits for social media companies drive mediated speech injustices. Tech companies will never self-regulate well: they operate for commercial purposes, so will always be slow to respond to calls of abuse while the reaction economy ensures hate remains profitable. As noted above (Fraser and Honneth, 2003), capitalism generates systematic social pathologies that ridicule marginalized and oppressed people's ways of life and blight the conditions for their self-realization. Meanwhile the right utilizes the mechanism of identity politics to invoke their own 'freedom of speech', which in turn deflects from the growing economic inequality that capitalism causes. And so we witness the transmutation of freedom into *un*social freedom.

We should also remind ourselves that such constructions of unsocial liberty by far right media, politicians and social media/ online spaces do not always achieve their intended outcome. In the UK 2022 leadership debates for the UK Conservative Party many of the candidates focused on anti-trans sound bites in an attempt to turn trans people into an electoral 'issue', a concern that research by Stonewall (2022) notes is not shared by the general public. Narratives that are hostile to trans people or challenge their existence don't resonate with most women. Stonewall also notes that in the 2022 Australian General Election, Scott Morrison's Liberal Party focused on trans rights, particularly regarding sports, as an attack on the Labor Party's trans-inclusive position. The Liberal/National coalition lost eighteen seats, half of which were previously safe or fairly safe, giving the Labor Party a majority. Attacking trans rights did not benefit the centre-right party, nor did it negatively impact the centre-left.

In the 2022 Scottish local elections, the Alba Party ran as an alternative independence party, with a pledge to 'push women's rights to the top of the agenda' by criticizing the SNP's plan to reform the Gender Recognition Act in the ways outlined above. Alba received 0.7 per cent of the vote and no seats. The Scottish Conservative leader, Douglas Ross, also campaigned on an anti-trans rights platform, arguing that 'trans women are not women'. The Scottish Conservatives lost sixty-two seats in the local elections, being displaced as the second-largest party by Scottish Labour. The trans-inclusive Scottish SNP, Labour, Liberal Democrat and Green Parties all increased their vote share and seats. In 2022 the Scottish government passed a new Gender Recognition Reform Bill, removing the requirement under the Gender Recognition Act 2004 for applications to have evidence of a diagnosis of gender dysphoria and aligning with international best practice and the consensus view of United Nations Human Rights bodies. In January 2023 the UK government announced that it would block the Scottish government's reform, arguing that it interfered with UK-wide equalities legislation. Meanwhile, trans people face indignity and repression as minoritized 'others' used for political point-scoring.

Concepts of freedom must not be abstracted and idealized as indisputable forms of democratic good. They are always interrelated with power and its mediations and hence with issues of inequality and so remain hotly contested. This means that we cannot fully appreciate interpretations of freedom of the press or freedom of expression and their relations to a democratic politics without appreciating the victims of injustices and systems of domination. We cannot understand the politics of (mis)recognition without understanding the politics of (re)distribution; we cannot understand the interpolation of the social into political discourse without extrapolating to the economic context in which it operates. As Cammaerts notes, 'freedom of speech and the right to offend are too often weaponized to protect racist and discriminatory language and to position these ideas as valid opinions worthy of democratic debate' (Cammaerts, 2022, p. 730), when in fact time and again they function as enablers of social injustices that support and sustain the interests of power and capital.

What can we do about it? Communicative freedoms ensured

The liberal model of freedom is premised on the individual: in liberal thought, we can only speak of individual freedom in a meaningful way if subjects are free to pursue their aims without hindrance limited only by the fact that these aims and actions must not impinge on the freedom of other subjects. As such, liberalism places the realization of individual freedom in a legal context meant to ensure that individuals can act without interference as long as they do not interfere with the equal claim of others to enjoy the same freedom. But the realization of human capacities requires the existence of social communities. Individual subjects can only realize their full capacities for freedom as members of a free social community – one in which shared intentions and mutual sympathy exist. Such a shared community needs to negotiate these goals democratically. Democratic will formation is an inter-subjective communicative act in which subjects cooperatively contribute to their personal, economic and political relationships with the goal of maintaining their community – it is not an individual endeavour. In other words, any form of freedom is relationally constituted. Relationality matters politically because it exposes the power dynamics involved in social relations, thus revealing the necessity of a justice-oriented approach to critical theories of democracy. We cannot address media freedom without understanding the victims of press abuse – just as we cannot understand freedom of expression without addressing the victims of hateful speech.

A turn to *communicative* freedoms helps us here. In the democratic way of life, institutions and structures are brought about by the subjects of the democratic process. They are the ones who correct and adjust the design and outcome by means of public deliberation. Citizens assembled in the democratic public sphere enable cooperation in all major social spheres to overcome exclusion by constantly pointing out that the realization of freedom, equality and solidarity is not possible under the prevailing social and economic conditions. As Cohen and Fung (2021, p. 61) note, 'equal, substantive, communicative freedom' goes beyond individual expression because it focuses not only on speakers or originators of messages but also on receivers and bystanders. By understanding communication as a collective endeavour, it moves beyond a sole focus on individual rights and censorship to creating the conditions and affordances that enable broad participation in the public sphere.

Creating the conditions and affordances for 'equal substantive communicative freedom' is no easy feat, but taking such an approach certainly forces a rather different perspective on both media freedom and freedom of expression. It broadens our understanding to one that goes well beyond a Californian ideology of equal access to platforms and individual freedoms of speech as the ultimate democratic aim, or one that focuses solely on the news industry's indefatigable right to publish whatever it pleases. Rather, it aims to consider the underlying structures and vested interests of both. Offering up individual freedoms may provide temporary respite for some but it will never address structural inequalities and enable full recognition and the flourishing of life for all. It may be a temporary diversion from structures of domination and manage their worst excesses (as with UK regulation for online harms) but it will never transform them. Similarly, when it comes to mainstream news organizations, regulatory tweaks may temper the impact of content distorted by the endless pursuit of ever more profit (by limits on things like media ownership or creating legal frameworks for ethical journalism) and shift our attentions to the foot-soldiers of journalism, but it will never transform the communicative infrastructures they must operate within.

In the US, one approach that aligns with a push for equal, substantive communicative freedom comes from the NGO Free Press. In 2020, they launched a project titled 'Media 2070', a Black-led coalition calling for media reparations to redress how white-dominant media companies, government media policies and philanthropic foundations have inflicted harms on Black lives throughout US history including the concentration of media power with white owners, supporting racist journalism, corporate media complicity in the slave trade and tech companies allowing white supremacists to use their platforms. The sorts of media reparations that members of Media 2070 suggest include directing philanthropic funding to media justice initiatives as well as media policies that limit concentration through a hypothecated tax on the profits of corporate media and tech companies that is then fed through to media justice work by democratic participatory mechanisms. In 2022, the US-based foundation Democracy Fund changed its strategy for funding news and information projects to support those who 'advance justice, confront racism and inequality and equip people to change and thrive' (Stearns, 2022) with a turn to media justice, community reporting and movement journalism that stands for equity and democracy. In the UK the Media Reform Coalition launched a guide for funding journalism using participatory grant-making to direct funding towards co-creational models of journalism (including defining harm and redress) that are independent of government and commercial interests, accountable, democratic and for everyone (Grayson, 2021). These sorts of initiatives take the notion of equal, substantive communicative freedom seriously and reject notions of freedom based on neoliberal premises that have too often entrenched social injustices.

Conclusion: Media freedom as democratic delusion

The notion of an ideal relationship between a 'free' news media and democracy is hinged on a conception of independent journalism in the public interest linked to notions of knowledge, political participation and democratic renewal. This normative liberal democratic understanding has been underpinned through legislative processes that incentivize truth (such as public interest defences, tax breaks, subsidies and distribution privileges) and protect from harm (such as libel and privacy laws) and codes of professional ethics in journalism upheld by trade unions, professional associations and regulatory bodies. But such legislative processes exist within a political economic context that has seen corruption and compromise come to the fore as political and commercial interests merge and expand. It is now abundantly clear that a media and tech system that may have many platforms and points of distribution but is dominated by a few powerful voices and a news media increasingly run to secure financial reward or political influence will never foster greater participation in political culture and deliver equal, substantive communicative freedom. In summary, arguing for press freedom and independent journalism in this context is a democratic delusion.

So where do we turn? Focusing on independence but retaining a (neo)liberal democratic framing only gets us so far. Reimagining liberal democratic frameworks towards *equal substantive communicative freedom* would need to take a rather different approach and recognize the multiple forms of *inter*dependence between media and political/private interests and seek to reconfigure this interdependence such that both are holding the other to account rather than existing in a relationship of vested interests. Communicative freedoms are always interdependent. In a reimagined democratic society the forms of interdependence between media and state/commercial practice would be oriented around a relationship based on democracy rooted in social justice and the common good and not the marketplace. Justice is a collective phenomenon and at the heart of what democracy can be. It should also then be at the heart of what a democratic media could become. Foregrounding interdependence and social justice acknowledges the power relations involved in communicative freedom and starts to build a wholly different type of *justificatory* democracy.

Equal substantive communicative freedom requires developing new ways of making media and tech policy that aren't captured by existing elites and that include a commitment to tackle the growing concentrations of power that dominate our media and communications systems – we need to prise open the continuing grip on our media of vested interests and proactively invest in co-creational democratic media. At a bare minimum this means:

- Proactive legislation for media plurality in the public interest, including an end to concentration of media ownership and the influence of billionaire media moguls as well as tech giant oligopolies' hold on political cultures (see Chapter 6).
- Public investment in alternative models of media ownership with democratic forms of governance for non/low-profit news in the public interest and for social justice, potentially funded through a form of hypothecated taxation on tech giants.
- The establishment of new publicly owned organizations that will provide an alternative to privately owned digital platforms, be democratically organized and run, develop innovative technological solutions to advance social justice and harness data for the public good (see Chapter 7).
- An end to all political influence over media organizations and operations (including public service broadcasting). Politicians should be banned from involvement in any appointments to any news media organizations or to any organizations that regulate them. All meetings between news organizations and government officials should be recorded, transcribed and published.
- All news publishers and platforms must be subject to effective regulatory mechanisms to uphold standards of ethical journalism and to enable people to hold them to account. The news industry or those who stand to benefit from it should never be actively involved in any way in mechanisms of accountability, either organizationally or in practice.

But creating the conditions for communicative freedoms means going beyond media policy to creating the conditions for a fairer, more equal society to exist. Previous chapters have argued that liberal democracy has been evacuated of meaning where concentrations of power (particularly in relation to media and tech industries) overwhelm public interests. In the next chapter I argue that where gross inequality exists, minorities and the disenfranchised are consistently excluded from political access, voice and mediated structures of meaning generation that 'reflect the merging of large capital and a political elite' (Tambini, 2021, p. 146) and preclude democracy.

5

EQUALITY AND INJUSTICE

Social, political and economic equality of all peoples in any political system is an essential principle of democracy. Political equality ensures that those with political power are authorized by and accountable to all those who are impacted by the decisions being made.

> When political equality is absent, whether from explicit political exclusions or privileges, from extreme social or economic disparities, from uneven or managed access to knowledge, or from manipulation of the electoral system, political power will inevitably be exercised by and for a part, rather than the whole. The demos ceases to rule. (Brown, 2019, p. 23)

This understanding of democracy takes us back to the differential distribution of power discussed in Chapter 2, the premise of which is that democracy and inequality are diametrically opposed. It also links closely to the concept of participation in Chapter 3 that considered differential access to knowledge and information resources. In the latter, I argued that political participation is not simply about access but also about social and communicative justice – the social and economic conditions necessary for the development and exercise of individual and collective communication capacities such that everyone can play a part in the shaping of society. It follows, then, that democratic health has a direct relationship to levels of equality (and all forms of equality are interrelated). A healthy democracy cannot exist when there are high levels of social, political and economic inequality. The more inequality you have, the more power differentials are at play and the less democracy will be able to thrive.

While liberty and equality have always been associated with notions of democracy, the relationship between both has long been contested and associated with particular political ideologies. According to Castoriadis (1980) the essential political issue is how to conceive of the balance between liberty and equality, which he sees as the defining difference between socialism and capitalism. Put simply, capitalism is often understood as valuing liberty through the free market, and socialism as valuing equality through the redistribution of resources. Castoriadis (ibid.) argues that these two concepts have been depicted as exclusionary when in fact they are complementary, and crucially so, for a just and democratic society to exist. The first question of liberty is whether equality of all in the participation of power exists. Capitalism presents the two concepts as inherently contradictory because it assumes that total equality and liberty are impossible together. Thus, the exploitation of the poor by the rich, of the colonized by the colonizers, is legitimized as the only possible system. If, however, we take the view that democracy is impossible unless everyone has the ability to change the social and political system of which they are a part, then democracy is impossible without equality. Similarly, Balibar (2014) advances the term 'equaliberty' to denote the interrelationship between equality and liberty – one can only be achieved on the grounds of the other – and if one is suppressed, the other will be too. Equaliberty then 'is nothing other than the demand for a popular sovereignty and autonomy without exclusions' (Balibar, 2004, p. 319).

However, while equality has long been argued as central to democracy, in the economic realm, austerity, unemployment, high personal debt, extreme poverty and inequality feature heavily across many liberal democratic states. In the UK (as elsewhere), the impact of these crises is particularly marked for working-class and minority communities, whose experiences are also inflected by the 'war on terror', lack of affordable housing, a rise in the cost of living, low pay, precarious employment and the lingering impact of the Covid-19 pandemic. In this context, an important question for liberal democratic theory is whether social stability and dialogic politics can prosper where poverty and inequality are apparent across so many intersecting fault-lines: young and old, Black and white, religious and secular.

Given that capitalism is fundamentally at odds with equality, the claim of democracy in capitalist states requires a transmutation of equality into meritocracy. Discourses of meritocracy abound in our mainstream media: from *Who Wants to Be a Millionaire?* and *The Apprentice* to *The X Factor* and *The Voice*: the underpinning rationale of these forms of reality TV is if you are talented enough, work hard enough and have ambition, you too can enter the class of wealth and privilege, you too can find fame and fortune. The principle of meritocracy disavows inequality because it is based on the notion of the 'level playing field' that is differentiated only by individual skill and effort. This logic is extended through the world of social media influencers – if you simply play by the rules of online engagement and increase your number of followers, you too can gain wealth and power; social mobility is yours for the taking. This perfectly embodies what Littler (2017) describes as 'entrepreneurial self-fashioning' (p. 190). The ideology of meritocracy obscures structural and systemic issues within the institutions of capitalism and allows inequalities in wealth to expand.

When meritocratic frames are normalized they can also capture and assimilate attempts to counter racism and sexism. For instance, a response to calls of institutional racism in media industries is often met with a tick-box approach to diversity politics – a few more Black and Brown people in the industry and on the screens and it's a job done. The door may be opened a little wider for a lucky few, but the multiple hurdles of institutionalized discrimination embedded within organizations are left untouched. Castilla and Benard (2010) also found that attempts to implement meritocracy in organizations leads to the kinds of inequalities it claims to eliminate. This is because explicitly adopting meritocracy as a value convinces subjects of their own moral certitude that avoids any consideration of structural prejudice or discriminatory behaviour. Meritocracy justifies the status quo because it claims that the world is just and everyone gets their just rewards in life according to their talent and how hard they work. It flatters by deception, transmuting material inequality into personal superiority, sanctioning the rich and powerful's own perception that they are indeed productive geniuses. Consequently, where people fail to succeed on this premise (because they are structurally disadvantaged) it breeds resentment and scapegoating. In the UK, this is most evident in forms of exclusionary ethnonationalism, where immigrants who 'come over here and steal our jobs' are blamed for enduring forms of inequality and poverty. And in Spain, France, Italy, Greece, Sweden, Finland and Denmark ethnonationalist movements have thrived in the face of social insecurity following the entrenchment of neoliberalism, a process in which the liberal individualism of meritocracy has played a part.

This chapter considers these debates in more detail, by bringing social, political and economic inequalities together into direct dialogue. It argues that while economic inequality is often the most talked about (and crucially important), social injustices are often where groups of people experience political disenfranchisement and where historically produced inequalities are manifest as differentiated political access, voice and treatment. The chapter ends by arguing that approaching the concept of democracy with an *egalitarian imagination* brings together economic equality with social justice. Because just as a politics of redistribution will be required in order to bring into being a people capable of self-rule, so democracy also demands recognition of and redress for social injustices. Both run counter to neoliberal politics and economics.

Where might an egalitarian imagination applied to our structures of media and communication lead us? One possible response is the concept of the commons. The notion of the commons stands in stark contrast to, and in criticism of, the privatization, deregulation and expropriation of neoliberalism (Ostrom, 1990; Hess and Ostrom, 2007; Hardt and Negri, 2009; Broumas, 2017), since it focuses on a more equitable, just and ecologically sustainable society. Literature on the commons outlines how commons resources (the air we breathe, the water we drink, the public services we share) can be inclusively managed through decentralized and participatory democratic institutions to prevent or limit corporate or state exploitation. This chapter ends by considering what a media commons that seeks to address (and redress) social, economic and political inequalities might look like.

But before we delimit what a politics of a media commons might be, we first need to address what we mean by inequality and how it is connected to power and poverty.

Inequality and poverty

Since the 2008 financial crash, the wealth of the richest 1 per cent in the world has grown at an average of 6 per cent per year compared to 3 per cent for the rest. If this rate continues, the world's richest 1 per cent will own two-thirds of the world's wealth by 2030 (House of Commons Library, 2018). This increase was exacerbated during the Covid-19 pandemic, with 2020 marking the steepest increase in global billionaires' share of wealth on record. Stiglitz shows how political and economic forces have combined in the interest 'of the one percent, for the one percent by the one percent' (2013, p. xxxix). The World Inequality Lab, building on the work of more than 100 researchers around the world, shows the richest 10 per cent of the global population currently (Chancel et al., 2022) hold 76 per cent of global wealth, compared to a 2 per cent share for the poorest half. Since wealth is a major source of future economic gains, and of power and influence, this signals further increases in inequality to come. At the heart of this explosion in economic inequality is the extreme concentration of economic power in the hands of a very small minority of the super-rich. The top 1 per cent is growing much faster than the rest: between 1995 and 2021, the top 1 per cent captured 38 per cent of the global increment in wealth. The share of wealth owned by the global top 0.1 per cent rose from 7 per cent to 11 per cent over that period as global billionaire wealth soared (ibid.).

Inequality has surged in many places around the globe since the 1980s. Therborn (2020) notes (commenting on a study that focused on the wage-earning capacity of men) that, in the US, while 95 per cent of boys born in 1940 earned more than their fathers at age thirty, only 41 per cent of the 1984 cohort did, with the main reason being not lower economic growth but higher inequality. The US has seen huge rises in living costs: between 1970 and 2015 family expenditure on housing increased by 57 per cent, on health insurance by 104 per cent, on childcare by 953 per cent and on college fees by 275 per cent, while men's earnings grew by 2 per cent (Warren, 2017).

In the UK, the Institute for Public Policy Research (IPPR, 2018) commission on economic justice revealed how the financial health of the UK is brutally divided along lines of income, geography, gender, ethnicity and age. But it is not only financial health that suffers. Inequality damages our societies, our economies and our democratic systems (Dorling, 2014). Wilkinson and Pickett's analysis (2009, 2018) is largely economic, but they make a compelling case that the relationship between economic inequality and the levels of trust, mental illness, obesity, children's educational performance, life expectancy, infant mortality, teenage births, murders, imprisonment rates, social mobility and community life are directly correlated to levels of inequality. All of these factors, in turn, impact on democracy because inequality makes certain political subjects less able to engage politically and participate in society and consequently less visible to politicians. Furthermore, Gethin, Martínez-Toledano and Piketty (2021) argue that the steep rise in economic inequality has seen a transition from class-based party systems to multi-elite party systems in Western democracies. In a study of fifty Western and non-Western democracies covering more than 300 elections between 1948 and 2020 they show that, whereas left-wing parties' support used to come from lower-income and less-educated voters, it has gradually become associated with more highly educated voters in nearly all Western democracies. They attribute this shift to the ascendancy of a global ideology that puts private property interests above all else, abandoning any sense that capitalism can be radically transformed. As leftist parties adopt neoliberal policies, class diminishes in political salience, and identity politics comes to the fore as social inequalities (relating to the likes of gender and ethnicity) take centre-stage. In the process, political systems have come to represent two types of elites: the rich and the well-educated. Consequently, as discussed in the previous chapter, the right focus on the derision of identity politics to garner the anger of the economically disadvantaged and once more deflect attention away from structural inequalities (of both the social and economic kind).

With concentrations of wealth come concentrations of power. Increasingly powerful and well-resourced business, financial and technological elites are influencing politics, economics and wider society through means that are invisible to most, behind closed doors and deliberately outside of the public sphere. Their extreme wealth gives them access and advantage. Hacker and Pierson (2010) in their book *Winner-Take-All Politics* systematically establish that the skewing of American incomes has primarily been due to major policy changes related to taxation that supports the ultra-wealthy; trade policies and business regulations that support the market; and the weakening of trade unions. In other words, these are decisive politics intended to organize society in ways that directly impact and benefit the mega-rich. In 1961 millionaires in the US paid 43.1 per cent of federal income tax. In 2011 they only paid 23.1 per cent. Between 2013 and 2018, the average tax rate for the 400 wealthiest Americans was 22 per cent. An investigation by ProPublica found that between 2014 and 2018, the twenty-five wealthiest Americans collectively earned $401bn but paid just $13.6bn – about 3.4 per cent – in taxes due to lower tax rates on financial assets and deductions from charitable donations.

Billionaires in technology industries pay the lowest income tax rate, an average of 17 per cent of their income, largely because their wealth comes from investment income. Bill Gates, whose income from 2013 to 2018 was an average of $2.85bn a year, paid an average effective federal income tax rate of 18.4 per cent. Laurene Powell Jobs, the widow of Apple co-founder Steve Jobs, earned an average of $1.57bn and paid an average tax rate of 14.8 per cent. In comparison, the average single worker earning $45,000 paid an average tax rate of 21 per cent. A married couple with one child who earned $200,000 paid a rate of 26 per cent (Kiel et al., 2022). The simple fact is that while the number of billionaires is rising and wealth taxes are falling in virtually all developed countries, there are severe and growing crises of health and social care because of a severe lack of state resources. And so inequality increases.

Inequality is always a political choice – it is not inevitable. This can be shown by looking at different countries' political responses to it. Following a series of deregulation and liberalization programs which took different forms in different countries, income and wealth inequalities have been on the rise nearly everywhere since the 1980s. But while certain countries have experienced spectacular increases in inequality (including the US, Russia and India), others (some European countries and China) have experienced relatively smaller rises. While inequality has increased within most countries over the past two decades, global inequalities between countries have declined. This points to the fact that over the past forty years nations have become richer but governments have become significantly poorer. Private wealth has grown as forms of taxation on wealth have decreased, but the share of wealth held by *public actors* is close to zero or negative in rich countries. In the UK public wealth dropped from 60 per cent of national income in 1970 to minus 106 per cent in 2020 – with huge implications for state capacities to tackle inequality – hence we see within-country inequalities increase. Although Europe has fared better than many parts of the world, the picture is still dismal. The *European Sustainable Development Report 2021* (Sustainable Development Solutions Network, 2021) ranks countries by a 'leave no-one behind' score that tracks inequalities along four dimensions: poverty, services, gender and income. Of the 34 countries that have been scored and ranked, Turkey comes last, the UK 24th, France 13th and Norway 1st. Those countries with less inequality have more robust social safety nets and progressive taxation policies.

Inequality is linked to, but also distinct from, poverty. The Joseph Rowntree Foundation defines poverty as 'when a person's resources are not enough to meet their minimum needs'. The UK is the fifth-largest economy in the world. Yet while poverty levels have remained fairly constant over the last decade – at roughly 21/22 per cent of the population (13 million people) – an unprecedented 68 per cent of families in poverty now live in a household where someone is in work (Schmuecker et al., 2022), indicative of low wages and precarious employment. Poverty is also strongly linked with disability and ethnicity, with people from Black and minority ethnic communities experiencing multiple forms of socio-economic disadvantage. In 2020 a report on levels of destitution (defined as when a household cannot afford two or more of the essentials we need to live such as shelter, food, heating and clothing) revealed that around 2.4 million people experienced destitution in 2019 – a 54 per cent increase since 2017, including 550,000 children. Inadequate benefit levels and debt deductions were identified as key drivers of destitution (Fitzpatrick et al., 2020).

In England between June 2010 and March 2016 welfare reforms enacted reductions of £26 billion in UK social security and tax credits spending, with 'deficit reduction' being the primary goal of government (Tinson et al., 2016). Young adults (16–24) were particularly hard hit with 'rapidly falling real wages, incomes and wealth' (Hills et al., 2015, p. 3). Since then, we have lived through the pandemic, where a £20 per week uplift was applied to Universal Credit (the combined system of UK welfare benefits). This additional payment was reversed in 2022 just at the moment when increases in living costs exploded due to high inflation as a result of Brexit, the pandemic and the war in Ukraine. A stark metric is the UK's level of absolute poverty, which is defined as being a household income less than 60 per cent of the median income level of 2010–11, adjusted for inflation – a measure that usually goes up only in times of recession. The Resolution Foundation (2022) forecasts that in 2023, the fall in real incomes means another 1.3 million people in the UK – including 500,000 children – will be pushed into this category, taking the total number in absolute poverty to 12.5 million. In 2020, it was already the case that almost a third of disabled people in the UK lived in poverty (Fitzpatrick et al., 2020). As noted in Chapter 3, when individuals are thrust into poverty, forced into holding down multiple jobs in order to earn a living wage in an endless individual battle for survival, they are more likely to be politically disenfranchised and less likely to participate in civil society.

Acknowledging that inequality is an active political decision is underlined from recent history. In the much-maligned 1970s, when trade unions were strong and the welfare state was a dependable safety net, income and wealth inequality were at an all-time low – and although poverty was an issue, it had not yet been allowed to run rampant (Thane, 2018). When Margaret Thatcher came to power in 1979, about 13 per cent of children lived in relative poverty; by 1992, the figure was 29 per cent (Joyce, 2014). When the Labour government took over in 1997 child poverty consistently declined, before increasing again after 2010 when the Conservatives returned to power. At the same time, the kind of precarious work that locks people into poverty has been allowed to increase exponentially, with the gig economy sending us back to an age of insecure, low-paid employment reminiscent of the workers congregating at the factory gates in the 1900s – only now the factory gates have become an app. Platforms such as Uber and Deliveroo increase precarity in the workforce, disrupt existing labour markets and exploit workers through the removal of benefits and refusal of decent working conditions. Thane (2018) notes that since 2010 the value of benefits and tax credits to working families has fallen by 10 per cent. Since the government's introduction of Universal Credit – replacing six benefits with one single monthly payment – rough sleeping and demand at food banks have risen. The Conservative government has argued that Universal Credit should be difficult to claim in order to increase incentives to work just as administrators of the nineteenth-century Poor Law justified low, punitive benefits as essential correctives to the innate idleness of the poor. The realization that the Poor Law perpetuated poverty and damaged society and the economy by driving people into low-paid work was one of the early pressures for state welfare. Yet since the 1980s the 'rolling back' of the state and welfare has returned us to a situation in some ways much like the 1900s, but with a contemporary technological twist.

Inequality and the rise of elites

In his first path-breaking book on inequality, *Capital in the 21st Century*, Piketty (2014) demonstrated that alongside rising income inequality, since the 1980s there has been a revival of a system of old closed elites, not dissimilar to the model of traditional aristocracies. This provocative claim punctured the complacent view that high earners could be justified as dynamic change-makers that result in 'trickle down' benefits for all and instead pointed to a bleaker picture in which elites feather their own nests and perpetuate their own privileges, just as they used to do in feudal societies.

A focus on the super-rich or the 1 per cent is distinct from approaches on institutional elites, even as they overlap, since the latter tends to discuss political resources and the power of elites rather than wealth. Institutional elites can be defined as those who control the key material, symbolic and political resources within a country, as argued by Reis and Moore (2005), and as those occupying commanding positions within the set of institutions that are most salient to national political influence and policy-making. Although occupational elites do not equate to a 'governing elite' or 'power elite' in general, in the case of media and technology industries the symbolic and political power they exert arguably exceeds many other industries or, at the very least, constitute a central organizing force in what Piketty and Goldhammer (2020) refer to as 'inequality regimes'. Because of the centrality of communications to political institutions, elite media occupations are significant in the sense that they constitute a key reservoir or recruiting market from which governing or power elites are drawn (and vice-versa).

Savage (2015) argues for the existence of a distinctive elite class which is not only economically privileged in terms of their income and accumulated wealth, but which also shows signs of social and cultural privilege and distinctiveness. Members of the 'elite' social class are part of the 6 per cent of the most economically advantaged in the country. Savage (2015) suggests the term 'economic' or 'wealth elites' to capture this phenomenon. The extended power of a growing wealth elite favours a policy environment of 'corporate libertarianism' (Pickard, 2014), where global corporations are given relative freedom to do as they please by governments who fiercely defend capitalist interests because, on the whole, capital is where their own interests lie. Meanwhile, chief executive salaries rocket: chief executives at the top US firms have seen their salaries increased by over 54 per cent since 2009, while ordinary wages have barely moved. In the UK in 2022, a FTSE chief executive would only have to work four days to surpass what a typical worker earns in a year (High Pay Centre, 2022). The chief executives of India's top information technology firm make 460 times the salary of a typical employee there. And women hold just 24 of the senior positions at Fortune 500 companies (Davis et al., 2020).

The growth of this sort of executive elite extends to the long-established revolving door between major news organizations and the government that has now expanded to include the tech giants. The former UK prime minister Boris Johnson worked for the national daily newspapers the *Telegraph* and *The Times*. Michael Gove, former secretary of state for levelling up, housing, and communities, was a *Times* journalist. George Osborne, former chancellor of the exchequer, became editor of the London *Evening Standard*. Nick Clegg, former deputy prime minister (2010–15) is now vice-president for global affairs and communications at Facebook. Clegg's former special adviser Verity Harding was hired as a policy manager for Google DeepMind, which works on artificial intelligence. Google also hired Theo Bertram, a former adviser to prime ministers Tony Blair and Gordon Brown, as public policy manager for Europe. Bertram then moved on to TikTok.

A report by Transparency International EU (Kergueno, 2021) noted that three of Facebook's five registered lobbyists had been working in EU political institutions before joining the social media company. While there is nothing inherently wrong with these appointments, the suspicion is that the revolving door of privilege often spins to benefit private gain. Google, Apple, Facebook, Amazon and Microsoft spent more than half a billion dollars between 2005 and 2018 lobbying Congress in the US and have been central to the crafting of bilateral and multilateral free trade agreements to their benefit (Mirrlees, 2021). These trends point towards the challenge of a renewed executive power where elite groups deploy their resources – their access to capital, their political influence and their ideological congruence – to dominate and dictate the terms of contemporary media and tech systems. Whether in the form of tax-avoiding corporations and offshore billionaires (in 2021 Oxfam estimated that tax havens cost governments around the world $427bn each year); data brokers and infrastructure empires (which harvest, consolidate, aggregate, analyse and sell your data for an estimated annual revenue of at least $200bn) (Reviglio, 2022); market-friendly politicians and captive regulators (an investigation in 2021 dubbed the 'Pandora Papers', revealed that hundreds of world leaders, politicians, billionaires and celebrities have used secretive offshore bank accounts and shell companies to hide billions of dollars from tax authorities in their countries), the end result is the increasing concentration of power and influence in ever fewer hands.

Another report, this time based on the UK, entitled *Elitist Britain* (The Sutton Trust, 2019) noted that the media, alongside politics and the civil service, form a triumvirate of sectors at the top of the socially exclusive list, with all three largely centred in London. Newspaper columnists, who play a significant role in shaping the national conversation, draw from a particularly small pool, with 44 per cent attending fee-paying private schools and 33 per cent coming through the private school system to Oxford or Cambridge (Oxbridge) universities. Looking at a variety of roles in the news media, including influential editors and broadcasters, they reveal a similar picture, with 43 per cent having been privately educated and 36 per cent graduating from Oxbridge. They note that trends in the sector, including budget cuts, the closure of many local media organizations, the increasing casualization of work and high numbers of unpaid internships, contribute to the ongoing under-representation of those from less-well-off backgrounds (correlated directly with ethnicity and gender) across the media. Ofcom's *Five-Year Review: diversity and equal opportunities in UK Broadcasting* (Ofcom, 2021) found that in 2020–21 the proportion of women in the television industry was 47 per cent (although only 16 per cent of these are aged fifty and over). When it comes to class disparity, workers are nearly twice as likely to have attended private school compared with the UK benchmark, while 59 per cent have grown up in homes where the main earner had a professional occupation. 72 per cent of all staff working in TV in the UK are white. The working structures of our media industries lay bare the embedded interrelations between economic, social and political inequalities.

Inequality and social injustices

Feminist scholars have long documented how inequality is inflected by gender. There are enormous gaps between women and men in terms of health, education, labour market participation and representation in institutions such as parliaments and the media. The gender pay gap is higher in more unequal societies, and, when you add ethnicity in to the mix, inequality increases further still. Women make up the majority of the world's lowest-paid workers and are concentrated in the most precarious jobs. Again, add ethnicity into the mix and the weight of inequality increases exponentially.

Piketty (2022) underscores that we are witnessing the greatest wealth concentration, inequality and impoverishment across the globe since the late nineteenth century, and these processes are rooted in ideology and politics. Like many (Chang, 2008; Robinson and Kelley, 2021; Rodney, 2018), he shows how inequality in Western societies is embedded in systems of world domination and colonial appropriation with the enormous wealth of European society in the nineteenth and early twentieth century a direct result of colonialism. Adding the injuries of capitalism to the ravages of colonialism, we see the further exploitation of culturally and socially constructed differences lived through the uneven and intersectional formations of race, gender, sexuality, class, disability and religion. Race-making practices are intrinsic to processes of capital accumulation because racism supplies the precarious and exploitable lives that capitalism needs to extract land and labour.

Capital accumulates by producing inequalities between those who control the means of production and workers without the resources to survive; between private captors of land and property and the landless and dispossessed; between creditors and debtors (Melamed, 2015). And as Danewid (2019, pp. 297–8) argues: 'race-making practices are intrinsic to processes of capital accumulation because racism supplies the precarious and exploitable lives that capitalism needs to extract land and labour'. Colonialism and unequal accumulation are intricately entwined (Arrighi, 2010) and continue in contemporary forms of neoliberalism based on inequality and 'financialized human capital' (Brown, 2015, p. 179). The manner in which dispossession is carried out today through the likes of urban gentrification cannot be understood outside these 'legacies of colonial expropriation' (Chakravartty and Silva, 2012, p. 369). Practices of racial capitalism (Bhattacharyya, 2018) are constantly remade in processes of othering and exclusion that work through class, gender, sexuality, religion and disability to ensure, as Brown (2015) argues, that when we are configured as human capital in all that we do, then we no longer relate to one another as equals and unequal capital accumulation can continue.

The structural relation between financialized human capital, racism and oppression foments fear, insecurity and anxiety that also, in turn, exacerbates racism and sexism and feeds the swell of far-right white supremacist movements that are resurgent in so many of the countries that make up capitalism's historic core. Finlayson (2021) argues that while contradictory and conflicting positions have emerged across the alt right (from conservatism through ethnonationalism to libertarianism), these are united in opposition to liberal ideas of the state. More specifically, what unifies the alt right is a belief in the value of inequality. Finlayson explains that for these groups: 'inequality is a core concept, understood as a natural phenomenon, scientifically verified and the necessary basis of civil order, essential to the maintenance of individual freedom, economic stability and cultural coherence' (Finlayson, 2021, p. 172). Such views are consistent with those of Hayek, who was openly critical of the attempts by welfarist states to equalize natural differences between individuals. However, Finlayson observes that contemporary forms of right-wing populism go further than traditional neoliberal advocates as they advance 'a broad-based challenge to the technocratic politics of third-way neoliberalism and globalization' and demand 'yet greater marketization of ideas and ideologies, culture and consciousness' (ibid.) in a blend of radical conservatism and libertarianism. The 'ideological entrepreneurs' of the alt right put their faith in the market to reveal the true capacity of individuals and the natural inequalities of talent – a form of meritocracy on steroids. In this manner the concept of social justice is dismissed entirely as a lie born of left-wing conspiracy.

The anti-equality offensive functions in perfect tandem with the social media economy of clickbait advertising, because the more gratuitously extremist and pugnacious the postings are the more they will provoke outraged reactions and the more the audience grows. To optimize performance, platforms have encouraged advertisers to group together related audiences to create affectively charged clusters that are encouraged to take the clickbait through a focus on their divisive views. Hate has become profitable (Angwin, Varner and Tobin, 2017). Buzzfeed News reported that Google prompted them to run ads specifically targeted at people typing racist and bigoted terms into its search bar and suggested additional racist terms to extend the ads reach like 'black people ruin neighbourhoods' (Kantrowitz, 2017). These race-making practices configure our media and tech infrastructures, which are themselves particular markers and makers of histories that embody the racialized exclusions they enact and the knowledges they produce. And so we see how economic, social and political inequalities intertwine in our mediated existences.

Data injustices

The structural and infrastructural injustices noted above are expounded by data that drive discriminatory practices – whose data are used to inform what political and policy decisions impacts directly on institutional strategies and policy decisions of governments and authorities. The subprime mortgage meltdown that ignited the 2008 financial crisis in the US revealed the deepening reliance of contemporary debt and financial power structures on the extraction of wealth from racialized communities. It also showed that such racialized debt regimes are ever more intensively digitized through racially encoded algorithms that determine creditworthiness (Noble, 2018) to access anything from a new job to a home loan and entrench status differentials (Benjamin, 2019). Milner and Traub (2021, p. 1) refer to this as data capitalism and algorithmic racism, 'an economic model built on the extraction and commodification of data and the use of big data and algorithms as tools to concentrate and consolidate power in ways that dramatically increase inequality along lines of race, class, gender and disability', stating that 'racial inequality is a feature not a bug of data capitalism'. They point to policy decisions as being the driver of data capitalism over and above technological progress.

Other research indicates how software analyses of large sets of historical crime data are used for predictive policing to forecast where crime is likely to occur, perpetuating a vicious cycle of excessive surveillance and scrutiny in non-white, poorer neighbourhoods (O'Neil, 2016) that is often strikingly unreliable and reinforces discriminatory policing practices (Angwin et al., 2016). And there are numerous reports of facial recognition systems that discriminate against those who are not white and/or male because the design, development, deployment and governance of AI is largely undertaken by white men – what Buolamwini refers to as 'excoding' (Buolamwini and Gebru, 2018). Techniques of surveillance are practised more intensively on marginalized populations – from workplace performance technologies that map not only when we work and what we do but also how well we perform based on criteria that benefit the employer not the employee; to street monitoring systems that support and direct policing and law enforcement in heavily racialized practices (Monahan, 2008). The under-representation of women and people of colour in technology and the under-sampling of these groups in the data that shapes AI (the pale male data problem) has led to the creation of technology that benefits a small portion of the world. Data-driven technologies target groups differentially. As facial analysis and recognition technology are adopted by government agencies, police and security systems, it is vital to interrogate and address these 'algorithms of oppression' (Noble, 2018).

Chun (2021, 2019) also notes how seemingly open and boundless networks are actually a series of poorly gated communities fostered by the market-logic embedded within most data capture systems. Networks segregate because their formulation is based on and perpetuates a reductive identity politics that posits race and gender as 'immutable' categories. Based on the concept of homophily, which assumes that people like to bond with similar people, 'Facebook packages into the idea that you are like what you like, and that you will like the things that people who are like you like' (Steyerl, 2019, p. 13). Chun analyses how algorithms based on homophily perpetuate the discrimination they 'find', arguing that:

Homophily . . . assumes and creates segregation; it presumes consensus and similarity within local clusters, making segregation a default characteristic of network neighborhoods. In valorizing 'voluntary' actions . . . it erases historical contingencies, institutional discrimination, and economic realities. (Chun, 2019, p. 76)

She goes on to expose how the history and design of social media are based on creating polarized networks of angry clusters (Chun and Barnett, 2021), even when the likes of Facebook claim that they operate on the principle of 'Fundamental Equality' and 'Voice' for everyone. By denying the oppression of racialized peoples and structural racism in society, they reproduce patterns of discrimination which are then seen as no more than a technical glitch that can be fixed through tweaking the technology (Siapera and Viejo-Otero, 2021).

What this research tells us is that increasing inequality is not simply a function of a global economy that rewards 'talent' as the necessary consequence of an innovating and dynamic economy. Rather, it shows that inequality and injustice have a clear politics and economics that structurally embed disadvantage and oppression into our societies through 'inequality regimes' that provide justificatory mechanisms for its continued existence. Piketty and Goldhammer (2020) refer to legal, education and fiscal systems as driving these inequality regimes, but we can also add datafication to this list as a further structural dimension that embeds and vindicates inequality. Other forms of mediation also contribute in no small part to these forms of vindication, where the myth of meritocracy continues to be peddled through channels of entertainment as well as dominant news narratives.

Mediating inequality and poverty

In 1982, way before the internet and the datafication of society, Golding and Middleton wrote the foundational book *Images of Welfare*, which looked at media coverage of welfare issues in the mid-1970s in the UK alongside a public opinion survey on attitudes to welfare and poverty. They showed how media reports largely scapegoated the poor, representing welfare claimants as scroungers and frauds: unworthy citizens undeserving of support. As Margaret Thatcher admonished 'shirkers' while espousing an ideology of economic self-reliance and New Labour focused on welfare reform in opposition to notions of 'worklessness', a cynical British public followed suit. Golding and Middleton (1982) revealed how, in general, the public tended to 'blame the victim', including among the poor themselves – claimants and the low-paid – growing a divisive resentment channelled towards others alongside them at the bottom of the ladder.

An anti-welfare rhetoric persists to this day (e.g. Jensen, 2014) and can be clearly identified in reality television shows dubbed 'poverty porn' (Skeggs and Wood, 2012). One of these, *Benefits Street* – based on a street in Birmingham, UK where 90 per cent of residents were said to be claiming welfare support – aired in 2014 and ran for five episodes. Jensen (2014) argues that poverty porn generates 'welfare disgust' (p. 278) and is an ideological assault on the welfare state, helping to forge neoliberal welfare as common sense. Tyler (2013) argues that the formation of 'national abjects' in the public sphere are technologies of social control through which the transition from liberal welfare states to neoliberal post-welfare states is affectively enacted. She analyses the stigmatization that comes through media representation, which illustrates the poor and working class as disposable populations and thus legitimizes the reproduction and entrenchment of inequalities and injustices. Tyler (2013) also notes how reality television production companies feed off exploitative production processes, harnessing the labours of unwaged participants with the unrealized promise of fame and fortune, as 'human capital' to produce immense wealth for global media corporations. For instance, the Love Productions company that made *Benefits Street* accrued £5.5m from the show in 2014, making it one of Channel 4's most popular, and most profitable, television programmes of the year.

Scholars have argued that the enduring representation of an underserving underclass helps enable 'structural conditions of a deep social, political and economic crisis' to be imagined as problems of 'individual behaviours' (Dowling and Harvie, 2014, p. 872) turning increasing levels of inequality and poverty into individual moral crises rather than political economic ones. Dowling and Harvie (ibid., p. 875) suggest that by creating scapegoats that can be blamed for structural consequences of financial capitalism, these dystopian visions of a broken Britain are used to 'politically justify austerity policies'. Representations of the poor in the US have also been shown to be racialized. A study by Dixon (2017) shows that in the US, Black families represent 59 per cent of stories about poverty in news and opinion outlets even though they make up just 27 per cent of poor families in the country.

The mainstream news media have also played their part in framing and fanning debates around asylum and migration. In an analysis of media coverage in five EU states (referred to in Chapter 2) Berry, Garcia-Blanco and Moore (2016) found that refugees and migrants have been consistently framed negatively as a problem rather than a benefit to societies. In the UK, the majority of the press were found to have consistently and aggressively campaigned against refugees and migrants. In other research on public reactions to the 2008 financial crisis, Berry (2019) notes how many UK respondents thought that the deficit had been created by immigrants sponging off the welfare state and bleeding the NHS dry (rather than predatory lending by the banks). He also points to the fact that research reveals Britons to be more in favour of restrictive asylum policies than Germans, Spaniards or Swedes (who had more favourable press coverage). While these attitudes cannot be attributed to media reporting alone, Berry et al. (2016) argue that the repetitive, negative, narrow and derogatory reporting by the British tabloid press plays its part in convincing the public that the main cause of their problems is excessive immigration. Mainstream mediations of the most economically disadvantaged have long since spun a narrative of the poor as morally as well as economically destitute, as unworthy of state support, public sympathy and policy intervention. They are simply disposable. Social and economic inequalities are used to reinforce each other as representational and datafied injustices combine to further engrain inequality regimes that justify their very reproduction.

Mediating meritocracy

The types of reality television referred to above really took off in the 1990s as the dominant format for mass market commercial television production. Whereas these formats began based on a camera-lens view of the 'real lives' of the public, the genre then morphed into a variety of forms of competitive game shows that required the participants' full immersion in a range of highly constructed situations. For entertainment, viewers watch participants pitched against one another, often exhibiting ruthless behaviour to get fellow competitors voted out week by week, with the ultimate prize of fame and possibly some fortune for the last person (or couple) standing. From *Big Brother* to *Love Island* the programmes scream, 'Look . . . this is how life really is, this is reality: an endless, ruthless competition for status, popularity and fame with no higher purpose than winning' (Gilbert and Williams, 2022, p. 54). Another sub-genre of reality TV gameshows – from *The Voice* to *Britain's Got Talent* and *Bake-Off* – sees singers, sewers, potters, carpenters, cooks and bakers pitted against one another in weekly knock-out competitions to show that talent will prevail. Regardless of how poor or disadvantaged you are, the message is clear: you too can become rich and famous if you just jump on the entrepreneurial bandwagon and self-maximize.

Former *Love Island* contestant Molly-Mae Hague was one of the lucky ones. After appearing on the show she landed herself the position of creative director of the fast-fashion giant Pretty Little Thing with a salary rumoured to be over £500,000. But her own success was on the back of garment workers in factories paid just £3.50 an hour in unsafe conditions. When questioned in a YouTube interview, Hague repeated the mantra of meritocracy in her defence:

> When I've spoken in the past I've been slammed a little bit, with people saying, 'It's easy for you to say that, you've not grown up in poverty, you've not grown up with major money struggles. So for you to sit there and say we all have the same 24 hours in a day is not correct. And I'm like, but technically what I'm saying is correct – we do . . . I understand we all have different backgrounds and we're raised in different ways and have different financial situations, but if you want something enough you can achieve it and it just depends to what lengths you want to go to get to where you want to be in the future. And I'll go to any length. I've worked my absolute arse off to get where I am now. I just think you're given one life and it's down to you what you do with it. You can literally go in any direction. (Harrison, 2022)

Yet, in reality, Molly-Mae's fortune was accrued through working-class exploitation of others – she may well have worked hard, but her achievements were not and are not available to all.

In the digital realm, influencer culture espouses the same illusion – material success can come to anyone who works hard enough, or so the story goes; there are no barriers to wealth, no obstacles to social mobility, no glass ceilings. All you need is a phone, an Instagram account and a large sprinkling of self-belief and you too can accrue 6 million social media followers and a bucket-load of lucrative deals. You can be your own 'boss-girl'. Celebrity has been democratized and is yours for the taking. The entrepreneurial self-brand sells itself on the dream that anyone can be just like them – buy into their scheme, like and subscribe to their cosmetics, fitness, fashion and lifestyle and join the online hustle culture. We are regaled to think of ourselves as companies of one – we are expected to invest in our own growth, accumulation, improvement and valorization of the self as 'capital' (Lazzarato and Jordan, 2012). While young people may find these promises alluring, the reality for most is precarious work on zero-hour contracts.

The success of online entrepreneurs also relies on tapping into the discriminatory nature of social media algorithms. Andrew Tate, a former *Big Brother* contestant in the UK who was ejected from the house after a video was revealed of him hitting a woman with a belt (the woman later denied any abuse had occurred), went from obscurity to global internet fame in a matter of months. Self-proclaimed king of toxic masculinity, he is characterized as a cigar-smoking playboy, and his video and social media content displays extreme misogyny, homophobia and racism. He was barred from Twitter for saying women should 'bear some responsibility' for being raped, but his account was reinstated when Elon Musk took control of the site. In August 2022 videos of him on TikTok have been watched over 11.6 billion times. In July 2022 there were more Google searches for his name than for Donald Trump or Kim Kardashian (Das, 2022). He set up a private online academy called Hustler's University (revamped and rebranded to The Real World in November 2022), to which subscribers (127,000 in August 2022) pay £39/$49 a month. To manipulate the algorithm in his favour and sidestep his own social media bans, his followers are told to flood social media with controversial videos of him to achieve maximum views and engagement in what is called an 'affiliate marketing programme'. Members, mostly boys and young men, are told that they can earn up to £10,000 a month through lessons on crypto investing, drop shipping and recruiting others to The Real World (with 48 per cent commission for each person they refer). To sign up the most people they are advised to stoke controversy to improve their chances of going viral in what amounts to a 'mediated network of misogynistic discourses and practices' (Banet-Weiser and Bratich, 2019, p. 5008) to the majority benefit of one Andrew Tate.[6] Meanwhile, research by the Centre for Countering Digital Hate (Hume, 2024) estimates that YouTube has accumulated approximately £2.4m in advertising revenue from misogynistic videos of Andrew Tate.

The ideology of meritocracy thus combines with that of the internet's libertarian premise, corralling us constantly with the message that social mobility is ours for the taking. It is also fuelled by the far-right anti-woke agenda, which argues that the whole notion of equality is a fabricated nonsense that is holding you back. It is no surprise that Andrew Tate has multiple associations with far-right activists including Stephen Yaxley-Lennon in the UK (the anti-Islam activist and former leader of the English Defence League, known as Tommy Robinson). But ultimately, the neoliberal promise of status and riches for the self-fashioned internet entrepreneur is hollow and fleeting. The reality is something quite different.

In the UK, babies born into disadvantaged households are more likely to have a low birth weight due to poorer maternal diets and higher rates of inadequate antenatal care. This is associated with worse health later in life. By the age of five, the inequalities are clear. In 2018, only 57 per cent of children with access to free school meals reached the expected level of development compared with 74 per cent of children not entitled to free school meals (Social Mobility Commission, 2019). Much of this is linked to the home learning environment. Studies show that how parents interact on a day-to-day basis with infants has strong implications for intellectual and cognitive development and verbal ability. For example, low-income children are less likely to have books read to them and are less likely to go on educational outings, such as trips to the zoo, the library or the park. A report from the Sutton Trust (Waldfogel and Washbrook, 2010) found that only 45 per cent of low-income children are read to daily at the age of three, compared with 65 per cent and 78 per cent of middle- and high-income children. This has important implications, as children who are read to daily at the age of three perform significantly better in vocabulary tests than those who are not. This gap continues to widen as these children enter adulthood, reinforced by educational disparity throughout school and university. In 2021 only 28 per cent of pupils entitled to free school meals entered higher education compared to 47 per cent of other pupils (DfE, 2021). Individuals with a degree earn an average of £210,000 more across a lifetime than those without. The impact of socio-economic factors on employment and income is particularly important for women, ethnic minorities, people with disabilities and members of the LGBTQ+ community. Almost two-thirds of white people from professional backgrounds end up in professional occupations, compared with 28 per cent and 37 per cent of people from Bangladeshi and Pakistani backgrounds, respectively. People from working-class backgrounds are 80 per cent less likely to get into professional jobs and even when they do they earn 17 per cent less than people from professional backgrounds (Social Mobility Commission, 2019). Economist Branko Milanovic argues that once you add gender and ethnicity earnings decrease again (Milanović, 2012). In other words, hard work and effort in no way reflect how much somebody earns.

In reality meritocracy is a fantasy. Many of the participants in reality TV shows remain unpaid (*Bake-Off* is unpaid with no cash prize for the winner; in *Big Brother* housemates are not paid but have the chance of a substantial cash prize if they win) or seriously underpaid (in 2022 *Love Island* contestants got £250 a week to be on the show, which works out about £3.50 an hour), yet all of them generate enormous profits for the production companies (Williamson, 2016).

The above discussion reveals how social mobility has stalled and inequality has surged from the late 1970s onwards. An analysis of ideologies of meritocracy, so prevalent across news and entertainment, exposes how economic inequality is narrated and justified through a variety of forms of mediation that combine with inequalities in the social economy marked by class, ethnicity, gender and disability. These industries may inform and entertain us but they also serve to legitimate a social order in which capital reigns supreme and only the super-rich benefit. It can also encourage people from disadvantaged backgrounds to believe that they are less deserving of success and to underestimate the extent to which they face structural obstacles of discrimination (McCoy and Major, 2007). And when the promises of meritocracy and libertarianism fail – when people are still poor and discriminated against – what then?

What can we do about it? Towards communicative egalitarianism

McChesney (2012, p. 1) points out that capitalism and democracy vie for opposite conclusions – one creates massive inequality and the other is premised upon political equality: 'in conditions of extreme economic inequality [democracy] is effectively impossible'. The rising inequality that we are now experiencing in many parts of the world endangers the remnants of liberal democracy we still have and also reveals that the various forms of representative democracy have not led to more economic redistribution and do not benefit the many. Leading economists around the world argue for the reduction of inequality as a global and national economic necessity. They point out that inequality is not inevitable; it is ideological and political and endures through what Piketty and Goldhammer (2020, p. 51) describe as 'inequality regimes': justificatory mechanisms for the institutional structures of inequality – the legal system, the educational system, the fiscal system – that organize and entrench inequality in societies. I am arguing for adding mediated representations, communicative mechanisms and practices and datafication processes to this list, as further structural elements that embed and vindicate economic and social inequality regimes. It follows then, to disrupt inequality and reconfigure democracy in egalitarian terms requires systemic change.

Economists also point to the ways in which government policies based on economic redistribution can reduce inequality, as clearly demonstrated with the rise of the welfare state between 1910 and 1920 and then again after the Second World War and into the 1980s with the development of state investment in education, health, pensions and social insurance. Piketty and Goldhammmer (2020) argue for a new 'participatory socialism', a system founded on an ideology of equality, social property, education, and the sharing of knowledge and power that supersedes capitalism and private property. They propose a universal minimum inheritance (or universal capital endowment) of about $180,000 per person paid out at the age of twenty-five, worker control over the boards of corporations and 'confiscatory' levels of progressive wealth and income taxation, including a carbon tax – with an individual carbon card to protect low incomes and responsible behaviour and to concentrate heavy taxation on the highest individual emissions. But no mention is made of how media and communicative systems are intimately interwoven with knowledge, education, carbon emissions and power.

Furthermore, as vital as more economic equality in a country is, it does not necessarily make it more democratic or less oppressive. Egalitarianism is about far more than economics and extends to the multiple ways in which social relationships are manifest. To achieve real equality, a whole range of relationships of power and domination must be rethought, such as gender and racial oppression. Fraser (2019) highlights the crucial relationship between a politics of recognition and a politics of (re)distribution and sees it as key to the revival of the idea of the working class as new counter-hegemonic bloc:

we will have to envision that class in a new way – intersectionally, if you will – as not restricted to the white, straight, male, majority-ethnicity, manufacturing and mining workers, but as encompassing all of these other occupations – paid and unpaid – and as massively encompassing immigrants, women and people of color. (Fraser, 2019, p. 39)

This will necessarily involve an acknowledgement of the residual power of white, heteronormative and male entitlement. While non-domination offers an extension of social power, strong egalitarianism also requires the elimination of the entrenched social, political and economic power of the privileged, largely white, capitalist class.

What might this mean for our media and communications systems? A just society is based on universal access to, and collective control of, a set of fundamental provisions that enable people to participate fully in social and economic life. Educational equality is key, as is the social state. But in the digital age, educational equality is now closely related to communicative equality, and increasingly one is impossible without the other. However, at the same time the issue of inequality cannot be reduced to equalizing access to communication services without eliminating other types of inequality. Otherwise, inequality is reduced to the ideology of freedom of speech and communicative participation that platform capitalism thrives upon. Indeed, social media platforms such as Facebook have established proprietary rights over a social commons found in online communities that enables them to extract enormous monetary value created by users (Muldoon, 2022) without giving users any control or ownership over platform architecture, protocols and rules. In effect, what was claimed as a democratic digital commons with open access, now used by half of the world's population, has been captured by global corporations for the private gain of a tiny minority of super-rich individuals.

Clearly, the principle of egalitarianism runs counter to the concentration of media and tech ownership endemic across the globe, with the tech giants now the largest oligopolies the world has ever seen. Mergers, takeovers and consolidations of media industries accumulate great wealth and great power in ever fewer hands. Limiting concentration of media and tech ownership is vital but only takes us so far. It may relax the stranglehold of power that certain global corporations exert but it does not necessarily alter the neoliberal nature of the system they operate within. If the current configuration of neoliberalism is exacerbated by wealth inequality, is more corporate, more capitalist, and has been built on and enhancing of colonizing and patriarchal interest, then a new politics is not simply about an extension of social democratic norms. A new politics must disrupt the day-to-day oppressions and injustices on which the current neo-liberal order depends. It must build economic power that is owned and governed by those whose live its effects. And it must reappropriate the spaces we inhabit for the social good of all and in particular for those who are currently exploited and excluded (Kelly and Howard, 2019).

Disrupting oppressions and reconfiguring spaces for communicative egalitarianism relates to publics and to the balance of power that different publics have in relation to various media industries. To date, approaches that have attempted to redress (the often severe) imbalances in power relations between media industries and publics have tended to stress either consumer rights (that focus on the individual and things such as privacy and complaints systems) or the rights of citizens (that stress democratic requirements of meeting the information and communication needs of communities) within the borders of nation states (that are themselves exclusionary and built on expropriation). This is evident in a discussion of what should be done about the phenomenal power over our data now exerted by the big tech companies. Prainsack (2019) argues that the response to big data society largely falls into two camps: those who want individual citizens to have more control over their own data, including the granting of individual property rights to personal data or implementing means of informing and consenting data subjects (Kaye et al., 2015) such as the European Union General Data Protection Regulation (GDPR). And those who advocate a collective control approach through the creation of digital data and information commons with an emphasis on collective ownership and control (Birkinbine, 2018; Hess, 2008; de Peuter and Dyer-Witheford, 2010). The hope in the latter is that the power dynamics between data givers and data profiteers will be equalized. However, as Prainsack (2019, p. 3) points out, such approaches can be problematic because they rarely tackle 'categories, practices and effects of exclusion' – whether this refers to exclusion from data and information entering a digital commons, using data in the digital commons, benefitting from the digital commons or participating in the governance of the digital commons. Exclusivity and exclusions, as we saw in Chapter 3, run counter to egalitarianism and equality. The same arguments can be put with regards to our media industries. Data for Black Lives has raised a call to action to abolish big data 'to reject the structures that concentrate the power of data into the hands of the few, and to instead put the power of data into the hands of people who need it most. Through movement building, data can be claimed as a tool for social change' (Milner and Traub, 2021, p. 30).

Egalitarianism means getting rid of inequalities, so it is also related to the internal plurality and power dynamics of organizations. An organization built on the principle of socio-economic parity must recognize ways in which the media and tech industries have held certain people back – Black people, old people, disabled people, working-class people – and will seek to counter those injustices by taking special measures to compensate for the social and economic inequalities of unjust social structures in full recognition of the different yet connected structural conditions of class, racial and hetero-patriarchal domination. In other words, it is about both recognition and redress. One approach that is more conducive to tackling social and economic inequalities along with the practices and effects of exclusion can be found in the concept of the commons referred to briefly in Chapter 2.

Within a critical theoretical approach, the commons are viewed as shared resources that are co-owned and/or co-governed by the users and communities according to their own rules and norms. This relates to physical spaces that are shared or pooled; the co-production of the resource; the means of maintaining that resource; as well as the mode of governance – how decisions are made collaboratively through collective problem-solving to distribute and use the resource. The commons are intended as social systems that do not systematically separate people from their means of livelihood. They are aimed at strengthening the collective solidarity of workers and offering mutual life support to all inhabitants. They are by definition sustainable. Where capitalism revolves around competitiveness and extractive relations and practices to nature and people, a critical approach to the commons requires a generative economy to ensure the sustainability of people and planet, working towards the accumulation of the commons rather than the accumulation of capital (Ostrom, 1990). As such, this version of the commons aims to shift the form of private ownership of the means of production from a global capitalist class to the inhabitants of a given space and to change the form of power that controls economic activity. In terms of media and communications systems we would have to apply these same criteria to reimagine how data and digital infrastructure are governed, owned and used to 'overthrow the data oligarchs and build a digital commons' (Lawrence, 2019).

Of course, it is not just a digital commons that we need but a media commons more generally (Grayson, 2021). The process of creating 'a media commons' demands that we confront inequalities and exclusions that exist and as they emerge. This has shifted debates to think more about the social practices, acts of provisioning and forms of peer governance of what has been termed *commoning* (Harvey, 2011). The acts of commoning have been associated with radical social epistemologies to address:

> possibilities of solidarity outside or against controlled and surveilled digital and material spaces; imaginaries of collectivities and communities of choice; configuration of new collective identities around joint action rather than origin and privilege; and acts of anti-systemic and radical redistribution of material resources, such as public space . . . and symbolic resources such as knowledge and digital skills (especially in digital commons). (Georgiou and Titley, 2022, p. 337)

Whereas a commons will usually be based around the common good and not be for private gain, not all commons extend this to being egalitarian, meaningfully democratic or even seek to support an intersectional shift in power relations (Kidd, 2020). Certain approaches to the commons may seek to give the same resources to everyone to provide equal opportunity, but are not necessarily equitable in that they do not recognize that each person has different circumstances and requires different levels of support. Hence, redress for structural injustices is left untouched and inequalities prevail.

To avoid the liberal pluralism of 'equal opportunity' that quickly slides back to meritocratic arguments requires a conceptual framing that Birkinbine (2018, p. 291) refers to as 'subversive commoning'. This insists on the necessity of a structural critique of capitalism as a system that entrenches normatively unjustifiable structures of domination that are unfair and unjust. Subversive commoning recognizes that social inequalities have been constructed from different histories and will require different responses. Here, ownership within the commons is based on a critique of the exploitations of capitalism such that it can bring about a change in social relations over time through the reproduction of mutuality, care, trust and conviviality.[7] A change in social relations will require our media and technology industries to be fully representative of the wider population, which means supporting marginalized people to become part of them. A substantive commitment to democracy inside media organizations would enable the broadening of a range of voices involved in decision-making that would, in turn, help ensure that our media systems meet a wider range of needs and serve a more diverse set of interests. To guard against any evaporation into the 'diversity washing' of liberal pluralism they must also be based on ownership models premised on genuine agency, equality and collectivism. We need to change the model of how our media and communication organizations are run and how media are produced so more people can participate – recognizing that high-quality media and communication systems are forms of public utility and a necessary part of people taking active roles in society for the public good. If we see our media or data as part of a shared public information and communications resource necessary for a healthy functioning democracy – a form of public utility – then we have to shift from viewing media or data as primarily commodities for corporate entities to being shared resources that can be not only co-owned but also co-governed by the users and workers according to their own rules and norms.

A politics of the commons responsive to the critique put forward here requires public forms of ownership and social control of finance – the commons as an alternative to capitalism rather than the commons as a substitute for the welfare state (Broumas, 2017). A politics of the commons requires the displacing of a fixation on economic growth to a focus on meeting social need and creating the conditions where we can all live together better – more equitably, more democratically, more inclusively and more sustainably.

Ideas relating data to commoning are now readily discussed by media and communications scholars: Pariser (2020) talks about building online public parks to reclaim the internet as a public space. Drawing inspiration from the ambition and vision of the early BBC and public television (PBS) and radio (NPR) networks in the US, Zuckerman (2020) has called for a 'digital public infrastructure' for the widespread adoption of new public service digital media tools enabling a diversity of platforms to serve a diversity of cultures, giving communities control over governance. Both propose funding from taxing digital advertising. Murdock (2018, p. 43) proposes building a digital commons 'with public service broadcasters as the central hub in an online space that would combine the holdings and expertise of established public cultural institutions with the energy and creativity of grassroots activity on the internet'. In a similar manner, Andrejevic (2013b) argues for a new public service media sector for the digital age to include social media, search and other information-sorting and communication utilities. These echo policy proposals from the former leader of the UK Labour Party, Jeremy Corbyn, who spoke about creating a British Digital Corporation (BDC), using non-commercial operating systems and software; alongside the development of a public search engine based on social value rather than ability to sell advertising – a modern, democratized public platform and network, fully representative of its audiences and completely independent of government and commercial pressures (see Chapter 7). In different ways, all of the above seek to remove the dominance of the media/tech giants and their data control with a shift away from media/data for capital accumulation to media/data for the common good.

Some of the best examples of 'media commoning' today can be found within independent and community media organizations that put recognition of marginalization, redress for social injustices and social and political change at the heart of their practice. In the UK, Bureau Local describe themselves as a 'collaborative, investigative network revealing stories that matter to communities across the UK'. In their *Manifesto for a People's Newsroom*, they state their collective promise as:

> We will report on inequality and the communities, institutions and services under pressure in the UK – those harmed, ignored and under-represented.
> We will do this by making our journalism open, inclusive and human-centred from start to finish.
> We will collaborate, co-create and share space, resources and experience with active members of a community – journalists, storytellers, experts and engaged citizens.
> We will harness data and evidence and use innovative techniques to find and tell stories so they are accessible for everyone.
> We are just one solution to the challenges facing local news and so we will focus our resources on stories where collaboration can make a difference.
> We will tell stories that matter to local people but are also part of a bigger picture in order to reveal threats to the public interest and challenge power at the highest level.
> We will do all of this to ensure that our journalism is useful to society and improves access to information – locally and nationally – on under-reported issues.
> We will work to ensure that our reporting lifts off the page, and then returns to our communities – and those with power – to spark change.
> (Bureau Local, 2022)

But collectives such as Bureau Local often rely solely on foundation grants or donations from individuals and struggle to survive. If communicative/data systems are part of inequality regimes, then reconceiving of them for egalitarian ends requires them to be seen as equivalent to other institutions, such as health and education, and funded accordingly as public utilities vital to the effective functioning of any democratic society.

Conclusion: The egalitarian imagination

The contemporary characteristics of advanced capitalism have brought to the fore structures of inequality and oppression that are part of our social order. They result in who owns what, the forms of labour we have, the nature of production, the means of exchange, the operation of the markets and the various stresses and injuries these exert on daily lives lived in debt, insecurity and in fear – all of which are deeply uneven. I have tried to reveal how structural and infrastructural inequalities are embedded in political, economic and social relations. Inequality is systemic; it is constructed and reconstructed through histories of injustice, norms and political choices and its injuries are connected and (re)productive.

Laclau and Mouffe argue that democratic revolutions enable relations of subordination that constitute the role of serf, slave or worker to be transformed into relations of oppression, that is, transformed into sites of antagonism. The discursive registers for this transformation are provided by the historical inauguration of democracy after the French Revolution in 1789–1799: '[o]ur thesis is that it is only from the moment when the democratic discourse becomes available to articulate the different forms of resistance to subordination that the conditions will exist to make possible the struggle against different types of inequality' (cited in Barnett, 2017, p. 121). According to this argument, developing the discourses of democracy in relation to forms of inequality becomes crucial for progressive social change to take place. This is not just a case of democratic discourse interpreting relations of subordination into relations of oppression around which people can be mobilized; rather, it extends to providing an entire discursive register of equality and liberty based on the constant contestation that institutes society. Radical democracy in this account is the further radicalization of the West's democratic revolution through the deepening and extension of the egalitarian imagination.

Applying an egalitarian imagination to our media and tech industries, organizations and institutions forces us to interrogate the question of who is doing what for whose benefit. Do these infrastructures organize and institute for the power of equality or the power of inequality? It will require building upon the struggles of labour through trade unions and other civil society groups and movements that focus on work and wealth, class and poverty and linking these to a broader intersectional politics of status and recognition associated with race and patriarchal heteronormativity. Foregrounding injustices also reorients our critical analysis towards an evaluation of the democratic qualities of public life. Systemic change means addressing the structural causes of poverty and socio-economic inequalities through redistributive mechanisms of wealth. It means foregrounding class, gender and racial subordination and political domination by sharing and redistributing power through processes of radically substantive democracy. Attempts to redress these injustices have come to the fore through the concept and praxis of the commons – part of an egalitarian imaginary to counter the injustices of racial capitalism and its contemporary neoliberal forms – with a focus on a more equitable, just and ecologically sustainable society. It introduces a new logic of decommodification of the social commons, where our institutions, industries and organizations of media and communications are reclaimed as part of the commons for the public good.

6

PUBLIC GOOD AND PRIVATE INTEREST

What happens to public life when the privileging of individual and corporate private gain is the norm? When deregulation for corporate gain takes precedence and media ownership is ever more concentrated in the hands of a few multinational and mega corporations, what does this do to the possibility of democracy? This chapter outlines the takeover of public life and expression by the ever-increasing concentration of corporate media and tech ownership now commonplace around the globe. It discusses how consideration of news media as public good for democratic gain has been overtaken by news production for private interest.

Commercial news production is primarily for profit. But of course, news is no ordinary commodity: it offers the possibility of directing the public conversation (both online and offline) and hence is of relevance to politicians keen to convince voters of the benefits of their particular policy formulations. The upshot of this state–market collusion is a media in bed with power rather than a media holding power to account. The news media industry has become a crucial power broker deeply entangled in a particular political-economic system made up of a combination of elites each seeking to advance or protect their own interests.

Unpicking how the distinction between private interest and public good has become blurred in news production is fundamental to a critique of how news media operate. Avoiding effective regulation (whether for media concentration, press standards or online harms) under the guise of media freedom and giving commercial journalism free reign (as discussed in Chapter 4) is about nothing more than enabling market dominance to take priority over all other concerns. Private gain over public good also feeds an elite political-media coterie that plays a powerful role in politics in many parts of the world. In the United States a celebrity-driven bandwagon gave us both the Hollywood movie star Ronald Reagan and the reality television celebrity and failed businessman Donald Trump as president. In the UK, the less glitzy but nonetheless powerful governing elite keep a revolving door spinning between major news organizations and the government, as noted in Chapter 5.

The revolving door spins not only for large corporate news organizations but also for public service media. In the BBC, Sir Robbie Gibb, a non-executive BBC board director, was a former director of communications for the Conservative prime minister Theresa May and former chief of staff to the Conservative shadow chancellor Francis Maude in the 1990s, as well as being a brother of the Conservative MP Nick Gibb. Emily Maitlis, a high-profile newsreader on the BBC until 2021, publicly described Gibb as 'an active agent of the Tory Party' and the arbiter of the broadcaster's impartiality code when she gave the 2021 annual McTaggart Lecture, suggesting he directly influenced BBC news content in the Conservative Party's favour (Maitlis, 2022). And in the summer of 2022 the UK Conservative government came under heavy criticism when it emerged that they had appointed Richard Sharp as the chair of the BBC shortly after he had helped to facilitate an £800,000 loan to Boris Johnson (the former prime minister). Sharp had also worked with the then prime minister, Rishi Sunak, as his boss at Goldman Sachs. Relations of power and influence are frequently interdependent. If public service media is to serve the people, then it must be fully accountable to those peoples and not be subject to interference and influence from the government of the day.

Elite influence on the BBC is not new and is illustrative of a governing caste of leading political figures, PR gurus, journalists, editors and media proprietors who all go to the same parties, attend one another's weddings, are godfathers to one another's children and defend one another's interests: former UK prime minister Tony Blair is godfather to two of Rupert Murdoch's children; Donald Trump's daughter Ivanka was a trustee of the nearly $300m fortune Murdoch set aside for the two children he had with his third wife, Wendi. Ivanka Trump gave up that oversight role in the December before her father's inauguration but well after election day. In other words, during the entire period when Murdoch's highly influential news organizations were covering Trump's campaign and transition, their executive chairman was entangled in a financial arrangement of the most personal sort. This chapter will outline the cost of this cosy establishment coterie, how it prioritizes private interests over the public good and what it means for the relationship between media and democracy. This analysis suggests that in order to recast and reclaim democratic media for the public good we need to conceive of it anew by rooting it in social justice and justificatory processes and outcomes.

The public good, media and democratic theory

The idea of collective solutions to collective problems is at the heart of any notion of the public in any form of democracy. And yet it is fraught with issues that often boil down to: who gets to decide what for whom? Who exactly is able to be part of what publics? In a liberal democracy, decisions by and about 'the public' are made through a political system of consensus orchestrated via elections where representatives are expected to voice the concerns of their constituents – a system that is often found wanting when election manifestos are abandoned once in power, or when the dominance of certain classes and ethnicities of privileged men in political office prevents anything remotely approximating representation of diverse people's views.

How we conceptualize the public good is also central to theories of democracy and is similarly conflicted. When people govern (in any organizational form), who decides what is for the good of the particular public they serve? Are public services in the public good or are they instruments of state power? Such questions are crucial when it comes to the provision of news and information, since well-informed publics are better able to hold those who govern to account and more likely to participate in decision-making processes about how society is organized (UNESCO, 2022b). Yet the notion of the public good is under-theorized in relation to media, where concerns tend to focus more narrowly and more legalistically around the notion of the public interest. Here debates often get caught in an unproductive stand-off between what is in the public interest (and who gets to define what people need to know) and what interests the public (what media people choose to consume). In other words, the focus is on whether we should be encouraged to have a healthy diet of credible and trustworthy news and information or be left to our own devices to binge on a barrage of junk food in the form of gossip and sensationalism.

These debates tend to end up in discussions of relative advantage and disadvantage located in economic theories of consumer sovereignty and the free market: market competition and economic imperatives will ensure that media corporations react to consumer preferences giving the public what they want (Hesmondhalgh, 2013). These debates, however, rarely take account of the issues covered in Chapters 3 and 5 relating to equality and participation and how people have differential access to information as well as vastly different resources available to them. Nor do they tackle the fact that issues of resources and access are structurally embedded in society and cannot be addressed by market preferences. McChesney (2003) also points out that market forces only respond to consumer demands insofar as they can reap the most profits. And as Nussbaum (2011, p. 54) notes, '[p]references are not hard-wired: they respond to social conditions. When society has put some things out of reach for some people, they typically learn not to want those things.' And part of this education is done by our media and communications systems driven largely by commercial returns.

However, if we shift our conceptual framework slightly from the public interest to focus on the public good, then a rather different philosophical purview emerges, one that invokes theories of social justice far more aligned to the arguments in this book. Rainer Forst (2013) provides a clear statement of the way in which the priority of injustice in critical theories of democracy is associated with a reassertion of an idea of public life as a field in which people are called upon to negotiate interactions by giving and sharing reasons (what Habermas called deliberative democracy). Developing the work of Habermas (1996) and Rawls (1999, 2001), Forst (2002, 2011, 2013) presents a theory of justice centred on the idea of justice claims as claims against domination, by formulating them as the 'right to justification' of social relations. Many theorists of the politics of recognition, such as Honneth (2004), Fraser (1995), and Tully (2004), seek to orient the critical theory of democracy towards an analysis of the many forms of reasoning that motivate claims of injustice. The prioritization of injustice rests on a commitment to the idea that harms, violations and wrongs are experienced felt, articulated and assessed in situations of intersubjective interaction. In other words, justice is a public phenomenon. And justice is at the heart of what democracy can be: 'For what is a democracy if it is not a normative order whose task is to generate generally binding norms that can be measured against the yardstick of justice and emerge from a practice of justification among political equals – and that must forbid policies that jeopardize this very status of equality' (Forst, 2019b, p. 380).

But who gets to define what the public good entails and how to bring it about is still fraught with difficulties. In Fraser's thinking, evaluations of the justice of social relations have two dimensions: both an objective one that assesses differential distribution of material resources to enable participation and an intersubjective dimension that assesses institutionalized patterns of cultural value by reference to norms of equal respect and opportunity (Fraser and Honneth, 2003). Fraser's view suggests that claims against injustice arise not so much as expressions of outrage against the violation of human needs for reciprocal recognition as from the denial of equal participation in the collective life of political communities. Forst underlines this by arguing that:

> justified claims to goods do not simply 'exist' but can be arrived at only through discourse in the context of corresponding procedures in which – and this is the *fundamental requirement of justice* – all can in principle participate as free and equal individuals. (Forst, 2013, p. 19)

In a later article, Forst (2019a) notes how the contemporary demise of democracy flouts the fundamental requirement of justice when claims to democratic rule degenerate into the claim to supremacy of an alleged majority. In other words, the ability of people to be political subjects is highly differentiated according to relations of power and domination.

For democracy to function for the public good, therefore, we not only need media oriented towards the public good such that everyone is able to participate in public life because they are well informed, we also need the participation of publics in deciding what this thing called the public good should be in the first place (while ensuring that those people who are most often excluded or minoritized take priority). Hence our systems of media and communication are vital for realizing social justice in general (Mansell, 2002; Noble, 2018). Seen in this manner, the public good is both process and outcome. Forst (2013, p. 28) spells this out by noting that in order to determine the material of justice, we need to appreciate how these understandings have come about – 'are they the result of deliberate action, of structures that benefit some rather than others and are upheld deliberatively, or are they the result of circumstances the responsibility for which cannot be ascertained?' Crucially, any theory premised on diminishing forms of injustice must first understand the historical and structural background of those injustices before setting out to do something about them. This makes clear that we are never talking simply of a singular public but multiple publics that are structurally differentiated. However, this need not take us down an indefinite road of relativism. Rather, it requires that we pay close attention to the different registers in which claims to justice are articulated. Seeing the public good as part of justice claims enables us to insist upon recognizing manifest injustices and the ways in which they are responded to and addressed. The ramifications for our media functioning for the public good are manifold. Not least, a media functioning for the public good should not only seek to keep the public well informed but also seek to explain the genealogy of social injustices in its own practices.

Seen from this perspective, if we assume that public service media should function for democracy and operate for the public good then our concern should be both with the content they provide and the extent to which they are democratically accountable to the public and justified in their approach. For Forst, being justified in their approach means embedding a 'basic structure of justification' (2013, p. 36) with specific rights and processes that include genuine possibilities for publics to intervene and exercise control. Justice and justification processes are related to power, and everyone must be able to participate on an equal basis with others to challenge illegitimate power. Forst (2011, p. 2) notes, 'this right expresses the demand that there be no political and social relations of governance that cannot be adequately justified to those affected by them'. As such, the public good seen through a justificatory lens insists on a political understanding of who determines structures of production and distribution. In a justificatory framework, citizens of public media services would not be passive recipients of goods but active participants of justice.

If we follow Forst's notion of justice as processes and practices of justification, then any social relationship that may impact upon the multiple forms of political participation (all of which are related to differential economic and social factors) should be justified reciprocally. As our systems of media and communications are so central to meaning-making and act as key sites of discursive power, so they should also provide the conditions for people to contribute equally to practices of justification. This would mean not only enabling people to represent themselves through media, but also facilitating people to play an equal role in the ways media organizations represent them, including through forms of democratic governance and accountability (Moss, 2018).

Forst argues that critical theory 'calls not only for justifiable social relations, but for a practice of justification' (Forst, 2001, pp. 168–9).

Once the structure and practices of justification are in place (that will necessarily be open to contestation, in order to guard against the reproduction of implicit power relations between and within differentiated publics), then the production and distribution of resources can be decided upon by means of democratic decision-making. Forst does not over-simplify this process by assuming that difficult processes of democratic practice will always result in consensus but argues that decisions will nonetheless have more legitimacy because of the justificatory processes that have been followed. This will build accountability and establish trust. A justificatory response to public media for the public good would then apply to both organizational factors (who is employed in what roles and with what decision-making powers), the nature of media content (including hegemonic and counter-hegemonic narratives of justification) and forms of governance (who is accountable to whom). This allows us to critically examine and address things like concentration of media ownership, lack of media plurality, dominance of particular elite perspectives, misrepresentation and under-representation of people or issues, limited funding for independent journalism, algorithmic personalization of media content, inequalities in media access and use . . . for the public good.

News media as public goods

There is a vast difference between thinking of the media as a 'public good' and thinking of them as public 'goods'. The 'public good' refers to a product or a service that is deemed (usually through largely unaccountable processes) to be for the public benefit and to which everyone should have access. Traditionally, 'public goods' are defined as services or commodities available to everyone in society without exclusion, and therefore no one is prohibited from using them due to cost, and one person's use does not inhibit another's. These include health care, education, roads, water, street lighting, libraries and parks. These are public because everyone needs them for basic living standards to be maintained and so are funded to a larger or lesser extent through the public purse. In some cases, public goods or services may be provided by the private sector (this is increasingly common in what has been termed the 'roll back of the welfare state'). But private provision of public goods is often deemed to be insufficiently profitable, resulting in major flaws in provision (and increasing levels of inequality) as private corporations try to squeeze ever more profit from public needs. A decrease in profits is often accompanied by an increase in market concentration as companies merge to reduce overheads or buy out the competition. Similarly, for democracy to function, all people in any one jurisdiction need to be informed about issues from a variety of perspectives. Yet in many places around the world, we rely largely on the private sector for the provision of media information and communication services. This has led to extensive problems.

Private interest: Mega media concentration

Scholars have long argued that plurality in media markets is a means of protecting democracy (Baker, 2006; McChesney, 2012). In Europe freedom and pluralism of the media are enshrined in the Charter of Fundamental Rights of the European Union (Article 11), and their protection is underpinned by Article 10 of the European Convention on Human Rights. In the United States a free press is enshrined in the First Amendment as a fundamental right. However, as noted in Chapter 4, freedom is a concept that is often weaponized by media corporations seeking to increase profits through buyouts and mergers in a bid to prevent restrictive legislation on ownership. Legislation that enables media pluralism is often fought against by media moguls keen to establish more market dominance. Furthermore, pluralism is defined differently in different countries, and assessments of what is deemed to be enough plurality differ substantially. Frequently, plurality is also concerned with the ability of the *market* to address democratic concerns. The assumption is that if we enable the market to function well and freely, then democracy will be well served. So long as dominance within a defined market is prevented, then there will be enough breathing space for a host of different organizations to provide a wide variety of information from a range of perspectives . . . or so the argument goes.

Attempts to hold market power in check are often implemented through national legal anti-concentration frameworks that include limitations on media reach; restrictions concerning capital control (limiting or prohibiting foreign ownership or control of media organizations and restrictions of ownership for specific actors such as politicians); requirements for transparency of financial information; fair allocation of state advertising; and public subsidies where deemed necessary (most often directed at the mainstream press). However, where these are present, they are modelled on legacy media and are usually concerned with audience concentration in a single media sector (e.g. the press *or* radio) rather than taking account of cross-media ownership. These kinds of anti-concentration frameworks fail to take into account more sophisticated analyses of media power and influence relating to content. In other words, they are structured entirely in relation to markets and the economic arenas in which they originate and not in relation to forms of power. They also generally leave untouched digital intermediaries (which form some of the largest oligopolies the world has ever seen). Consequently, to date, legislation to tackle media concentration has, on the whole, been fragmentary, piecemeal, unable to keep pace with technological innovation and spectacularly unsuccessful in terms of serving the public good. For the most part and to different degrees around the world, we have seen a consolidation of corporate power, an increase in state interference and a reduction in independent journalism (Trappel and Meier, 2022). Where media ownership rules have resulted in reduced market concentration levels, as in Germany and Greece, or the deregulation of media ownership restrictions resulting in increased concentration, as in the Netherlands (Papathanassopoulos, 2018), none of these frameworks address the actual diversity of providers or the plurality of types of media content they offer. And media research has often failed to point this out, thus reproducing arguments based on market needs rather than the public good.

Threats to media plurality emerge from a range of processes including the lack of transparency in media ownership (particularly when this is across media sectors and difficult to track); from highly concentrated markets, in terms of both production and distribution (with concentration of the latter massively increased in the digital age); from the poor economic sustainability of the media industry (where commercial and owner influence becomes more prevalent due to a desire to keep profit margins high and shareholders happy); and from the influence of commercial interests on editorial content (from sponsorship deals and advertisers in a context of a drop in classified advertising revenue with the shift to online) (Trappel and Meier, 2022). Noam (2016) undertook a worldwide study of news media concentration and discovered that it was very high in most countries with an average of four companies controlling over half of all national media industries, exposing an astonishing level of control by private corporations of our knowledge and information ecologies.

The Media for Democracy Monitor project (Trappel, Nieminen and Nord, 2011; Trappel and Tomaz, 2021a, 2021b) show the enduring high levels of media concentration at the national, regional and local levels across eighteen countries and administrative regions (Australia, Austria, Belgium, Canada, Chile, Denmark, Finland, Germany, Greece, Hong Kong, Iceland, Italy, the Netherlands, Portugal, South Korea, Sweden, Switzerland, UK). They point to how the globalization of media business alongside deregulated media policies have exacerbated the issue. The Media Pluralism Monitor (MPM) run by the Centre for Media Pluralism and Media Freedom has assessed media plurality in thirty-two countries (twenty-seven EU Member States and five candidate countries) on a regular basis since 2013/14 (Centre for Media Pluralism and Media Freedom et al., 2023). In 2021 MPM documented that only one country (Germany) is at low risk of the perils of media concentration, fifteen countries are at medium risk (Austria, Belgium, Croatia, Denmark, Estonia, Finland, France, Italy, Latvia, Lithuania, Luxembourg, Portugal, Sweden, the Netherlands, the Republic of North Macedonia – many of which were very close to the border of high risk) and sixteen are at high risk (Albania, Bulgaria, Cyprus, Greece, Ireland, Malta, Montenegro, Hungary, Poland, Romania, Serbia, Slovakia, Slovenia, Spain, the Czech Republic, Turkey).

In the vast majority of the countries covered by the MPM2022 they found no efficient mechanisms to protect editorial autonomy and help prevent undue external interference in editorial decisions (either by owners or politicians). Furthermore, they note that in half of the countries they surveyed, there is evidence that the appointments and dismissals of public service media management are, to some extent, politicized (Rebillard and Sklower, 2022).

Among so-called 'free' countries in Freedom House's *Freedom in the World* report (Puddington and O'Toole, 2020), 19 per cent (sixteen countries) have experienced a reduction in their press freedom scores between 2014 and 2019. The report highlights that this aligns with a general reduction in political rights and civil liberties across many countries traditionally perceived as democratic. In the US, Donald Trump's relentless denigration of any press that doesn't support him as 'fake news' has contributed to diminishing trust in the mainstream media (see Chapter 7). When he was president, Trump repeatedly threatened to strengthen libel laws, revoke the licences of certain broadcasters and damage media owners' other business interests. Although the US constitution offers protections against such actions, his stance on press freedom has had reverberations around the world. Elsewhere, Viktor Orbán's government in Hungary and Aleksandar Vučić's administration in Serbia have consolidated media ownership in the hands of their supporters. Indeed, in Hungary, the Freedom

House 2019 report states that nearly 80 per cent of the media are owned by government allies (Puddington and O'Toole, 2020).

When notions of public good centre around both knowledge production and public accountability, the need to reveal and challenge the practices and policies of those with power and private interest in media is clearly key. Protecting journalists from persecution for standing up to power is also a condition for journalism for the public good to be possible. The MPM singles out Turkey as the only country that is high risk in this regard, with a large number of imprisoned journalists, a lack of independence within the judiciary and abusive use of the criminal justice system with regards limiting freedom of expression. The prosecution and intimidation of writers, journalists and social media users for insulting President Erdoğan has grown. In 2021 seventy-one fines were imposed on TV networks critical of the government, whereas no fines were imposed on pro-government networks in the same period (Inceoglu et al., 2022). Journalists have extensively been prosecuted and imprisoned on charges of terrorism, insulting public officials and/or committing crimes against the state.

However, as I have argued in Chapter 4, journalistic independence is also threatened by commercial interests. Indeed, when the 'business' of news takes over and knowledge is treated like any other commodity to be sold for profit, then commercial gain subsumes any notion of journalism for the public good.

Private gain on steroids

The digital age has unleashed unbridled concentration and unprecedented capital accumulation, as noted elsewhere in this book. Digital platforms rarely produce their own news content; rather they use their enormous reach and influence to disseminate the content of others, including news organizations. The algorithms used to decide which content is circulated to whom change constantly, are opaque and are predicated on profit maximization. Where content is deemed popular it is circulated further. This is not only a threat to diversity of content but also privileges those media players that already have a large market share – such as mainstream news providers. It also operates against content from smaller countries and minority languages. The dominance of the likes of Google has created enormous gatekeeper power while also increasing the possibilities of abuse of that power. In their defence, tech giants frequently shelter behind the shield of 'freedom of speech', claiming to enhance the democratic participation of the many while seeking to protect their dominant business model from regulatory intervention. Meanwhile, dis/misinformation proliferates (Pickard, 2020).

A review of media plurality in the UK undertaken by Ofcom in 2022 highlights concerns about the impact of online intermediaries, and in particular social media platforms, on media plurality. Their analysis indicates that people who most often use social media to access news are 'less likely to correctly identify important factual information, feel more antipathy towards people who hold different political views and are less trusting of democratic institutions than people who use TV and newspapers most often as a source of news' (Ofcom, 2022c, p. 2). Global digital communication platforms also fall foul of some of the same sins of legacy media concentration, but on steroids. As Trappel and Meier (2022, p. 153) point out, digital platforms can also be seen to follow a platform owner's agenda; be governed undemocratically; amplify voices of undemocratic, misogynistic and racist hate speech; block legitimate content; algorithmically determine communication flows in non-transparent ways; operate globally and avoid regulatory requirements of nation states; and so benefit from 'weaknesses of democratic control and jurisdiction'.

Like legacy media, digital media can also use their enormous power and dominance to corrupt politics and influence political decision-making through algorithmically manipulating content or exerting pressure on political processes through extensive lobbying. The Corporate Europe Observatory (Schyns, 2023) reveals how the European Union's attempt to regulate artificial intelligence has faced intense lobbying from US tech companies. Via years of direct pressure, covert groups, tech-funded experts and think tanks – and a last-ditch push by the US government – tech companies succeeded in securing reduced safety obligations, sidelining human rights and anti-discrimination concerns and gaining regulatory carve-outs for some of their key AI products. The Corporate Europe Observatory notes that three-quarters of all Google and Meta EU lobbyists have formerly worked for a governmental body at the EU or member-state level.

In whose dominion?

Many of the above issues relating to ever-greater media concentration: the diminishing power of journalistic independence and increasing prevalence of media owners' strategic agendas, as well as large media conglomerates becoming political actors, came to the fore in the Fox and Dominion lawsuit in 2023. Dominion is a voting equipment company in the United States that sued Fox News for defamation, whilst demanding $1.6bn for knowingly broadcasting false and outlandish allegations that they had been involved in a plot to steal the 2020 election from Donald Trump – in other words that they had been involved in the rigging of an election. It is important to note that Fox News regularly averages the highest viewership of any cable news channel in the USA. The broadcasting of an outright lie on the Fox News channel is thus said to have contributed to threats against election officials across the country and helped fuel the violent attack on the US Capitol by far-right Trump supporters (Martinson, 2023).

In its defence, Fox News, like many other Murdoch-owned news organizations before it, raised the shield of press freedom, claiming that they were protected by the First Amendment. The final out-of-court $787.5m settlement (more than half of the company's total profit in the year prior) led Fox to state that its willingness to settle showed their commitment to the 'highest journalistic standards'. In other words, it admitted that it had indeed been telling lies but simultaneously claimed that the press should be free to do so. At the time of writing, another voting equipment company, Smartmatic, is suing Fox News for $2.7bn. Abby Grossberg, a former Fox employee, also alleged that she was coerced into giving misleading testimony against the lawsuit, as well as being subjected to gender discrimination during her employment at Fox. She later made an out-of-court settlement for $12m. Meanwhile, a Fox shareholder is currently seeking damages, arguing that executives breached their fiduciary duty to the company by broadcasting election conspiracy theories.

These cases reveal that many at Fox News knew the rigged election claims were false (including Rupert Murdoch) but were driven by short-term ratings and market share. Lawyers for Dominion Voting Systems argued that Fox executives elevated election conspiracy theories because they feared they were losing their audience after Donald Trump's 2020 presidential election loss. Internal communications gathered for the Dominion lawsuit showed how employees at Fox expressed serious doubts about, and at times were scornful of, Mr Trump and his allies as they spread lies about voter fraud and questioned the legitimacy of Mr Biden's election. These messages told the story of a frantic scramble inside Fox as it started losing audience share to competitors, like Newsmax, that were more willing to report on and endorse false claims about how Dominion was plotting to steal the election from Trump.[8]

The Dominion lawsuit was reminiscent of the now infamous quote from the CBS executive chairman Leslie Moonves, who once said that Donald Trump running for president 'may not be good for America but it's damn good for CBS . . . bring it on Donald, keep going' (Wang, 2016). The case showed how Fox News wanted Trump to win the election and to capitalize on Trump's popularity by inventing a story. In other words, sensationalism sells, and lies and smears are profitable. Trump's outrageous attention-seeking behaviour is far more profitable than Joe Biden's more sober approach because it draws audiences.

Ultimately Dominion won one of the largest ever publicly disclosed settlements for a media libel case. The company has claimed that this pay-out has held Fox accountable. However, the case never went to court, and as a result Fox was never forced to give an on-air apology or correct the lies that they broadcast to viewers about Dominion. Moreover, consistent polling showed that large numbers of Republicans continued to believe the 2020 election was tainted (Greenberg, 2022). Thus, relying on defamation law to address mediated injustices is always going to be problematic. Defamation law is not designed to deliver truth and can equally be weaponized by the rich and powerful against people who raise factually grounded criticisms. One of these techniques is the use of 'SLAPPs' (strategic lawsuits against public participation), a term coined by George Pring and Penelope Canan in the 1980s to indicate an abusive or meritless lawsuit filed by a wealthy party against someone for exercising their political rights or freedom of expression in relation to matters of public interest (where 'the public interest' is a legal term). The purpose of SLAPPs is not to seek justice but to use frivolous legal claims to harass, intimidate, silence and drain the financial and physical resources of their less-affluent opponents – including journalists – thereby discouraging scrutiny of matters that are generally deemed to be in the public interest.

The key aim of a SLAPP is to prevent publication on matters of public importance, such as academic research, whistleblowing, campaigning or investigative journalism. Claims of defamation or invasion of privacy are the causes of action most associated with SLAPPs. To end or prevent a SLAPP, those who speak out on issues of public interest frequently agree to remain silent, apologize or 'correct statements'. In the MPM2022 a growing number of SLAPPs were reported in various countries, such as Bulgaria, Croatia, Malta and

Romania. Anti-SLAPP laws have come into play in certain jurisdictions but are more common in the US (as of April 2022, thirty-two states and the District of Columbia have anti-SLAPP laws), as well as in Canada and Australia, to allow individuals to get lawsuits against them dismissed at a very early stage if that lawsuit qualifies as a SLAPP. What SLAPPs show us is that libel and privacy law (as with anti-trust laws) are not above the influence of power and wealth. Wealthy litigants will use the law to their strategic advantage and always seek out-of-court settlements to avoid a guilty verdict (as with the Dominion case above). Thus, in a context of the increasing concentration of media ownership and subsequent rise in political power of media moguls, media law (as well as media policy and regulation more generally) is wholly inadequate as a means to ensure news and journalism function for the public good.

In this complex intervolving of corporate and political power, the situation has worsened as commercial pressures on legacy media industries have increased and the driving force for commercial news ventures is ever-more focused on maintaining and growing capital accumulation. The solution to this conundrum may not be as complicated as it seems, however: to enable news to function for the public good you have first to remove the profit motive and shift thinking to a non-market horizon. Only then will journalism get close to being free of corporate influence and the public good be well served.

One model that is produced largely not-for-profit is, of course, public service media. But the public provision of media services comes with its own problems. These relate largely to government funding and subsequent interference in media freedoms that extend to the electoral incentives any one government may have to put pressure on public media organizations to provide distorted information in their favour. This is discussed further below in relation to the BBC.

The BBC as a public good

The BBC plays a central role in the UK media landscape (and beyond). It is (theoretically at least) accountable to and paid for by its users, and has a remit to represent and deliver content and services for all communities across the UK via a universal payment mechanism. Without the need to attract advertising and deliver shareholder value, it is free from market pressures to cater to particular demographics, and many argue (e.g. Barwise and York, 2020) that the BBC therefore has a virtuous impact on the broader media ecology of which it is part: by delivering high-quality information, education and entertainment, it sets professional standards for its rivals, raising standards overall. It is an important investor in, and driver of, the wider creative economy and has long acted as a training ground for talent and a laboratory for technological innovation.

In 2023 the BBC Annual Accounts (BBC, 2023a) noted that 90 per cent of adults and 80 per cent of 16–34-year-olds in the UK use the BBC each week. A study by Ofcom (Ofcom, 2020) noted that public service broadcasters account for nine of the top twenty news sources in the UK. The BBC's Royal Charter in 2016 (Department for Culture, Media and Sport, 2016) noted that the BBC has the highest audience share of any UK provider in both television and radio. The annual Ofcom news consumption survey for 2022 noted that the BBC remains the news organization with the highest cross-platform audience reach (76 per cent) among those following news and that BBC1 remains the most selected for 'single most important' news source, even as the proportion choosing it (53 per cent) has declined since 2018 (when it was 62 per cent) (Ofcom, 2022b). A 2020 Reuters Institute report also found that BBC News was the most trusted national/international news brand in the USA (Newman, 2020).[9]

The BBC and other public service broadcasters have always been more trusted than the tabloid press in the UK, and for good reason. This became clear during the Covid-19 pandemic, when the BBC had record audiences and was the first port of call for the UK public seeking news and information (BBC, 2021). In recent years, however, levels of trust in the BBC have fallen across the political spectrum, and particularly on the left. The Reuters Institute shows the percentage of those identifying with the left who mostly trust the BBC dropped from 75 per cent in 2019 to 60 per cent in 2020 (particularly after the 2019 election, when impartiality of coverage was challenged) (Newman, 2021).

Much of the dip in trust on the left comes from perceptions of a lack of independence from government and a subsequent political bias in news and current affairs that draws attention to the BBC's apparent inability to uphold its own editorial standards of impartiality and accuracy. The BBC's Royal Charter states that it is independent of government. But it is clearly not, and there are many opportunities for the government to influence how the BBC operates. The licence fee is renewed every ten years, and in the last two decades governments have imposed substantial cuts. As noted at the beginning of this chapter, the government appoints the BBC's chair and the majority of the BBC board, and the BBC board chooses the director general, who tends to be aligned with the government – Greg Dyke was close to New Labour and the new director general, Tim Davie, once stood as a Conservative candidate. Research on the BBC's news and current affairs in 2007 and 2012 found that it over-represented the views and perspectives of the government of the day, and that this was more pronounced under the Conservatives (Berry, 2013). In the BBC's annual plan for 2019/20 (BBC, 2019) it acknowledged that its reputation for impartiality had been weakened and developed new editorial guidelines in an attempt to restore trust. Alongside these new rules on impartiality, came new guidance on the use of social media designed to limit employees of the BBC involved in news and current affairs from expressing political opinions on social media platforms (BBC, 2020).

In 2023 a fresh scandal on impartiality went viral when Gary Lineker, a freelance football pundit who hosts the BBC flagship football programme *Match of the Day*, tweeted his own critical views on new government plans to stop asylum seekers and refugees crossing the Channel in small boats. He was then asked to step down from his role presenting *Match of the Day* when he refused to apologize. In its revised Editorial Guidelines, the BBC states that it 'is committed to achieving due impartiality in all its output. This commitment is fundamental to our reputation, our values and the trust of audiences.' It also says '[we] must always scrutinize arguments, question consensus and hold power to account with consistency and due impartiality' (BBC, 2023b, p. 44). This is complemented by in-depth guidelines, which provide for 'controversial subjects' including 'political controversy'. For BBC staff and regular BBC presenters or reporters associated with news or public policy-related output, the guidance says that 'it is not normally appropriate for them to present or write personal view content on . . . matters of political controversy, or "controversial subjects" in any area' (BBC, 2023c, p. 279). The BBC has also updated guidance on individual use of social media (BBC, 2024, p. 2), which states that 'anyone working for the BBC is a representative of the organization, both offline and also when online, including on social media'. It adds: 'everyone who works for the BBC should ensure their activity on social media platforms does not compromise the perception of or undermine the impartiality and reputation of the BBC, nor their own professional impartiality or reputation and/or otherwise undermine trust in the BBC.' This is unlikely to prevent government ministers attempting to influence pundits with large audiences to adopt their policies. Lineker has spoken about the government minister Michael Gove inviting him to dinner to sell him Brexit. Gove clearly thought it was appropriate to encourage a BBC pundit to adopt pro-government policies. Yet when Lineker tweeted in favour of Remain, the same politicians who wanted him to back Brexit cried foul, claiming that he was breaching BBC impartiality guidelines.

The BBC's decision to suspend Lineker over his outrage on the small boats policy was controversial for three related reasons. Firstly, questions were raised as to whether the guidelines apply to Lineker in general, since he is a freelance broadcaster, and not responsible for news or political content. Secondly, it was unclear whether his tweet fell within the ambit of the impartiality section, as the tweet was published on his personal account, which does not include an official link to the BBC or *Match of the Day*. And thirdly, and perhaps most importantly, it drew attention to the definition of *due* impartiality to which the BBC subscribes. Due impartiality is meant to address concerns of false equivalence when the parameters of the debate appear to be loaded in one direction. So being impartial in a debate on climate change does not require the views of climate change deniers to be presented when 99 per cent of the science suggests otherwise. In this instance, the Migration Bill, designed to stop small boats carrying migrants and refugees across the Channel, begins with the home secretary stating under Section 19(1)(b) of the Human Rights Act that she is unable to confirm if the bill is compatible with the European Convention on Human Rights. The UN Refugee Agency, among others, said that the bill breaches the UN's 1951 Refugee Convention by preventing people who arrive irregularly a chance to seek asylum in UK, amounting to an effective 'asylum ban'. Similar widespread responses have led to the Bill being tagged as 'the Illegal Migration Bill' (Clyne and Savur, 2023). When the majority of evidence points in favour of the accused's perspective, how is *due* impartiality breached? Many pointed out the apparent double standards applied to Lineker's oppositional comments on government policy versus Alan Sugar's vocal support for the Conservatives (Alan Sugar presents the popular BBC gameshow *The Apprentice*). The row highlighted a longstanding tension in impartiality clauses, which come into conflict not only with the freedom of expression of football pundits but also the ability of journalists to practise a journalism of integrity amidst a conception of due impartiality that bends to the prevailing politics of the government in office – in this case the ultra-nationalist, anti-immigration agenda of the Conservative Party.

So if the BBC is such a force for the public good, why has it found itself embattled on all sides? There is a long and documented history of every government in power, whether on the left or the right, accusing the BBC of political bias. But Boris Johnson's Conservative government (July 2019–September 2022) was one of the most hostile to the BBC in living memory. Johnson made it clear that the funding and remit of the BBC was up for grabs and moved to privatize the publicly owned Channel 4 – a thoroughly unpopular proposal that 96 per cent were against in a process of public consultation and which was later dropped when Rishi Sunak took over as prime minister. During the Johnson era the government also explicitly sought to restrict media challenges and scrutiny by refusing to put forward ministers or representatives to go on news programmes such as Radio 4's *Today* programme (Fenton, 2020). It is also worth noting that Johnson's then chief advisor, Dominic Cummings, believed that the demise of the BBC was crucial for Conservative success. In a 2004 blog in his think tank New Frontiers Foundation he set out his plan to discredit the BBC and create a new US-style media landscape in the UK. He said this was essential because the BBC was the 'moral enemy' of the party, stating that '[t]he Right should be aiming for the end of the BBC in its current form' (Mason, 2020). He admitted that this would be a long battle and that the right should immediately begin the fight online – the latest of these attacks is a campaign called 'Defund the BBC' – founded by a Conservative activist working as an intern for a Conservative MP (James Yucel). Other Conservative think tanks such as the Institute of Economic Affairs and the Taxpayers' Alliance also frequently argue against the BBC and for its privatization.

Campaigns to defund the BBC have run alongside severe funding cuts in recent years, which have caused its editorial culture to become more conservative and risk-averse. Licence fee income is currently 30 per cent lower than it would have been had it kept pace with inflation (Chalk, 2020). The BBC has been through extensive cost-cutting and resource-stripping and now has far less to spend on local news, regional broadcasting, children's broadcasting and technological innovation. In June 2020, the BBC announced a newsroom reduction of 450 staff to deliver £80m of recurring savings. In July 2020, it announced a further seventy news roles would be made redundant, with losses across the wider BBC, and taking the total headcount reduction to around 900 (Watson, Harrington and Hind, 2020). In 2022 there were further cuts to regional radio news (with a loss of forty-eight jobs), to regional programming and CBBC and deep cuts to its World Service output – with a net loss of 226 jobs in the UK and 156 overseas that could extend to over a 1,000 job cuts over the next few years (Waterson, 2022).

A situation in which public media are threatened both ideologically and structurally by the government of the day undermines their ability to act as a 'fourth estate', holding power to account and acting as an independent intermediary between the people and the state. Radical reform is necessary if the BBC is to function in the public good and meet the challenges of twenty-first-century media and politics.

What can we do about it? Building a media commons[10]

Chapter 4 outlined the basic need for proactive legislation for media plurality to prevent and limit concentration of cross-media ownership, investment in alternative models of non-profit news and new publicly owned digital infrastructures and effective and fair regulation for news publishers. This chapter has built on this framework for a democratic media for the public good by arguing for public media to entail structures and practices of justice and justification with genuine possibilities for all people to intervene and exercise control of media that is made in their name and that in turn makes publics (through practices of recognition and representation). Democratic media for the public good requires that people are not simply represented 'in' media but are 'of' the media. Below, I outline what this could mean in terms of acknowledging structures of *inter*dependence (between state and media) and creating structures of *intra*dependence (between the public and media), achieving actual accountability, meaningful democracy and substantive equality.

Structures of inter- and intradependence

Chapter 4 argued that communicative freedoms are always interdependent and that acknowledging the relations of power between the likes of public service media and the state and in turn public service media and government in order to orient them towards social justice is necessary for communicative freedoms to prevail. As such, acknowledging that state funding of the BBC involves financial dependency enables government interference to be identified and removed without arguing for private capital as the only route to independent media. Guaranteed, stable and adequate funding dissipates political interference and provides insulation from the market-based approach that has eroded the BBC's public service ethos. While the government holds (and frequently pulls) the purse strings, it elicits the conditions for ideological amenability at the very least and, at the worst, it exerts undue pressure for ideological complicity. The BBC's major source of income, the licence fee, was frozen from 2010 to 2017 by a Conservative-led government as part of its 'austerity' programme. Consequently, the BBC had to bear the cost of free TV licences for the over-seventy-fives, effectively making the broadcasting house responsible for providing a welfare benefit. This caused a dramatic reduction in the BBC's income over the course of a decade. In 2020 the BBC scrapped the licence-fee concession for most over-seventy-fives by introducing means testing. The remaining subsidy outlay cost around £250 million a year – roughly the same as its budget for all of its online content (Woodhouse, 2022). The more the government hold the threat of further funding cuts, the greater their power over the BBC becomes. So government control of the licence fee is a problem.

Futhermore, the BBC licence fee is a flat tax that disproportionately falls on low-income groups. The Media Reform Coalition recommend that the licence fee system be maintained but be radically reformed, with rates set by an independent, democratically constituted, non-market regulator acting solely for the public good. They suggest that the traditional TV licence should be replaced with a digital licence fee, based on internet access rather than possession of broadcast-receiving equipment alone and that the fee should be pegged to households' council tax bands (premised on the value of property), to avoid payment falling disproportionately on lower-income groups and to increase equity. To be inclusive of everyone, such a system would also have to be underpinned by universal public digital infrastructure with high-quality broadband available to all.

Funding is also vital to enable public media to develop and innovate as new technology becomes available. Public media should do more than produce programmes; it should develop technology for the common good. The resources available for this are tiny compared to the private sector. Big Tech typically spends 7 to 21 per cent of net sales on research and development (Fleck, 2022). The BBC, meanwhile, typically spends less than half of 1 per cent of its revenue on research and development, while regulatory restraints require that despite its commitment to technological innovation it must demonstrate that any innovation will not negatively impact on the private sector. In a public media system based on justificatory mechanisms for equality this requirement would be switched to a demonstration that it had positively contributed to the public good with evidence drawn from the public rather than the market.

Acknowledging the forms of interdependence between media and state/commercial practice and orienting them toward social justice also requires managing structures of governance. Removing interference in the BBC could be further ensured by replacing the BBC's Royal Charter with a proper legal structure for public service media, so that its remit and constitution can be properly scrutinized by parliament rather than unilaterally changed by government. As long as the government remains responsible for appointing the chair and four directors to the BBC board, for setting the level of the licence fee and for the periodic renewal of its Royal Charter, governmental influence over the BBC will continue, further undermining its capacity to deliver impartial news and information. These procedures must be abolished if governmental influence over the BBC is to be removed. Rather, members of the BBC board should be directly elected by citizens and BBC staff.

Chapter 5 introduced the idea of the media commons as a means to envision communicative egalitarianism. Public service media would form one part of a media commons. A media commons would require forms of *intra*dependence between those who manage media systems/organizations and make media content and those who share in the media environment where such content is circulated – recognizing that as our mediated worlds help define all of our social and political existences, so they should be open to forms of co-creation and co-governance. *Intra*dependency is a way of foregrounding that public institutions operating for the common good be defined by and work with the people who share in mediated life-worlds. In relation to the BBC, rather than returning to the top-down, statist model on which it was founded, it would become a modern, democratized public platform and network, fully representative of, open to and accountable to its audiences and protected from government and commercial pressures. Broadcasting in the UK was originally regulated according to public service principles. That model has been increasingly marginalized as the BBC has become more and more subject to market-based regulation. Currently, BBC activities have to be balanced with consideration for competition through 'public value' tests. They are also subjected to 'market impact assessments' by Ofcom, the communications regulator that has been criticized for privileging consumer over citizen's interests and whose chair is also appointed by the government (Barnett, 2021). Regulation of the BBC must move away from a 'market failure' model – in which the BBC is expected to provide what the market will not – to a model in which the *intra*dependencies between public media and the public good are prioritized.

*Intra*dependency firmly situates public media with and for the public good and appreciates that we all have a stake in the mediated existences of one another. As such, everyone should have the chance to participate in defining, creating, managing, leading, governing and owning anything that is important to the future of the media commons and in the determination of its interests, needs and values. Indeed, those people most affected by critical decisions in media spaces must be included in the process of making them. *Intra*dependency asks that we recognize and repair the damage that has been done, and the inequities that have been created, by our current, market-based, heavily mediated societies. In other words, that we insist upon justificatory mechanisms that foreground the prioritization of dealing with injustices in any provision for the public good – to do justice to those who are differentially subject to domination, exploitation and oppression. This will require systems that provide actual accountability.

Actual accountability

Justificatory mechanisms for accountability speak to collective and relational modes of being in the world and go far beyond orchestrating adequate systems of complaints. They point to a move away from complaints mechanisms bound up with elite power (which are frequently impenetrable to people on the ground and often impose particular perspectives as global truths) to one where people are conceived of as active agents in reciprocal debate and decision-making about matters affecting their lives. This means that claims of injustice against media organizations should be subject to judgement and evaluation through an inclusive public process of deliberation in which the validity of those claims is scrutinized. Reciprocity is fundamental to democratic processes because it is based on ensuring equal recognition of the other through eradicating forms of domination and oppression; and is one of the first requirements of justice. Justificatory mechanisms of accountability won't be achieved by tweaking regulation in liberalism's image; they will require a fundamental shift in the relationship of our media systems to the multiple publics they serve.

The BBC is officially accountable to the public that owns them, but to date this has translated into an opaque and largely ineffective complaints system that functions across the broadcaster's own internal complaints mechanisms and those of Ofcom's, leading to confusion, delay and sometimes contradictory rulings (Grayson, 2022). The BBC has no duty to involve the wider public in decision-making and has never tried to use digital technologies to give audiences a meaningful say in how they are run. There have been lots of proposals for how the BBC could be transformed into a far more democratic 'mutual' structure. The Cooperative Society (McCarthy, 2015) suggested setting up Audience Councils, and the BBC itself, very briefly (with a one-day experiment), flirted with the idea of setting up citizens' juries to oversee the coverage of Brexit (Hind and Mills, 2019).[11]

The Media Reform Coalition (2021) suggests a network of Citizen Media Assemblies that could develop a set of ways for people to participate, such as elections for regional boards, selecting citizens' juries to monitor coverage of controversial issues and auditing commissioning, for example to ensure that people from minoritized groups are well represented. By being connected to assemblies rooted in communities, an independent regulator could be responsive to evolving ideas of what is harmful and what constitutes meaningful redress – and these could be regularly consulted on and revised. Beyond this kind of formal regulation, deeper forms of accountability would also be encouraged through participation with measures to ensure that the workforce was fully representative of wider society (see below) and premised on social justice.

The BBC remains a highly centralized organization, built around a London-based managerial and editorial structure despite strengthening regional production through the opening of Salford's Media City in the northwest of England. But to fully reflect the diversity of the UK's nations, regions and communities and make the BBC more accountable to the broad British public it serves, programme-making and editorial functions need to be further devolved to the nations and regions. The Media Reform Coalition (2021) suggest that this can be achieved by establishing a system of localized, democratic management and commissioning, with national and regional boards elected by staff and local licence fee payers in the same manner as the BBC board. Concurrently, the role of the BBC board and executive committee would be restricted to corporate-wide oversight, coordination and strategic planning. This would not denigrate national coverage, which would still be overseen by the Citizen Media

Assemblies, but enrich and deepen content, making it increasingly relevant to the lives of diverse, differentiated publics.

Meaningful democracy

Justificatory mechanisms also translate into internal forms of democracy within media organizations. In particular, how do workers in media organizations get heard and partake in organizational decisions? Media workers need processes and practices of justification through trade unions as well as broader representation on decision-making bodies. Journalists also need to be empowered to do their job properly – to thoroughly investigate issues and help their audiences understand who has power and how that is shaping their perspectives. The UK National Union of Journalists has long argued for a conscience clause for journalists, which would allow them to refuse unethical assignments and better resist market pressures (DeLong, 2012). When media organizations are more democratic, and have strong union representation, they are more likely to be able to produce independent journalism. The need for meaningful democracy is interconnected with the requirement for substantive equality.

Substantive equality

As Chapter 5 argues, extensive forms of inequality across all sectors of society have led to the systematic ordering of those who are allowed and able to be heard and partake in decision-making that affects the ways in which they can live and consequently who is represented on our screens and in our media. If viewing publics do not recognize media representations as adequately reflecting their realities, then broadcasters lose credibility while maintaining definitional authority over those who are (mis)represented, resulting in their credibility diminishing further still. The BBC has acknowledged the need to address its institutional lack of diversity, both in its programming and its workforce. It has a Diversity and Inclusion Strategy and is committed to Project Diamond, an industry-wide initiative to monitor diversity across the sector. But after decades of diversity initiatives, the BBC's staff still does not fully reflect the society we live in.

The Puttnam review on the Future of Public Service Television (Puttnam, 2016) suggested that Ofcom should supplement its occasional reviews of public service broadcasting with a regular audit of public service content to ensure diverse programming with detailed data on the representation and employment of minority groups and a comprehensive account of the changing consumption patterns of younger audiences. The report provides evidence that minoritized ethnic, regional, national and faith-based communities are dissatisfied with their visibility and portrayal on public service television. It also points out that the television workforce is not representative of the wider UK population, with systematic under-representation of disabled people, those from poorer backgrounds and minoritized ethnic communities at the top levels of the industry. Although the BBC claims this has changed in recent years, the manner in which they collect and combine data has also changed, making it impossible to determine whether the claims are accurate. Again, justificatory mechanisms for addressing data collection and monitoring would help establish how misrepresentation and under-representation is occurring in both content and workforce at all levels, and how to seek urgent systemic repair.

Ensuring adequate diversity will require complete transparency about the makeup of the public service media workforce. This will mean publishing rigorously collected equality monitoring data at the programme and production level for all content producers, whether in-house or externally. Delivering on diversity will also mean addressing the casualization of the BBC's workforce over the last three decades. Precarious working conditions narrow the range of people able to produce programmes, disproportionately impacting on those from lower-income families, women, minoritized groups, and those with disabilities. The BBC cannot claim to be representative of its audiences while maintaining exclusionary employment practices.

Building a media commons

It is important to underscore that developing democratic media for the public good is not restricted to forms of public service media as we currently know it. Our public service broadcasters are only one part of the media ecosystem. To counter the increasing concentration of media for private gain we also need to grow a media commons with public investment in alternative models of media ownership with democratic forms of governance for non/low-profit news for the public good and for social justice. This will require sustainable sources of funding that will prevent these smaller and often local media from falling prey to the pressures of commercialism and help to preserve their journalistic integrity. News organizations with democratic intent require a political and social environment that enables journalism to perform its role as a public good. This can be hindered by commercial pressures, state interference and influence in the media, as well as by restrictions on freedom of expression (see Chapter 4). Such organizations also need to be sustainable in a digital environment that has enabled mega-media concentration to advance. Financial viability of news media gives journalism the environment, resources and autonomy to function as a public good without editorial pressures to prioritize particular products, political parties or politicians (UNESCO, 2022a).

There are now several bodies (including UNESCO, EU, UK Department for Digital Culture, Media and Sport Select Committee, International Fund for Public Interest News Media; the Institute for Nonprofit News in the US, the UK Public Interest News Foundation) that have recognized that new policies and measures are urgently needed to ensure that journalism can function as a public good. These include forms of public financing for non- or low-profit news for the public good; enhanced support for genuine public service media and philanthropic investments in public interest news production (Scott, Bunce and Wright, 2019). To fulfil the requirements for structures and practices for justification, funding would itself need to be administered democratically by organizations that are separate from government, using forms of participatory grant-making. Eligibility for funding would also need to be dependent on media organizations evidencing existing processes and practices of intra-dependence, accountability, democracy and equality.

Reimagining publicness in new and justificatory ways

The relationship between what we used to call 'the public' and the collective is being rapidly reconfigured – our public institutions and lives are being ever-more repurposed for private gain. Our communicative spaces have been taken possession of by private interests that do not encourage users to engage collectively but rather to compulsively share and circulate content that ultimately drives profit for private mega-corporations. The right and the corporate interests they represent want to see public media severely diminished. They want either to place information and culture behind paywalls – with wealthier groups well served and others priced out of our public lives and collective culture – or, alternatively, to allow free access with the relentless and intrusive surveillance of every aspect of our lives via algorithms for commercial advertising and data analytics in order to serve private interests.

Trappel and Meier (2022, p. 161) note that despite a raft of media policies over the last thirty years directed at media ownership within the European Union and in individual European countries, oligopolistic media structures that are harmful to democracy remain firmly in place. Rather, faced with the multiple challenges of digital platforms, 'national governments seek to protect and promote their legacy media without obliging them to refrain from potentially undemocratic business models and practices'. The combination of a concentrated legacy media and oligopolistic digital giants is a toxic form of capitalism that chokes publicness.

The argument that an unregulated free market in the media is one that better serves democracy is one that Rupert Murdoch has often used against the BBC. The BBC, he claims, has an unfair market advantage because it is publicly funded, with the majority of people in the UK still using it as their main source of news. This, he argues, prevents other media from growing. What he really means is that it prevents his own media from exerting even more of a stranglehold on the UK's media environment. If we are to avoid the wholesale takeover of public expression by private gain, if we believe that information and knowledge production are for the public good and necessary for democracy and if we accept that our mainstream systems of media and communications play a key part in sustaining regimes of inequality discussed in Chapter 5, then we need to foreground justificatory mechanisms to reclaim publicness for the public good in our systems of media and communications.

Foucault (2010) argues that neoliberals formulated competitive markets as needing political support such that all governing is oriented for markets and by market principles, while markets must be built, facilitated by, propped up and rescued by political institutions. This is precisely what we have seen in the denigration of and attacks on public media in the UK. He goes on to argue that this entrepreneurializes the subject, converts labour to human capital, repositions and reorganizes the state away from the public good and towards the valorization of markets. This neoliberal alignment of state and markets has indeed led to the increasing privatization of public goods from health services, schools and universities, transport systems and postal services to water supplies and energy provisions – and the same can be said of our public media systems. Legal frameworks such as privacy and defamation law are ill-equipped to deal with the consequences and are often part of the problem, as access to the law is also determined by wealth inequalities. Globalization, namely, the deregulation of constraints on transnational movements of money, products, service and labour, has further weakened the possibility of nation states being able to tame the market through national forms of regulation.

In targeting intensified market logic as a major barrier to public media for the public good, we should be wary of suggesting that once upon a time all in the garden of democracy was rosy until neoliberalism set out systematically to roll back its democratic qualities. Neoliberalism may have weakened the relationship between mainstream media and democracy, but this degeneration has a far longer history (Curran and Seaton, 2010). The lack of diversity in and accountability of the press has been recognized for many years and, at least in the UK, there is a long history of failed attempts to reform the press that started with the first Royal Commission on the Press in 1947 and continued through to the Leveson Inquiry that followed the phone-hacking crisis of July 2011. At each stage, recommendations made were largely rejected by a press that consistently promised to behave better and then consistently failed to do so. Governments, always keen to maintain good relations with the press, have time and again bowed down to industry pressure.

Opposition to the mainstream media's amplification of neoliberal 'common sense' ought not to be based, therefore, on the idea that there once existed a meaningfully independent and representative democratic media determined to maintain a check on official power. Tom Mills' (2016) history of the BBC demonstrates how its relationship to the state was compromised from its very inception: from its involvement in the general strike through its relationship with the security services to its coverage of foreign interventions and its framing of economic issues. This is a history marked by deference to the state, a lack of diversity – both geographical and cultural – which it is only just now starting to acknowledge, and perhaps address and a paternalistic political agenda that is intertwined with a legacy of imperial, corporatist and neoliberal affiliations. Arguably, this is a broadcaster that has, throughout its history, served the state more effectively than it has served the public.

So the main reason the BBC is embattled *is* fiercely political. But this does not detract from the dire need for an intradependent and financially secure public media sector – precisely to act as a counterweight to growing government influence over the media, the 'clickbait' logic of commercial organizations and the private sector concentration in the tech and media sectors. However, the sort of unexamined liberalism that we see in the glib defence of the BBC at all costs simply because it is situated in the realm of public media is yet another democratic delusion and can only weaken its support. The acritical defence of public service broadcasting merely serves to reveal a liberal refusal to acknowledge a range of issues while promulgating an extremely narrow (and increasingly outmoded) conception of public service media. While this is understandable in the face of a right-wing tirade that is all too willing to place the BBC at the centre of the battle field in the 'culture wars' along with a political-economic crusade to de-public everything, this acritical approach negates the significance of our media systems being embedded in our political systems and reduces collective agency to very narrow group of the public largely drawn from white privileged parts of society. Defending the BBC at all costs also prevents the reimagining of publicness in new and justificatory ways that would enable the critique of liberalism and its failures.

Conclusion: Democratic public media for the public good

Private interest is driving our communicative frameworks and informational provision and not the public good. The prioritization of private gain by media and tech firms and the subsequent hollowing-out of publicness is accompanied by an attack on social solidarity, social justice and social redistribution that has devastated public institutions including the BBC. The promulgation of vested interests in private media seeks to undermine the notion of universal service – a people's media – and shrink the public imaginary along with the notion that we have a society that we must care for together. Public media is about far more than delivering a range of content as efficiently as possible. Rather, it speaks to a value system premised on intradependency, actual accountability, meaningful democracy and substantive equality – a media system for all, for the public good.

The constraints of an overly concentrated market, the fetishizing of economic relations and practices as the only way of doing things and the sheer difficulty of thinking beyond a capitalist market and liberal democratic state all stymie social transformation. Systems of knowledge production and information exchange that our media and communications systems are part of should be viewed as public utilities essential to democracy's well-being. Raymond Williams once stated that democracy must refer to 'popular power' and an arrangement in which 'the interests of the majority of the people [are] paramount and in which these interests [are] practically exercised and controlled by the majority' (Williams, 2014, p. 96). A democratic communications system would be one that thrives on intradependency and is genuinely in the hands of its users as opposed to one controlled by billionaires and bureaucrats. 'The principle', as Raymond Williams wrote some fifty years ago, 'should be that the active contributors have control of their own means of expression' (Williams, 1976, p. 121). But as we try to reimagine our way out of capital accumulation at all costs, we need to be wary of simply returning to forms of liberal media thinking about public communication that have not encultured an alternative value system to capitalism and have not aided inclusive collective political agency. In the next chapter these concerns are deliberated on further through the notion of trust and its demise.

7

TRUST AND DISTRUST

Journalists and politicians have long languished at the bottom of tables of the most trusted professions. Cries of illegality, corruption, misrepresentation and abuses of power have been levelled at both as long as they have existed. But with the abundance of news and information now available online and the proliferation of what has been termed 'fake news', alongside the development of Artificial Intelligence/Machine Learning (AI), the stinging loss of accountable knowledge is being felt more than ever. Whereas previous chapters outlined the media's role in the demeaning of democracy, this chapter shows how one of the consequences of this is that the exercise of political power is starved of informed debate, accountability and legitimation, leading to greater exposure to deal-making, corruption, spinning and indifference to critique and truth. This brings disrepute to the political process and undermines perceptions of the meaning and value of democracy as both concept and practice. In other words, fault-lines in the delusion of (neo)liberal democracy are exposed.

The chapter first addresses the demise of trust in news and journalism with a call for any interrogation of trust to be deeply contextualized and understood in relation to social, political and economic power, as well as better conceptualized and analysed as a cultural construct. It then goes on to discuss how issues pertaining to the decrease in trust are evidenced in government and media/tech responses to the Covid-19 global pandemic, which revealed deep problems with political institutions, crumbling public services as a result of years of austerity and an opportunistic news media and tech industry desperate to make commercial gains from a state of crisis. I go on to argue that trust in news and journalism requires a shift from news as a commodity for the accumulation of capital to news and journalism as a means of building social and political commons via forms of co-creation, co-ownership and co-governance in ways that seek to rectify power inequalities, enhance accountability and constantly create new publics.

Decline in trust in news and journalism

Several surveys have pointed to a general decline in journalism's authority and legitimacy in many places around the globe. The Reuters Institute Digital News Report (Newman, 2023) (based on six continents and forty-six markets) notes that overall trust in the news fell by a further 2 percentage points (aggregated across markets) since 2022. In the same Reuters' survey, Finland came top of the league with 69 per cent of people surveyed saying they trusted the news in general most of the time, while Greece sank to the bottom of the league with just 19 per cent (during a year marked by debates about press freedom). In the same survey in 2022 they noted that interest in news more generally has fallen sharply across nations from 63 per cent of those surveyed in 2017 to 51 per cent in 2022 (Newman, 2022). This trend continued in most countries surveyed in 2023 with people (especially women and younger people) becoming increasingly disconnected from news, particularly in those countries characterized by high levels of political polarization and as concerns about false and misleading information remain a constant worry. These concerns exist alongside confusion over an apparent abundance of online choice, with the combined effect leading to less engagement with news in general rather than digital media plugging growing democratic deficits, with less than half those surveyed (47 per cent, aggregated across markets) now not engaging with news at all. While many studies (see, for example, Ofcom (2022a)) show increasing levels of news consumption through third-party platforms as well as increasing levels of distrust in social media as a source of news and information, the 2017 *Digital News Report* from the Reuters Institute also stated that 'the vast majority of news people consume still comes from mainstream media and that most of the reasons for distrust also relate to mainstream media' (Reuters, 2017, p. 19).

However, the Reuters Institute study has been heavily criticized for its methodology (including querying whether a quantitative questionnaire can really interrogate the complex nature of 'trust'); for its analysis (particularly the lack of country-specific contextualization and understanding); and its overall purpose (the survey itself has been used to attack independent media and intimidate journalists). Its annual *Digital News Report* has been accused of being no more than a popularity contest that enables governments and politicians to embolden their attacks against news organizations that attempt to hold them to account (Mendoza, 2022), facilitating the rise of anti-media populism (Krämer, 2018) and feeding a 'bandwagon of hate targeted at legitimate journalists' (Soriano and Tandoc, 2022). In other words, studies dependent on overstretched comparative generalizations can have far-reaching consequences, and trust is much more complicated than these studies often allow for.

Part of this complexity is apparent in the highly politicized context of 'fake news'. In 2018 – two years after 'fake news' entered general discourse in 2016 amidst the election of Donald Trump in the US and the Brexit Referendum in the UK – the Edelman Trust Barometer noted that 63 per cent of people globally said that the average person does not know how to distinguish rumour from falsehood. The same survey also revealed that 33 per cent of people are reading or listening to the news less and 19 per cent are avoiding the news altogether because it's too depressing (40 per cent) or because it is too one-side or biased (33 per cent) or controlled by hidden agendas (27 per cent). A total of 66 per cent of people said that news organizations were more concerned with attracting a big audience than reporting (Edelman, 2018). The 2023 Edelman Trust Barometer noted that in the UK only 25 per cent of the population said they trusted the media to do what is right (a ten-point drop from 2020), and only 27 per cent trusted the government (a seven-year low); 57 per cent of people felt that their interests were not represented in British politics, and 70 per cent felt that government prioritized its own supporters over those in most need. In the US, Republicans came out as much less trusting of the media and government (25 and 26 per cent) than Democrats (63 and 61 per cent) (Edelman, 2023). Similarly, in 2022 a Gallup poll in the US noted that just 7 per cent of Americans have 'a great deal' of trust and confidence in the media, and 27 per cent have 'a fair amount'. Meanwhile, 28 per cent of US adults say they do not have very much confidence, and 38 per cent have no confidence at all in newspapers, TV and radio (Brenan, 2022).

As more and more people access their news via the internet and social media (Ofcom, 2022c), the 2023 European Broadcasting Union survey, which was based on thirty-three countries in Europe (including EU states as well as acceding and candidate countries), found that the majority of European citizens do not trust the internet or – and even more so – social networks. They also note that public service broadcasters remain the most trusted news in more than 60 per cent of countries in their survey. They align trust in broadcast media with a free and independent media landscape and state that the more citizens perceive public service media in their country to be free from political pressure, the higher the level of trust in the information provided by national media in general. In addition, the more citizens think that their national public service media are independent, the more they trust the news it produces. Radio and TV continue to be the most trusted media throughout Europe. By contrast, social networks appear to be least trusted in thirty-two countries (86 per cent). They also note a positive correlation between trust in news and the degree to which citizens are convinced that their national media cover a diversity of views and opinions, arguing that citizens seem to value a national news media landscape which upholds ideals of impartiality in the news (European Broadcasting Union, 2021).

So it would seem that there is a problem with trust in news and journalism. However, the vast majority of surveys on trust are quantitative, and it is important to keep a close eye on the limitations of the questions posed and the difference in terms used to collect data. Given that each survey takes a different approach to what they are measuring, it is impossible to compare one with another or to really interrogate the meaning of trust to each respondent. In 2023, the Reuters Institute reported on a qualitative analysis of trust in digital news based on forty-one focus groups in Brazil, India, the United Kingdom and the United States, populations which account for more than one billion internet users and places with a wide range of media systems and contexts – strategically selecting participants from disadvantaged communities (based on race, caste, religion, class and place) to understand how they may differ from dominant groups in their expectations around news (Arguedes et al., 2023). The analysis supported other research in the field that notes a general scepticism towards all news media and a deep suspicion about bias and commercial or political influence in news production, only in this instance these ideas emanated from identifying as part of a group that is marginalized or situated far from the centres of power with the stakes of under- or misrepresentation often being far higher than those of privileged audiences. Moreover, the analysis underscored that this kind of under- or misrepresentation constitutes palpable sources of harm to those who are already disadvantaged in society. So lack of trust in news cannot be understood without first understanding the levels of social and political marginalization people feel in general. But again, this report did not allow for a detailed understanding of the news and information ecosystem in each country that would allow us to make meaningful conclusions relating to levels of inequality and marginalization.

While these surveys and focus groups are often problematic for their lack of conceptual clarity and are rarely comparable to each other, they do give us some hints as to why trust in journalists, journalism and news in general has declined. They tell us that news audiences often believe that, despite the claims of journalism to be an institution that supports and strengthens democracy, too often it is found guilty of the opposite – of being unrepresentative of marginalized groups and discriminatory, or of valuing commercial imperatives above journalistic integrity. However, such studies also have a tendency to encourage a reductive news-centric approach that evades a broader and deeper understanding of the news as part of the social and political context within which it exists. Distrust is not simply related to the changing contexts of news. Rather, it is firmly situated in a broader and more general political economic context that requires much more sustained consideration. For example, discontent with democracy has been associated with perceptions of whether or not the economy is considered to be working well. According to Pew (2019), in twenty-four out of twenty-seven countries surveyed, people who say the national economy is in bad shape are more likely than those who say it is in good shape to be dissatisfied with the way democracy is working. In twenty-six of twenty-seven nations, those who believe that in their country most people cannot improve their standard of living are more likely to be dissatisfied with the way democracy is working (Wike, Silver and Castillo, 2019). In other words, when levels of social and economic disenfranchisement are high and inequalities in general are widespread, then levels of discontent and distrust are likely to be higher too.

All of which points to the need to begin with the concept of trust itself.

Concepts of trust

Both political theory and development theory and practice see trust as a key component of the social contract and therefore related to democracy. Literature on trust makes a distinction between horizontal trust (the trust that the members of a community have in each other) and vertical trust (the trust that the members of a community have in the institutions presiding over that community). As with related concepts of 'confidence' and 'risk', approaches to trust are bound up with issues of uncertainty in social, economic and political life and with increasing markers of inequality across multiple aspects of social, economic and political life. As the divide between the top 1 per cent of the global elite and the rest increases, the more estranged the majority of people feel from the minority elite, and the more trust diminishes. So it follows that the more news organizations are seen as part of or at least entangled with elite power, then the less trusted they will be – this is hardly surprising. But there is a broader and deeper context that needs to be taken into account. The emergence of global markets has helped to produce key changes to relationships in society (Waters, 2001). The market is far more than simply the mechanism through which demands are met. It is a system of values and relationships. The marketization of the public sphere has led to a severing of trust from confidence – the difference between supporting the public good (and inspiring trust) through holding power to account, and doing well (and inspiring confidence) through market success. It is on the basis of 'inspiring confidence' (showing that you can do a job well) that the likes of Facebook and Google changed their news algorithms to address concerns of 'fake news' to prioritize large-scale, legacy news organizations, even though for many of these organizations levels of trust in them remain low.

The concept of trust has generally been seen as involving three components – a trusted object (usually a certain actor or institution such as a journalist or news organization); a trusting subject (a citizen or media audience); and expectations that the object will act in a manner that will have certain expected outcomes (such as acting in the public interest when it comes to news journalism). Zucker (1986) also refers to three different kinds of trust: characteristic-based trust, which is tied to a person's social or cultural background; process-based trust, which is tied to past or present exchanges, as in reputation; and institutionally based trust tied to forms of certification or legal constraints (such as press regulation). Anheier and Kendall (2000) argue that in modern societies we have shifted from a more particularist trust based on the individual to a more generalized institutional trust. When societal trust levels are low, then trust in institutions (such as media organizations) may require more direct reliance on government guarantees (through regulation that both sustains the media activity and holds it accountable) or through things like involvement in labour unions and other organizations that retain independence from government control and commercial influence. These are able to create networks of trust that in turn build a level of confidence in media and communication systems functioning fairly and appropriately and being held to account when they fail through incompetence or corruption. In either trust or confidence, the ability of an organization to operate without pressures from vested interests (whether they be political or commercial) is key.

There are also conceptual differences between trust and trustworthiness. While trust relates to subjectively held beliefs regarding the future actions of a certain actor, organization or institution (and is hence more values-based); trustworthiness refers to the actual existing qualities that characterize this actor, organization or institution (and based on which the actor may or may not be deserving of trust). Typically, trustworthiness is conceptualized along two dimensions: intentions (the goals an organization pursues through its actions – such as whether or not a news organization has democratic intent) and competence (the organization's ability to fulfil a given set of goals – such as whether or not it has the financial resources to employ enough skilled journalists). Consistency and predictability are also key markers of trustworthiness and so the ability to enact democratic intent consistently and with predictability are important aspects of trustworthiness in news.

The literature on trust (e.g. Misztal, 1996; Hardin, 2006; Luhmann, 2018) also notes that a person can form evidence-based opinions about the ability of the governance system to promote trustworthy conduct (and prevent breaches of trust) through a mix of incentives and safeguards (which can be formal or informal in nature). An important consequence of this is that trust in actors themselves may not be necessary, provided that people can reasonably trust the governance system itself and the mechanisms that uphold the system. So where we might expect a degree of citizen cynicism towards news and journalism, where a system of independent governance and accountability exists, then trust is more likely. Similarly, where there are low levels of trust in politicians but the ability of systems of governance to protect the rights of those who are excluded from political power are visible, then trust may be maintained. Where neither exists, then trust diminishes. This was evident in relation to the discussion on the BBC in the previous chapter, where low trust in politicians is matched by low expectations of BBC governance that has been shown to be subjected to government influence. And so trust in the BBC declines.

Any discussion on issues relating to trust quickly reveals the importance of perceptions in trust-building processes. So for trust at any level to exist – related to any actor or institution – the news and information economy is a crucial factor, including what type of information is available to whom, about what and through which channels. If the news and information economy is driven by and prioritizes the narrow interests of capital and foregrounds the importance of markets, then this can undercut public trust in the public sphere more generally.

In a digital media landscape, it is also vital to understand the specific configuration of news and information intermediaries that can orient a given public in the identification, prioritization and interpretation of information. This raises concerns about echo chambers (Sunstein, 2017) and filter bubbles (Bruns, 2019), which may close people off from a more diverse range of perspectives, as well as celebrity influencers (Soriano and Tandoc, 2022), which may intensify possibilities for information manipulation. Additionally, digital platforms may simply overwhelm citizens with incessant information pollution such that it becomes impossible to establish confidence in systems of governance that are constantly called out as lacking in content moderation or failing in fact-checking, leaving people disoriented and unable to find a means of trusting anything in the public sphere.

What is clear, from a host of literature on trust from different fields, is that it is deeply contextual and embedded in histories of political culture and the integrity of news and information ecosystems more broadly. Elsewhere in this book I have discussed convergent shifts in cultural production, journalism, political communication, marketing and data mining – all of which have contributed to the emergence of a mediated regime facilitated by deregulated, commodified, affective and ever-faster forms of 'communicative capitalism' (Dean, 2009). Here, we find political discourse commandeered by the stuff of entertainment while mainstream news stands accused of trafficking in trivialities and repackaged public relations material. This direction of travel, traceable across at least the last forty years, to subjugate *all* areas of mediated activity to market logic and competition through ever more commercialization, privatization and restructuring, has prepared the way for what Will Davies has referred to as 'post-truth politics' based on an over-supply of 'facts' and an under-provision of meaningful analysis (Davies, 2016). This is the context in which we see trust in news and journalism falter.

Yet, as mentioned above, other issues pertaining to social and economic inequalities are also of critical importance. These came to the fore in the Civil Society Futures Inquiry in England (also referred to in Chapter 3), which involved participatory action research in nine areas[12] over a period of two years (Civil Society Futures, 2018).

In this study, participants made it clear that, although it had never been easier to express views and opinions, very few people felt heard let alone responded to or involved in any decision-making affecting their lives. For them, politics had become something done to people and places and not by people in those places. They felt, acutely, that decisions about them were being made without them. People told us how their jobs were insecure and lives precarious, that social services were being withdrawn from those who are most unprotected – the poor, the homeless, the undocumented – yet those in power neither recognized nor responded to the consequences this had in the places they lived. They recounted a loss of confidence in the institutions that are supposed to represent them and saw the political system as one that ignores them and consistently fails them. As one respondent noted, 'People are just that tired . . . they've seen that no one's been listening to them' (Newcastle community workshop); or another: 'It's called an election but we might just as well throw darts and see what happens' (Penzance focus group). Few people we spoke to believed that actually existing democracy could solve their problems. Feelings of irrelevance and lack of agency were linked to felt experiences of inequality. Participants spoke of their own power over their lives as depleted. They expressed a sense that existing democracy does not work for the majority and never will unless there are new forms of governance in which everyone can challenge and change the social and political system of which they are part.

It is against the backdrop of these conditions in which a series of political 'earthquakes' took place, including the election of Donald Trump and the decision taken by UK voters in 2016 to leave the European Union. These events brought to the fore an economic dislocation that has been experienced and intensifying since the 1980s, revealing deep class, generational and ethnic divisions. These same circumstances contribute to decreasing levels of trust in certain systems of news and information that are so often seen to be unrepresentative, out of touch with people's lives and heavily implicated in the systems of dominant power they claim to hold to account. In 2023 the Edelman Trust Barometer reported that the media was distrusted in 56 per cent of the twenty-seven countries they surveyed and it had dropped in twenty-one of those countries since the previous year. They note that government and media are seen as the largest sources of false or misleading information by 46 per cent and 42 per cent respectively of people globally (excluding China and Thailand). They also revealed a clear class divide with those in lower socio-economic groups expressing far less trust than those in higher socio-economic groups in the majority of countries. They point to distrust, lack of shared identity and systemic unfairness as drivers of polarization, followed by economic pessimism, societal fears and distrust in media (Edelman, 2023).

Fake news or fake democracy?[13]

So the collapse in trust in news media has not happened in isolation and is related to the same backlash against entrenched interests that has eaten into the credibility of neoliberal political parties and politicians. Given that the mainstream media in many places are seen to be ever-more closely entangled with elite power, so they are also implicated in the same mire of corruption and scandal. This is part of a wider narrative about the degeneration of the liberal 'centre' and its failure both to stand up to, and to distinguish itself from, the market forces that have eviscerated, evacuated, hollowed out, reined in, commodified, trivialized and generally contaminated those spaces with which democracy has been traditionally associated.

Of course, it is neoliberal forces, rather than liberal democracy more generally, that are most frequently associated with this degeneration. For millions of people, it is the neoliberal logic and the narrow instrumentalism of allegedly self-correcting markets that has ridden roughshod over permanent jobs, communities, egalitarian structures and democratic aspirations. It is the emphasis on economic efficiency that has depoliticized much government decision-making, transforming social, political and moral dilemmas into technical and often technological problems, leaving little room for public participation – as the participants in the Civil Society Futures (2018) project made so clear. Neoliberal global capitalism has subsumed political power into market power as nation states, circumscribed by increasingly deregulated and untaxed or low-taxed capital, are left with decreasing resources to tackle the social issues global capitalism creates (Wood, 2005). As transnational capital escapes the boundaries of the nation state (with the tech giants the latest and largest example), the power of capital becomes ever more diffuse, polluting the atmosphere and impacting all forms of life and nature in a bid for profit maximization and accumulation, while being seemingly impossible to locate, challenge and hold accountable.

It is hardly surprising that news media have been unable to hold global capital to account when they too are global corporations ensnared by the market with profit as their ultimate endgame.

However, profit is hard to come by in a largely unregulated digital market, where tech giants extract value from content created by news and information organizations without compensating them for it. With the veneer of liberal watchdog now stretched perilously thin across the mainstream news media, it should come as no surprise that neoliberal rationality has been so successful in occupying the terrain of the liberal centre. The issue may be less that we are now suddenly surrounded by fake news – a concept that has been used in a variety of ways to fulfil a variety of political purposes (what Farkas and Schou refer to as 'the politics of falsehood' (2019), but rather, that we have been living for too long with fake democracy beholden to the interests of capital.

Colin Crouch, referring largely to Western Europe, famously described this situation as 'post-democracy', a situation in which 'politics and government are increasingly slipping back into the control of privileged elites in the manner characteristic of pre-democratic times' (Crouch, 2004, p. 6). Crouch describes a paradox of contemporary Western European democracy: that despite the surfeit of apparently democratic-sounding developments – the collapse of deference, increases in transparency and literacy and more formal opportunities to engage in democracy – we nevertheless have to be persuaded to vote and to exercise civic responsibility. The media themselves are partly to blame with their attachments to power and their use of sensationalism and soundbites that 'degrade the quality of political discussion and reduce the competence of citizens' (Crouch, 2004, p. 47). This is amplified in a digital age, where clickbait too often drives content. This sham sovereignty is not incidental to but intertwined with neoliberal capitalism, of which, in many parts of the world, our mainstream media industries are very much a part, alongside the thoroughly marketized notion of 'media freedom' they shield behind in order to continue to reap profits.

As discussed elsewhere in this book, actually existing democracy– both in its rhetoric and its political practices – has very successfully used discourses of equality (see Chapter 5) and autonomy (see Chapter 4) to commodify individualism and to constrain freedom. It has promised sovereignty and self-governance through market exchanges and constitutional guarantees, but instead we are left with a junk democracy that celebrates super-sized forms of digital participation and engagement with all political nutrients removed. Citizens have been recast as consumers and collective decisions transformed into questions of individual choice. We have been fed the delusion of democratic communications in a 'free' media while editors and top politicians cosy up to one another and feather each other's nests. Power remains heavily centralized, and the most powerful networks are firmly closed to an elite class who dine at the same tables, are educated at the same institutions and share many of the same corporate values and ideological agendas. This coterie of media and political elites trade in a common currency of emotion and lies (Tsipursky, 2017) – what Dahlgren has referred to as an 'emerging new epistemic regime, where emotional response prevails over factual evidence and reasoned analysis' (Dahlgren, 2018, p. 25). We now have a mainstream journalism that fails to perform what is assumed to be the central role of media in a liberal democracy: its willingness to interrogate the power relations that shape our world. This is not exactly new: 'the truth' has long been a contested and problematic term, and news production has a ragged history of political entanglements. But it has been brought to the fore partly because of the quick-fix, rapid-fire, clickbait-focused strategies, and also because media organizations themselves appear to be ever-more implicated in power relations that they often have little reason to illuminate or to challenge, a form of elite capture that is becoming increasingly apparent to disillusioned publics.

In addition, there is an ongoing struggle by the commercial mainstream press to find new 'business models' in the digital age, to claw back some of the control over capital accumulation they once had. Both digital intermediaries and more traditional content providers are jostling to command and monetize public attention. There is, in other words, a political and economic hustle between two sectors that are heavily interconnected. The bewildering market power wielded by the likes of Google and Meta has not come at the expense of the influence of mainstream press and broadcasters. Google, Meta and X (formerly Twitter) are, if anything, *reinforcing* the agenda-setting power of the mainstream news brands by facilitating their increased circulation. In an attempt to respond to calls to limit the circulation of 'fake news' Google ranks news providers in relation to what it considers to be the most 'reliable' indicators of news quality. According to Schlosberg, this means 'they rely on quantitative measures of quality, which produces their own bias in favour of large-scale and mainstream providers' (Schlosberg, 2017). Such measures rely on what Google refers to as 'importance', which is calculated in terms of volume of a site's output on a single topic, at once privileging concentration of news providers (the bigger the better) and concentration of news output (favouring topics that are widely covered elsewhere), a measure that in Schlosberg's words 'single-handedly reinforces both an aggregate news "agenda", as well as the agenda-setting power of a relatively small number of publishers' (Schlosberg, 2017).

News-gathering and news-ranking algorithms change frequently and are largely opaque. In 2019, the VP of Google News, Richard Gringras, wrote that 'The algorithms used for our news experiences analyze hundreds of different factors to identify and organize the stories journalists are covering, in order to elevate diverse, trustworthy information' (Gringras, 2019). While the majority of these factors remain unknown, Google states that they include prominence, geographic relevance and freshness of the content as well as estimates of the trustworthiness and authoritativeness of the publishing organizations. In response to concerns over Fake News Gingras stated that '[t]o reduce the visibility of [harmful misinformation] during crisis or breaking news events, we've improved our systems to put more emphasis on authoritative results over factors like freshness or relevancy' (Gringras, 2018). What this means in practice in unclear. What we do know is that elevation up the Google hierarchy does not rely on the intent or factual accuracy of any piece of content but rather on judgements of established news sites that it deems more generally trustworthy, which are most likely to be those with volume and scale.

In other words, capital accumulation of one major corporation reinforces capital accumulation of another major corporation – a spiral of amplification of news that has already secured a market dominance in a thoroughly commercialized context, each reinforcing the other's version of what they claim to be real, legitimate and authoritative news. However, in much of the popular press – in the UK at least – this press has consistently been found to be riddled with distortions, misrepresentations and illegitimate news. Yet Google's algorithms amplify these so-called reliable sources of news and reproduce their dominance. So it is hardly surprising that they become difficult to distinguish from the likes of the 'actual' fake news industry.

An Ofcom plurality report (Ofcom, 2022a) notes that there are real concerns about the impact of online intermediaries, and in particular social media platforms, on media plurality. It found that people who most often use social media to access news are less likely to correctly identify important factual information, feel more antipathy towards people who hold different political views and are less trusting of democratic institutions than people who use TV and newspapers most often as a source of news. Other studies have shown that people who use social media to access news tend to express lower levels of political trust. Furthermore, an increase in social media use as a source of news at the national level is associated with a decrease in trust in the news media in general. This all paints a depressing canvas, and the picture doesn't get any rosier when we add AI/ML to the mix.

AI and the engineering of news from nowhere

Text-generating AI, the latest of which is GPT (Generative Pre-trained Transformer), pull together what is available to them on the internet, including the entire gambit of facts, half-truths and lies, and pieces them together in what looks like a cohesive narrative. GPT is fed reams of data in the form of vast volumes of text from scanned books and the Web; from this, it extracts statistical patterns and abstract linguistic conceptualizations. Through a process of computer-generated learning, GPT uses these patterns and concepts to estimate what word is most likely to follow any preceding collection of words. In practice, this means a user inputs some text as a prompt, and GPT extends this one word at a time for as long as the user likes. AI cannot attest to the credibility of an argument or accuracy of an observation; it is only mimicking similarities discovered in data available to it; but it is much cheaper and faster than hiring a journalist. It has been used to create profile pictures of non-existent journalists (using an AI-powered method termed deepfake), source quotes, summarize reports, suggest questions for interviews, write headlines or entire articles based on a user's prompts. AI-powered journalism may well (quickly) become a form of supercharged churnalism that doesn't just take one press release and repeat it but pieces together articles from millions of digital texts to create a (relatively) seamless report. This is not so much what Fishman (1990) once referred to as 'manufacturing [of] the news' as a way of explaining how the routine methods of gathering news determine the ideological character of the product, but rather the wholesale commercial *engineering* of the news. And before we know it, news from everywhere becomes news from nowhere.

As noted in Chapter 5, given that AI functions on the texts it finds based on past patterns which it then replicates, it can also endlessly reproduce systemic inequalities and structural discrimination that exist (Bolukbasi et al., 2016; Chun and Barnett, 2021; Mitchell et al., 2021). Geoffrey Hinton (referred to by some as the 'Godfather of

AI') quit Google in 2023 in order to speak freely about the dangers of AI (Metz, 2023). That same month IBM CEO Arvind Krishna told Bloomberg that up to 30 per cent of the company's back-office roles could be replaced by AI and automation within five years (Ford, 2023). The economic consequences of AI could be far-reaching. Susskind (2018) notes that between 1990 and 2007 – before the introduction of smartphones – industrial robots alone eliminated up to 670,000 American jobs. Between 2000 and 2010 the US lost 5.6 million manufacturing jobs, 85 per cent of which were attributable to technological change. In 2016 analysts at McKinsey estimated that 'currently demonstrated technologies' could be used to automate 45 per cent of the tasks that we pay people to do (Chui, Manyika and Miremadi, 2016). Others have sounded similar warnings (Agrawal, Gans and Goldfarb, 2023; McAfee and Brynjolfsson, 2016), adding that this could also lower workers' political influence and representation (Acemoglu, 2021; Gallego and Kurer, 2022), while the threat of replacement helps to intimidate workers. As people are made to feel that they are disposable, new forms of exploitation emerge (Dyer-Witherford, Kjøsen and Steinhoff, 2019). And no one is there to push back. AI doesn't go on strike.

In a cash-strapped news industry the temptations of AI will be manifold and the path has already been charted. In June 2020 dozens of news production contractors at Microsoft's MSN were sacked and replaced by AI. These staff were not reporters in the traditional journalistic sense, but they did exercise some editorial control – it was their job to curate stories from other news organizations (the sorts of practices that are referred to above as extracting value from legacy news organizations), writing headlines and selecting pictures to accompany the articles. These roles are now performed by algorithms that identify trending news stories and try to optimize the amount of page views any particular content receives.

Dyer-Witherford, Kjosen and Steinhoff (2019) note that AI is an instrument of capital and exploitation. It has an inbuilt logic to produce surplus value. Its purpose therefore is to contribute to a capitalist social order. Whereas, Google explicitly states that it is not driven by commercial imperatives in relation to news, when it comes to advertising algorithms the opposite is true. Google is the largest advertising company in the world. It posts ads by placing them on its own site and on external sites in the Google Display Network. The more ads Google places, the more money it makes – it doesn't differentiate between those that are trustworthy and those that are not. In doing so, Google is providing a financial incentive for these sites to bring in as much web traffic as possible, even if it comes by way of mal- or disinformation. In September 2019, a UK nonprofit called the Global Disinformation Index (GDI) released a report analysing ad placement on fake news sites. They collected a list of 1,700 websites that had been flagged by fact-checking organizations for publishing content that included fake news. They found that Google was serving up ads on 70 per cent of these sites. They estimated that the fake news industry brought in nearly a quarter of a billion dollars in the year 2019 – of which Google was responsible for $87m (Global Disinformation Index, 2019). This means that Google was responsible for almost 40 per cent of the fake news industry's revenue that year. This was almost the same share of ad revenue that Google was responsible for among mainstream legacy news sites. In other words, in terms of the advertising market Google does not differentiate.

Facebook also built its massive platform by designing algorithms to maximize user engagement at all costs (Hao, 2021). Many studies (Anspach, 2021; Kim et al., 2021; González-Bailón and Lelkes, 2023) have concluded that algorithms designed to maximize engagement also increase polarization and amplify far-right content. A study of the US 2020 election found that far-right content generated more engagement than any other partisan group, and far-right misinformation generated 65 per cent more engagement than far-right factual content. This means that any recommendation/ranking algorithm with engagement as the metric it aims to maximize will prioritize far-right misinformation above all else (Edelson et al., 2021).

In other words, 'fake news' is not an exception to but the logical result of a market economy that privileges short-term rewards and commercial impact. The rise of programmatic advertising and the domination of advertising by Google and Facebook are not peripheral developments but part of a structural readjustment of the media. In these circumstances, 'fake news' is indicative of a much larger issue relating to the structure and economics of social platforms that encourages the spread of low-quality content over high-quality material. Journalism with a civic value – journalism that investigates power, or reaches underserved and local communities – is discriminated against by a system that favours scale and 'shareability'. Giansiracusa (2021, p. 10) refers to the datafication of journalism – the page views and clicks we sprinkle across the internet as the 'digital fertilizer' feeding a burgeoning garden of misinformation and fake news. As the weeds take over, Vogl (2022) argues that the capital accumulation strategies of new platforms and social media are pushing people into fragmented, opposing and conflictual communities, where their feelings of grievance and rejection generated by capitalism are redirected into attacks on migrants, foreigners and others.

'Fake news' then becomes an interminable shape-shifter morphing into whatever form suits the proponent's purposes, whether this form refers to falsehoods deliberately concocted to undermine democratic processes (such as elections and referenda), traditional journalism with its long history of misrepresentations, exaggerations and distortions (including 'yellow journalism' and sensationalist claims such as Saddam Hussein's Iraq being able to launch weapons of mass destruction within forty-five minutes), or to what Tambini describes as '[n]ews that challenges orthodox authority' and that departs from an elite shared consensus (Tambini, 2017, p. 5).

Those critics who have attempted to offer typographies of fake news (Hameleers, Brosius and de Vreese, 2022) note two main categories: misinformation and disinformation. They note that misinformation has been characterized as 'inaccurate information' (Fisher and Karlova, 2013) and is sometimes used as a general term for information that is inaccurate without being deliberately harmful or misleading (e.g. Vraga and Bode, 2020). In other words, it doesn't have an explicit political agenda and could be seen as an 'honest mistake', easily remedied. It is this sort of interpretation that leads Creech (2020) to note that many journalists address fake news as a technical problem of the digital age and call for technical fixes focused on getting 'social media companies to clean up their sites, monitor content with the public interest in mind, and tweak algorithms' (Waisbord, 2018, p. 1868).

Disinformation, however, is characterized as 'deceptive information' (Fisher and Karlova, 2013), that is deliberately false and misleading (Wardle, 2017) and often aimed at mobilizing people against 'centre parties, governments and elections', hence is seen as polarizing and divisive (Bennett and Livingston, 2018, p. 122). This form of fake news has been designated as a danger zone of infowar by professional journalists keen to distinguish their work from it (Bratich, 2020). In these instances, Lim (2020) describes how a 'securitization of "fake news"' (p. 7) has taken place to legitimize laws in countries such as Malaysia, Singapore, Cambodia, the Philippines, Vietnam, Kenya, Burkina Faso, Venezuela, Honduras, France, Hungary and Russia (Lim, 2020; Human Rights Watch, 2021; Neo, 2022; Tenove, 2020; Tully, 2022). Farkas (2023) explains how the articulation of fake news as a national security threat is connected to the rise of new forms of state censorship, linked to lower levels of public satisfaction with the overall state of democracy and increased support for free speech restrictions. In Malaysia, Lim (2020) shows how an 'Anti-Fake News Act' made it illegal to distribute false or partly false information and imposed penalties ranging from fines to imprisonment of up to six years. Human rights advocates stated that the legislation was '100 percent intended to muffle dissent . . . the punishment is extremely high and what amounts to fake news has been loosely defined' (Paulsen, 2018 as cited in Lim, 2020, p. 5). While the Malaysian Anti-Fake News Act was repealed in 2019 after public pressure and a change of government (Lim, 2020), it was then revised and reinstated during the Covid-19 pandemic in 2021 under the banner of fighting the virus. In other words, who gets to define what counts as 'fake news' is highly politicized and can be used to quash opposition to prevailing power relations.

Wardle (2020, p. 8) also talks about malinformation to describe genuine information that is shared with an intent to cause harm, such as when Russian agents hacked into emails from the Democratic National Committee and the Hillary Clinton campaign and leaked details to the public to damage reputations. She states that, '[w]e are increasingly seeing the weaponization of context and the use of genuine content – but content that is warped and reframed . . . anything with a kernel of truth is far more successful in terms of persuading and engaging people'. Malinformation is arguably harder to detect and often a response to search engines and social media companies getting tougher on fake content.

Disinformation and malinformation, however, do not exist in splendid isolation. They are also part of a political-industrial complex linked to political funders, think tanks, movements and parties all aiming to disrupt formerly authoritative information flows that may have come from governments of liberal democratic nations or their mainstream media. That the legitimacy of each has consistently been found wanting has left both struggling to claim the high ground. The long history of growing disillusionment with liberal democratic institutions of the press and politics is at the heart of this demise. Liberal democracy is no longer a centring force organized around majority consensus but rather an elite practice seen to be protecting vested interests. This was epitomized in 2019 during the UK election debates when the Conservative Party changed their Twitter account into a false factchecking service 'factcheckUK' in a clumsy attempt to gain political ground that revealed them to have no regard for the truth at all. These sorts of manoeuvring, spinning, brand management and indifference to facts all serve to bring more disrepute to, and grow contempt of, political parties and further perturb people about the meaning or value of democracy.

In this situation, claims made about the dangers of 'fake news' are hardly innocent but part of a coordinated attempt by the centre ground to construct a narrative that contrasts 'professional journalism' (based on contested claims to ethical responsibility and objectivity) with 'fake news' (anything that departs from or challenges established protocols). This was evident in Hungary when politicians called for free speech restrictions during the pandemic, stating that fake news was a matter of national security that required legislation 'to protect citizens' life, health and security' (Varga, 2020). This is likely to involve the resurrection of the same newsroom agendas and the same authorities of 'truth-telling' and expertise that have so often failed to make sense of the world for so many people and that, at least in part, paved the way for the rapid rise of the 'fake news' that mainstream media so deplore.

Where does this discussion leave us? Fake news is a political and economic phenomenon that is indicative of a much deeper fear around democratic and social decay and can be mobilized to both detract from this democratic demise and to add to it (Bratich, 2020; Monsees, 2023; Wright, 2021). Corrosive commercialization, concentration of ownership, technological change, decline of public trust and growth of tech giants have all challenged mainstream news' status as authoritative purveyors of knowledge. When both politicians and journalists are the least trusted people in society, it is relatively easy for one to push the other into the spotlight of the accused – yet both are trying to assert their dominance. Trump may cast the term about as a derisory label for any news outlet that doesn't agree with him and we may easily spot the rhetorical device. But when news organizations allow automated engineering of news content through AI on grounds of 'efficiency' and cost savings, it may not be so straightforward to identify. If the lie is exposed – that news has always been manufactured and to a certain extent captured by the political economic context it resides within (such as neoliberalism), then the professional paradigm of news crumbles. If we realize that politics circulates on a political economy of lies for electoral advantage, then liberal democracy is found out. Each is pointing the finger of liar at the other to retain political and/or economic power.

Amidst the furore of fake news came another crisis – the global health pandemic of Covid-19 – where access to reliable information quite literally became a case of life or death and the necessity of governments to respond adequately to the health requirements opened up opportunities for some to make quick economic gains. The consequences of these dodgy deals further exposed where the interests of political elites lie, their deep entanglement with global corporate power and the chasm between them both and the public at large.

The pandemic, media power and privilege

There is still much that remains unknown about the global health pandemic that began in China in 2020, yet its consequences are likely to be felt for decades to come. As of 9 July 2024 the World Health Organization (WHO, 2024) noted 7,052,472 deaths globally. From school closures to devastated industries and millions of job losses, the social and economic costs have been manifold. The pandemic shone a light on systemic, structural inequalities in society while intensifying them, with a grossly disproportionate impact on racialized minorities who tend to be poorer, have worse living conditions and work in the care services (Nolan, 2021). In October 2022 the WHO reported that the high levels of anxiety, stress and depression among care workers has become a 'pandemic within a pandemic' (WHO, 2022). Mental health issues as a result of isolation, loneliness, uncertainty, socioeconomic distress, bereavement or personal infection have been extensive. The pandemic uncovered and engendered more inequality (Davies and Gane, 2021), enabled more militarism (Khisa and Rwengabo, 2023) and was used to legitimize authoritarianism and close borders with dramatic consequences for democratic rights (Pelizza, Milan and Lausberg, 2021).

Provost and Kennard (2023, p. 220) note how corporate power also challenged government policies enacted to protect people amid the pandemic. In 2021 the Chilean government was sued by French shareholders of a consortium controlling Santiago's international airport, demanding compensation for lost profits due to fewer flights and complaining about policies requiring additional sanitary measures. What we witnessed, and as many predicted (Morwoski, 2020; Klein, 2020) was neoliberal forces seizing their opportunity for an extensive transfer of wealth to the rich facilitated by ruling classes declaring states of exception; we also witnessed enhanced surveillance and control through the global police state in the name of limiting the virus through mass testing, tracing and identification – all the time entrenching digital capitalism. Platforms exploited the emergency of the pandemic more than any other type of business, whether in relation to social relations, home-working, home-schooling, the gig economy, retail, health monitoring or news and information (Milan, Treré and Masiero, 2021).

The pandemic laid bare the workings of a renewed executive power (see Chapter 2), where elite groups deploy their resources – their access to capital, their political influence and their ideological congruence – to dominate and dictate the terms of contemporary media and tech systems. Whether this is in the form of tax-avoiding corporations and offshore billionaires (a new billionaire was created every thirty hours during the pandemic (Oxfam, 2022)); data brokers and infrastructure empires (with the pandemic accelerating the adoption of digital technologies leading to an increase in the amount of data being generated and collected for market analysis); market-friendly politicians and captive regulators; the end result is the increasing concentration of power and influence in ever fewer hands. As Robinson (2022, p. 34) notes, the impacts of the pandemic 'were integral to ongoing processes of domination and resistance . . . and accelerated a new wave of restructuring and transformation of global capitalism'.

Other giants of global capitalism, such as pharmaceutical companies, engaged in a global lobbying blitz to ensure corporate dominance over required medical products (Fang, 2021). The bid to share Covid vaccine recipes around the world failed. Big Pharma went to great lengths to curb efforts to share pandemic-related patents and waive intellectual property rights, including threats to the leadership of Belgium, Colombia and Indonesia that if they supported such proposals then investments in research and development in their countries would be withdrawn (Furlong, Aarup and Horti, 2022). Ultimately, attempts to introduce a special World Trade Organization waiver (known as the TRIPS waiver) necessary for the rapid creation of generic pandemic medicine failed due to aggressive lobbying from Big Pharma (Fang, 2021). The assault against the creation of generic vaccines resulted in an unprecedented explosion in profit for a few select biopharmaceutical drug interests. Pfizer and BioNTech generated a staggering $37 billion in revenue from its shared mRNA vaccine in 2021 alone, making it one of the most lucrative drug products of all time. The high cost of vaccines and concentrated ownership meant supplies in 2021 were hoarded in the European Union, United Kingdom, United States, Canada, Japan and other wealthy countries, while much of the developing world was forced to wait for excess vaccines the following year (Intercepted, 2021).

In the UK, elite power was very clearly on show when the clamber to deal with the pandemic was seen by many as a business opportunity too good to miss. Well-positioned firms hustled to profit from the provision of public goods and services when British politicians scrambled to procure the necessary personal protective equipment, ventilators and Covid-19 tests for tackling the virus. The *New York Times* (Bradley, Gebrekidan and McCann, 2020) analysed 1,200 UK government contracts worth $22 billion to reveal that 50 per cent went to companies either run by friends and associates of the ruling Conservative Party, or to those with no prior experience of providing these sorts of goods, or to companies/individuals with a history of controversy (from tax evasion and fraud to corruption and human rights abuses). About $5bn went to politically connected companies: some had former minister and government advisers on staff, while others were Conservative Party donors. During the procurement process, Matt Hancock, then secretary of state for health, created a 'VIP lane' for favoured companies endorsed by officials or politicians, which then, according to the National Audit Office, became ten times more likely to win contracts than those outside that group (National Audit Office, 2020). Those allowed into the VIP lane were given a secret email address.

UK national newspapers, like other businesses, experienced the financial consequences of the economy's demise during lockdown. The News Media Association (which represents most of the largest and wealthiest media organizations in the UK) lobbied government for their own bailout. The result was government underwriting of large corporate media to the tune of £200m through advertising and paid-for content under the rubric of 'we are all in this together'. This content was designed to look like any other article but had been paid for by the government to extol the good job the government was doing. The only difference was a small tag with an additional health warning that 'this advertiser content was paid for by the UK government'. In the UK, this is particularly ironic given that the press campaigned extensively against effective (independent) regulation on the basis that it would lead to unwarranted state 'intrusion' into the industry. Meanwhile, virtually none of the payout went to small independent news organizations, even though they lobbied for their fair share.

At the same time as they were propping up corporate power the UK government explicitly sought to restrict media scrutiny by refusing to put forward ministers or representatives to go on news programmes such as Radio 4's *Today* programme and barred certain journalists (with more interrogatory approaches) from asking questions at their press briefings in order to discredit critical reporting – actively seeking to punish and freeze out watchdog journalism. In 2023 a parliamentary inquiry found Boris Johnson, the Conservative prime minister during the pandemic, guilty of lying to parliament about his own breaches of Covid-19 laws. Johnson resigned from his role as a Member of Parliament shortly before the report was published. The day after the report was published he was given a job as a columnist in the *Daily Mail* national newspaper.

And so we come back to the importance of the conditions required to enable democracy. It will never be enough to turn to tech solutionism – better design, more responsible approaches to data, better algorithms – when the problems are social, political and economic as well as technological.

What can we do about it? Resocializing the political for a news media commons

We are right not to trust our media and systems of communication when they consist of giant corporations and wealthy elites. What we see is a corporate media that is largely insulated from democracy, and a media and tech industry that set the rules of how they should operate in order to profit from them. The frightening truth is that because of what Provost and Kennard (2023) call the 'corporate coup' of our media and tech worlds, the actual truth of what is going on in the world is likely to be much worse. Power is hidden from view rather than held to account. Fake news, however defined, is doubtless a major problem, but allowing all of our attention to be subsumed by it as the cause of all our ills distracts our attention from the problems of fake democracy, which a demise of trust points us to.

A focus on fake news in relation to trust and distrust also suggests that if we could just find an effective way of filtering out the dodgy stuff, then everything will be fine – but it won't. Or, if independent fact-checking sites were attached to every news outlet, then the problem would be solved – but it wouldn't. All these measures do is address the end product of news that has already been through a news-gathering and selection process, framed in particular ways with certain sources deemed 'authoritative knowers' or truth-tellers, set within a dominant paradigm of newsworthiness that has long been criticized. Talking about media representations of sexual violence, Banet-Weiser and Higgins (2023, p. 4) draw our attention to what they call the 'mediated economy of believability . . . in which public bids for truth are made, evaluated and authorized', noting how certain bodies have always been more believable than others – an economy where whiteness, men and wealth win out. Fact-checkers and fake news algorithms offer no more than a sticking plaster approach to a much larger, deeper, multi-layered wound, one in which who gets to decide what is dodgy and what is not has plagued our dominant processes of news and knowledge production for too long and is embroiled in the neoliberalization of truthism that is part of the problem. The privatization and marketization of news has a long history wherein the prevailing norm is that news and information is for sale and is tailored to the desires of the consumer (over the information needs of any democratic society). Audience maximization is the end-game (over democratic sustenance). Concurrently, in many places around the globe, people (especially those who are marginalized or minoritized) have experienced political disaffection and disenfranchisement. Those who feel the pain of disenfranchisement the most trust the least, because as bodies they are positioned as less worthy of consideration and have suffered multiple forms of misrepresentation and under-representation over many years.

Trust (and distrust), then, is intricately related to social, political and economic power and exists as a cultural construction rather than an epistemological pillar in the shifting sands of reality. So building trust networks will necessarily involve acknowledging and rectifying power inequalities in order to enhance accountability and cultivate and grow trustworthiness. In many places around the globe we can identify instances where forms of mediated democracy based on these premises are ethnographically emergent, where democracy is understood as the sharing of rule and the constant creation of new publics, new forms of mediated civil society where narratives are emerging that speak to a citizens (or even a solidarity) economy– a sense of collective human power against the habitual feelings of powerlessness and isolation.

In Mexico, Rhizomatica is an organization that began in 2009 with the purpose of making 'alternative telecommunication infrastructures possible for people facing oppressive regimes, the threat of natural disaster or the reality of living in a place deemed too poor or isolated to connect' (Rhizomatica, 2015). It attempts to use innovative applications of technology for community organizing and for bringing about personal and collective autonomy. It has worked with communities in Africa and Latin America to build autonomous cellular networks, develop radio technology for safe and reliable long-distance communication without the internet and deploy alternative energy infrastructure and bio-economy projects. Their mission is to support communities to build and maintain self-governed and self-owned communication systems. In Oaxaca, Mexico they helped create a regional community telecommunications cooperative, Telecomunicaciones Indigenas Comunitarias (TCC), which encompasses all of the member communities with mobile networks and provides a platform for mobilization around regulatory issues, resource and profit-sharing, economies of scale for interconnection with existing telecommunications infrastructure (telephone and internet), technical capacity-building and maintenance. TCC was one of the first fully licensed, community-owned and -operated telecommunications networks based on community norms and specific organizational structures established by indigenous communities.

If we turn to other literature from community and alternative communication in Latin America (e.g. Sánchez and Gómez, 2023) and also North America (Kidd, 2019, 2020) we also find many indigenous and environmental movements using decolonizing practices of communication that reject commercial forms of media. These communities turn instead to forms of media borne of the collective participation of inhabitants with a focus on the conditions of production and social reproduction of life as a counterforce to the dispossessions and decimation of indigenous populations and the dominant capitalist, hetero-patriarchal and colonial world system. These movements seek to build different forms of communication infrastructure that aim to coordinate

> processes between media and related entities, and thus weave networks that seek to provide joint responses to common problems, ranging from the exchange of information and experiences to the implementation of technical training initiatives through the agreement of actions and programmatic definitions. (Munoz Gonzalez, 2018, p. 11, cited in Sánchez and Gómez, 2023, p. 114)

Once more, as discussed in Chapter 6, we see communication through the lens of social justice, which foregrounds a need for a means of organizing communications as a kind of shared 'commons' – a shared resource, which is co-owned and/or co-governed by its users and/or stakeholder communities, according to its own rules and norms. This is related to physical spaces that are shared or pooled, the co-production of the resource, the means of maintaining that resource as well as the mode of governance – how decisions are made collaboratively to distribute and use the resource. All of these practices are based on an ethos of collective social transformation. It puts the commons and not the market at its epicentre, with civil society becoming the place where the institutions of the commons are located. The principle of the market then changes from one focused on the accumulation of capital to one which serves the accumulation of the commons – for the public good. What I call *resocializing the political* (Fenton, 2016) is at the heart of this endeavour. Politics has become so disconnected from, and distrusted by, the majority of people that it needs desperately to reconnect with the social – to rediscover forms of substantive relationality. A process of resocializing involves mutual recognition and information, dialogue and shared radical praxis. Resocializing the political means just that: political actors that are part of the communities that are dealing with the problems they face through establishing community banks and soup kitchens, tackling corruption, resisting evictions, and developing media cooperatives; organizations premised on equity, inclusion and social justice that recognize the intradependencies of the work they do, care deeply about the communities they are embedded in and seek to work with and be of benefit to and accountable to those communities.

The Civil Society Futures (2018) research foregrounds that the further people feel at a distance from decision-making, the more arbitrary domination feels and the more vulnerable people feel to those who hold power. This obvious point is hugely significant because it indicates just how much *relationality* matters politically – for agency and for understanding and for seeking the means to non-domination. Relationality is also about the ordinary, everyday experience of politics and culture – it is part of what creates meaning through conversation, collaboration, public forms of art, creativity and meaning-making. Relationality is a key part of knowledge production related to processes of generating and circulating news and information. It is by definition participatory and constitutive of our understanding of places, situations and circumstances. If we do not attend to the resocializing of the political, the dangers are huge: democratic participation must offer the sense of solidarity and belonging that surpass darker political forces that promise to look after their own and lock others out. Although deepening social and economic divisions have made the process of overcoming this alienation ever harder, it has also increased the urgency for the crafting of other forms of social attention that can respond to the harms caused through democratic depreciation. This stresses the need for practices of care, listening and the active seeking of understanding – whether this be through reimagining forms of news and journalism or community organizing.

The question we are left with, in a context of ever-decreasing trust, is how much of our collective lives should be directed and controlled by powerful people and corporations – not least Big Tech. It was Williams (1961) who pointed out that a key contribution of the Labour movement was in its creation of social institutions (unions, cooperatives, the Workers' Educational Association, mutual support arrangements, like the forerunners of the NHS in Welsh mining communities) that prefigured a different and more just society. We need to rethink news media operationally in ways that embrace mechanisms of genuine citizen participation and community organizing.

In Scotland, Greater Govanhill is a free, not-for-profit community magazine produced both in print and online with an accompanying radio show and podcast. It states that it believes in 'doing journalism differently . . . Journalism that serves the community and brings about positive change' (Greater Govanhill, 2023). It runs workshops, training and events to enable local residents to feed into the magazine, empowering marginalized people to tell stories in their own words. It engages in 'solutions' journalism and refuses an exploitative approach to personal stories seeking to avoid sensationalism in favour of in-depth coverage. In 2022 they joined forces with The Ferret – an online investigative journalism cooperative in Scotland, to open a community media hub in Govanhill. The 'community newsroom' is a space for community-based journalism to collaborate with investigative journalism – a space where people can engage directly with journalists. Its first project was an investigation into health inequalities in the area.

In Brazil, Agência Pública was founded in 2011 as a non-profit newsroom by women reporters. Their work is republished free of charge under a Creative Commons licence. They state that they 'investigate public administration, including all levels of government and legislative houses, the social and environmental impacts of companies, their corrupt and anti-transparency practices; the Judiciary, its effectiveness, transparency and equity; and violence against vulnerable communities in urban and rural areas' (Agência Pública, 2024). To foster a journalism of integrity, they provide mentorship programmes for journalists, offer micro-grants for reporting and organize events and discussions about journalism. They distinguish themselves from mainstream journalism by uniting social responsibility with journalism that has editorial independence, promotes human rights, the right to information and improving democratic debate. They describe their journalism as grounded in unbiased and cautious reporting supported by primary sources, gender equality and a cooperative environment that cultivates ethical and skilled journalists (Agência Pública, 2021).

Conclusion: News *is* relational

A journalism of integrity that is fully accountable, democratically organized and for everyone – that works with people and for people, in appreciation of the intradependencies between news production and democratic, socially just societies, understanding that society works best when forms of substantive relationality flourish – is the way to rebuild trust. As with the Govanhill magazine, news outlets need to declare practices that have brought the journalism profession into disrepute as professionally and socially unacceptable. They need to be willing enthusiasts for independent and effective regulation so that its practices are open to challenge and subject to scrutiny. Until journalists are willing to recognize that freedom of the press must be balanced by freedom of the public to assess and challenge the nature of that communication, trust in journalism is unlikely to be rebuilt. Until journalism is able to hold its own institutions of power to account; to expose its own malpractices, and is willing to challenge some of the most obvious abuses of media power, *dis*trust in news journalism is likely to grow. And if we want to ensure that big data is captured for the public good and that technological innovation of the future helps solve rather than intensify our most urgent problems, from climate destruction to gross inequalities, then we must radically transform the governance and ownership of digitally generated data and its underlying infrastructure: news and data of the people, by the people for the people.

8

HOPE AND HOPELESSNESS: DEMOCRACY AND THE MEDIA RECONFIGURED

Ernst Bloch (1995), in *The Principle of Hope*, famously wrote '[t]he most tragic form of loss isn't the loss of security; it's the loss of the capacity to imagine that things could be different'. Bloch rejected the cultural pessimism of his peers at the Frankfurt School, preferring to put his faith in the transformative power of working-class activism and new social movements. In 2009 Mark Fisher affirmed this tragic form of loss by also famously writing that 'it is easier to imagine the end of the world than it is to imagine the end of capitalism', addressing what he called 'capitalist realism . . . the widespread sense that not only is capitalism the only viable political and economic system, but also that it is now impossible even to imagine a coherent alternative to it' (Fisher, 2009, p. 2).

Social, cultural, political and economic theorists must surely carry some of the blame for this emptiness. We may critique capitalism but we have spoken far too little of what it could be replaced with. Bloch hints as to where we should start the search:

> Actual utopia . . . signifies that utopian possibilities are established in the concreteness and openness of the material of history. . . . This is the objective, real possibility which surrounds existing actuality with tremendous latency, and affords the potency of human hope its link with the potentiality within the world. (Bloch, 1995, p. 17)

For Bloch, hope is not a dream-like state of being; rather, it smoulders in the embers of materiality. Vestiges of hope are to be found in the remnants of history and the fragments of contemporary practices burning with possibilities of democratic futures that could be lived otherwise. The very notion of democracy pulsates with hopefulness, with the possibility of what could be. In this book I have approached the problem and prospects of democracy in the spirit proposed by Pierre Rosanvallon (2008), seeking to reframe democracy's universalism not as a thesis to be confirmed or refuted, but as a difficulty and a desire to be excavated and explored. Indeed, one could argue that this is the only form in which the concept of democracy can be interrogated; anything more didactic would in itself be profoundly anti-democratic. It should be clear from the preceding chapters that whatever form of democracy we place our bets on, it is always historically located, contextually dependent and ethnographically emergent. This directs our attention to the situated disputes and the structures of expectations that inform and shape political contestation of which our systems of media and communications play no small part.

In his last book, the late Erik Olin Wright (2019) concludes that in order to transcend capitalism and move towards a more just and sustainable socio-economic system, capitalism needs to be not only openly contested and opposed but also eroded *from within*. Movements, initiatives, collectives and networks operating within but counter to capitalism can offer forms of prefigurative politics that can, he argues, foster capitalism's demise. But prefigurative politics has also been criticized for not attending carefully enough to existing relations of intersectionality between racialized people, class, gender, sexuality and disability that may impact individual access to, and participation in, prefigurative initiatives and movements. In fact, some critics have pointed out that prefigurative politics is deeply exclusionary, attracting mostly Western, white, middle-class, highly educated individuals (Fenton, 2016).

So a search for democratic hope beyond capitalism must begin from the premise that understanding current contexts requires appreciation of political cultures and histories of subject production as well as the economic conditions that led to them. Throughout the chapters of this book I have argued that the democratic crisis we face is multifaceted and linked to the economy, society, politics and technology – all of which are linked to a crisis of ecology (which is addressed further below). As Fraser (2022, p. 78) puts it, '[c]apitalism . . . represents the sociohistorical driver of climate change, and hence the core institutionalised dynamic that must be dismantled in order to stop it'. She also argues that capitalism is deeply implicated in other forms of social injustice: from class exploitation to racial-imperial oppression and gender and sexual domination, all of which are wholly de-democratizing and each of which I have demonstrated are alive and kicking in our global corporate media and tech systems.

Creating cultures of democracy is vital to its health and vitality. Our systems of media and communications create the conditions for much of this culturing to take place. Media and communications capitalism is far more than an economic system of production and exchange, it encultures the social relations of production and exchange and cultivates common-sense understandings that support capitalism as a way of life. This is one reason why the so-called 'culture wars' (referred to in Chapter 4) are seen as so crucial to those on the right desperate to protect wealth accumulation at all costs.

The fullest possible realization of the sort of democratic egalitarian values expressed throughout this book can only be achieved by looking beyond institutionalized global capitalism, by transcending the current system, although, in order to see above and beyond capitalism's enclosures, we may need to stand on the shoulders of the counter-movements, networks and initiatives that are working within them. Systemic change means addressing the structural causes of poverty and economic inequality through redistributive mechanisms of wealth. It means foregrounding class, gender and racial subordination and political domination by sharing and redistributing power through processes of radically substantive democracy. These factors introduce a new spatial logic of de-commodification of the social and political commons where our media institutions and technologies of communication are reclaimed as part of a media and communications commons for the public good.

But before we turn to the smouldering embers of hopefulness, we need to first encounter the wildfires of climate catastrophe and environmental breakdown, where hope is not easy to come by and hopelessness prevails.

Climate catastrophe

Bauman (2003) argues that we are living in a world dominated by fear instead of hope – fear of collective disaster (pandemics, war, terrorism, climate catastrophe) and fear of personal disaster – the humiliating fear of falling among the worst-off or otherwise ostracized. As liquid moderns, he argues, we have lost faith in the future. And why wouldn't we? In 2023 the Intergovernmental Panel on Climate Change (IPCC) noted that climate breakdown is accelerating rapidly, that many of the impacts will be more severe than predicted and that there is only a narrow chance left of avoiding its worst ravages. Vulnerable communities who have historically contributed the least to climate change are disproportionately affected both within and between countries, low- and middle-income countries suffer greater impacts than richer ones, and there are high concentrations of global greenhouse gas emissions among a relatively small fraction of the population in rich countries (Chancel, Bothe and Voituriez, 2023). Hans-Otto Pörtner, a co-chair of Working Group 2 of the IPCC, states that '[a]ny further delay in concerted global action will miss a brief and rapidly closing window to secure a liveable future' (Intergovernmental Panel on Climate Change [IPCC], 2023, p. 33). Yet concerted global action appears a long way off. The IPCC report (2023) reveals that national plans to mitigate climate change will not limit global warming to 1.5 degrees Celsius and exceeding it will be catastrophic for millions of people and other species around the planet through extreme weather events, rising sea levels and environmental breakdown. Even at 1.5 degrees Celsius of warming 950 million people across the world's drylands will experience water stress, heat stress and desertification, while the share of the global population exposed to flooding will rise by 24 per cent (IPCC, 2023). The IPCC report is clear about causation: human activities, through emissions of greenhouse gases, have caused, and continue to cause, global warming 'from unsustainable energy use, land use and land-use change, lifestyles and patterns of consumption and production across regions, between and within countries, and among individuals' (IPCC, 2023, p. 4).

While more people than ever are worried about environmental disaster, the media are failing dismally to keep up (Brevini and Lewis, 2018). In the US the major broadcast networks – ABC, CBS, NBC and FOX – spent just 142 minutes on climate change in 2018, according to one calculation from the progressive group Media Matters (Macdonald and Hymas, 2019). And about half of Americans hear about global warming in the media once a month or less, according to surveys by climate communications programs at Yale and George Mason universities (Leiserowitz et al., 2018). At the global level, in 2022 media coverage of climate change dropped 11 per cent from 2021, although coverage was up 38 per cent from 2020 and 7 per cent from 2019 according to the Media and Climate Change Observatory at the University of Colorado in Boulder, which has been monitoring worldwide media coverage of climate change and global warming since 2004 (Nacu-Schmidt et al., 2023). Although research also indicates that coverage is becoming more scientifically accurate in certain media (McAllister et al., 2021), other research notes that too often coverage has been dominated by the high drama of newsworthy events (Painter, 2013) framed as climate disaster – wildfires, flooding, forced migration – but with little by way of analysis of causation or critique of an economic system that is hell-bent on endless and excessive growth, productivity and consumption enmeshed in (contemporary) histories of colonialism and extractive capitalism. As Cottle (Cottle, 2023, p. 271) notes, journalism's response in general has been 'diluted, disaggregated and dissimulating', presenting:

> a world-view of 'business as usual' against a background assumption of 'life as normal', and does so notwithstanding the evident incursions of accelerating and deepening crises now impacting life chances and indeed the chance of life itself for millions around the planet.

Representations of climate catastrophe and environmental breakdown are one thing, but materially contributing to them is another. The tech industry consumes massive amounts of energy to power data centres, servers and other IT infrastructure, most of which comes from fossil fuels (Maxwell and Miller, 2012). In 2020 data centres alone accounted for 45 per cent of greenhouse gas emissions in the global IT sector. Cooling data centres also require large amounts of water (data centres with several thousand servers can consume between 11 million and 19 million litres of water per day) often straining water supply in water-scarce areas and contributing to water pollution (Brevini, 2021). In-built obsolescence also leads to vast amounts of electronic waste containing toxic substances, which are sold to poorer nations, thus damaging their environment and health. The manufacturing of electronic devices involves the extraction of raw materials and hazardous substances that release pollutants into the air and water. Producing electronic devices requires a large amount of minerals and metals that require mining, with the environmental impacts of deforestation, soil erosion, water pollution and loss of biodiversity (Ghoshal, 2023).

The work of ecosocialist thinkers (Huber, 2022; Lawrence and Laybourn-Langton, 2021; Vettese and Pendergrass, 2022; Foster, 2022) interrogates the role of capitalism in the ecological crisis we are now in. They argue that nature has been plundered by capitalist enterprises that view it as no more than a raw resource for capital accumulation, a resource that can be expropriated without any care for its restoration or renewal. Here expropriation of land and exploitation of labour work hand in hand, as both are commandeered into firms' operations to lower production costs and raise profits. Both are also interwoven with racial oppression through coerced and/or underpaid labour, as well as with colonialism and the dispossession of stolen indigenous lands and looted minerals (Estrada and Lehuedé, 2022) that continues in the mining of rare earth resources, such as neodymium, dysprosium, praseodymium, terbium, gadolinium, lithium and lanthanum to support 'green' innovations in mobile electronic technology (Dutta et al., 2016). Capitalism is a way of organizing nature for exploitation (Moore, 2015) and appropriates nature most often from the places where people have been robbed of the power to defend themselves and their land. It is a capitalist mode of production that has led to a metabolic rift between humans and nature, and it is only through forging a non-capitalist relationship with nature that we can begin to address the planetary ecological crisis we are in.

Ecological questions are always also questions of political power just as they are also issues of imperial domination, racial oppression and indigenous dispossession. In her bid to encourage us to see capitalism as more than a form of economy, Fraser (2022) refers to these social, ecological, political and racial/imperial dimensions as the non-economic enabling conditions of a capitalist society, conditions which are highly differentiated and structural. These non-economic realms are often the site of conflict and contradiction and provide resources for anti-capitalist struggle but they too are part and parcel of capitalist society and are co-constituted by its economy. In what she terms 'cannibal capitalism' she describes how:

> the accumulation of capital relies on nature – both as a 'tap' which supplies material and energic inputs to commodity production, and as a 'sink' for absorbing the latter's waste . . . capital disavows the ecological costs it generates, effectively assuming that nature can replenish itself autonomously and without end. (Fraser, 2022, p. 118)

Despite consistent linking of environmental destruction and climate catastrophe to capitalist modes of production, very little media coverage of environmental concerns links the debate to global capitalism (Bødker and Morris, 2022). More often, we see notions of green capitalism such as carbon offsetting or replacing how we power the production of goods and service with renewable alternatives that are not proven on a mass scale but seek to keep billionaire investment portfolios intact. Technological advancement alone will not fix our problems. The mineral resources required to satisfy a capitalist hunger for big cars, big houses, lots of meat and cheap air travel are connected to the industrial extractivism that continues to devastate entire regions of the South. The production of electronic devices that work with AI also require extraction of raw materials with huge social and environmental consequences. The use of AI and other digital technology does not lead to a de-materialization of the economy, as some hope. It leads to more consumption and more ecological destruction.

Different forms of political economic thinking are beginning to emerge that are trying to link political, social, economic and ecological crises. Oxfam have been at the forefront of raising awareness around levels of poverty and inequality both within and between nations (Oxfam, 2019). In 2012 they also launched a report by Kate Raworth on 'Doughnut Economics': a model based on Earth-system science that consists of two concentric rings – the social foundation (the inner circle) and the ecological ceiling (the outer circle) – that together encompass human well-being. If the boundaries of the inner circle (the social foundation) are not met, then we find hunger, ill-health, illiteracy, etc. If the boundaries of the outer circle (the ecological ceiling) are exceeded, then we get climate change, ocean acidification and loss of biodiversity. Both reflect deep inequalities of income and wealth, of gender and race, of exposure to risk and of political power. The area between the outer and inner rings represents a safe and just space within which to exist. The Doughnut model (Raworth, 2017) highlights the dependence of human well-being on planetary health and adeptly puts the case for economic theory and policy-making to shift away from an obsession with economic growth and capital accumulation to human nurturing and regeneration by design. Yet the model does not in itself take us beyond capitalism.

Other theorists such as Braidotti (2017, p. 9) argue for rethinking subjectivity 'as a collective assemblage that encompasses human and nonhuman actors, technological mediation, animals, plants and the planet as whole' in a bid to work towards a more egalitarian relationship to non-human others and reject the dominant position of the human as the ruler of creation. Other posthumanist thinkers such as Cudworth and Hobden (2018, p. 136) suggest an alternative to neoliberalism that is 'terraist' – a 'politics for all that lives' – since we are all part of a relational landscape with other living things. In relation to our systems of media and communications, this points us towards being less dependent on technologies that seek to endlessly reproduce, exploit and control nature for profit and turn more towards cultivating concern for egalitarian relationships across human and non-human life. Similarly, Lawrence and Laybourn-Langton (2021) argue that decarbonization must mean reparative equity, social ownership and public plenty and that economies (including our media and tech economies) need re-embedding in nature, social relationships and fairness.

As political protest against climate disaster grows around the world, so global inequalities between the rich and the poor, the powerful and the powerless increase and environmental degradation continues apace. Democratic delusions may be plentiful but, try as it may, capitalism cannot consume us. From within the growing and multiple forms of ecoactivism around the globe we see a range of movements insisting that we face climate catastrophe and environmental breakdown in ways that are degrowth and anti-consumerist. Indigenous peoples are in fierce battles to defend their lands and ways of life from corporate extractivism and colonial takeover (TallBear, 2019). Meanwhile, the Movement for Black Lives demands that resources be diverted away from racist policing and invested in communities of colour to enable them to deal with the environmental racism that burdens Black and Brown communities with damaging toxic deposits (Wilson, 2021).

Nurturing the seeds of these prospects for hope so that they can germinate and take root puts ordinary people, as opposed to elites, back in the picture; it allows the reimagining of the sorts of institutional and regulatory frameworks, including those that apply to our systems of media and communications, that may be required to support such a radical repositioning; it suggests social and economic forms that can be integrated into forms of democracy that can fulfil the principles outlined in the chapters above, a political commons that is concerned with developing an alternative politics that can advance freedom, equality, collectivism and ecological sustainability while avoiding corporate, financial and market domination. Rethinking the media in these terms and as part of a complex of social, political, economic and ecological relations may well help lead us to a reinvention of our democratic futures.

Building a democratic media for a transformative democracy

The basic premise of this book is that democracy and capitalism are incompatible, and so long as the majority of media and systems of communication are based on capitalist principles, they cannot be democratic themselves or serve democracy well. When capitalism has become so all-encompassing and so corrosive, it impacts every single aspect of society. To prevent democratic and environmental destruction, we must confront capitalism. The problem is that many of the emergent examples of living otherwise that I have referred to in this book – such as commoning, cooperativism or degrowth – do not necessarily address capitalist power but, rather, settle in small pockets of alternative approaches that threaten to merely make capitalism more bearable. They may recognize labour rights, anti-racism, anti-imperialism, feminism, pro-democracy and environmental struggles but they have not yet found a way to conjoin these differing approaches in a counter-hegemonic project. Given the centrality of our media and tech systems to knowledge production and the nourishing of our political imaginations, reconceiving media and tech for democracy is a vital part of any quest for a conjoined counter-hegemony. This requires, at the very least, a consideration of the major themes related to democratic well-being that I have covered in this book.

Power

I have tried to present a counter-hegemonic conceptualization of power as a democratic and relational means of cultivating freedom – the power of everyone to realize their capacity to participate in the shaping of social, political, economic and cultural life. A counter-hegemonic approach to power directs its attention to the ways in which each person's capacities are limited or constrained and whose interests are being served by the exercise of power in different situations. Seen in this way, democracy is a form of power. Power and democracy are not mutually exclusive but interdependent on each other.

We have seen the hollowing-out of public power of so-called democratic states right through our institutionalized societal order (Fraser, 2022). Mega-global media and tech corporations refuse public powers of territorial states and evade taxation for corporate gain. Concurrently, capitalism has relied on the public powers of the state to provide a legal framework to legitimate private enterprise and market exchange. Foucault (2010) argues that neoliberals formulated competitive markets as needing political support such that all governing is oriented for markets and by market principles, and markets must be built, facilitated by, propped up and rescued by political institutions. This requires the ongoing and active denigration of a politics of the public good. As this book goes to print, we are witnessing attempts across the globe to rein in the market domination of the tech giants with laws that will attempt to release capital to more players, enforce contracts and adjudicate disputes. But where these have come into play, such as in Australia with the News Bargaining Code, they have been criticized (Brevini, 2023) for being non-transparent and for serving large corporate enterprises over smaller independent news outlets in a manner that maintains the privileges of money supply for global capital. In these instances we see how capital accumulation relies on public power to guarantee property rights, enforce contracts, adjudicate over disputes to maintain order and manage dissent – precisely what is happening with the new attempts at controlling digital markets.

While such attempts at partial reforms are important because they render visible, albeit momentarily, the exploitation and expropriation that certain forms of media and tech industries result in, they will never be transformative. Or, worse, they enable a form of order and confidence to develop around systems of sustained accumulation that bend and adapt to ensure their pursuit of capital remains relatively unhindered. A legislative approach that wishes to tweak and tame these global media and tech industries will find itself in an endless game of whack-a-mole – as one problem pops up you knock it back down only to see it resurface elsewhere, because the underlying issues and systemic causes remain unaddressed. What we surely know is that when capitalism hits a road block it quickly reroutes. So when Meta are told that it will face fines of £390m because of inappropriate use of private data (for profit), it is not particularly worried, because it knows that it will find some other loophole to circumvent consent.

Similarly, anti-trust regulation is directed at markets and market dominance and not forms of power that structure our social, political, cultural and ecological worlds. Tinkering with media and tech policy will not solve the democratic crisis they are so deeply implicated in. As Coeckelbergh (2022, p. 49) argues in relation to AI, '[t]he real problem is that AI and robotics are used within a capitalist system, which uses these technologies not for the emancipation of the people but for the sole benefit of making the capitalists even richer than they already are'. For Dyer-Witherford, Kjosen and Steinhoff (2019) AI represents the power of autonomous capital, leading to commodification and exploitation – the culmination of the alienation of workers under capitalism. To say that competition laws can control digital markets is to effectively declare them out of the purview of state control and in the hands of corporate capital. Rather than a few new reformist policies we need new political projects and ways of living that can build a counter-hegemony and create a new common sense that is anti-capitalist.

Capitalism has both an economics and a politics and is part of capitalist societies. Social change requires changing the entire socio-economic system as well as the media and technology industries since their entanglement with capital is so intrinsic to their form and practice. Taking a counter-hegemonic approach to argue for *democratic media and communications systems that work for democracy* seeks to democratize power and, in this way, to redress powerlessness.

Participation

Conceptualizing democracy as something that refers to the rule of everyone by everyone – a form of collective self-determination – infers a type of participation that involves building something together in a constant process of reflection and renewal. This form of participation will involve cooperation among equals with deep disagreements about what constitutes the common good. This requires the enabling of diverse publics to participate collectively and fairly (especially those who are socially, economically, politically or technologically disadvantaged) in a democratic society, a democratic politics and a deliberative democracy in which our media and communications systems play such a key role. This approach to participation has an egalitarian principle at heart, one that seeks to permanently challenge and transgress its instituted forms, unsettle universalism through constant recognition of difference and permanently struggle for routes to equitable participation and communicative justice.

Participation is differentially inscribed in capitalist societies because capitalist societies are premised on exploitation and expropriation. Nation states confer participation to some and refuse it to others, as we have seen with the refugee and migrant crisis. A multistate political system ensures capital accumulation of the global North through military and financial means. Global media and tech oligopolies entrench systems of oppression and exclusion through processes of marginalization, exploitation and cultural imperialism that correlate with intersectional issues of race, social class, gender and disability. While communicative spaces have proliferated and 'participation' in them increased exponentially, they have been commandeered by private interests whose main objectives are to encourage compulsive use and content circulation for profit. If our objective is to assess the actual conditions for democratic politics in which media and technology play a key part then we must begin with how recent structural developments concerning neoliberal economics, state and corporate power and political engagement have affected our communications environment before we can identify the ways in which media and communications can play a role in the radical critique of neoliberal democratic frames and the regeneration of communicative democracy for communicative justice.

Freedom

Freedom of any kind relates to power and to participation. Both states and corporations can facilitate the sharing of power and equal participation or restrict powers and participation to certain organizations, groups or individuals. The crucial question is: in whose interest do these constraints or freedoms operate? Whose interests, needs and values take precedence in any given situation are often a marker of the social order of the day. This is one of the reasons why it is helpful to consider the concept of freedom (as well as participation and power) in relation to the concept of justice when considering its relationship to democratic theory. We need new and richer conceptions of media freedom, freedom of expression and freedom of association that are critical, emancipatory and address issues of communicative justice.

Bauman (2003) argues that today's societies are integrated around consumption rather than production. Freedom is modelled on freedom to choose how one satisfies individual desires and constructs one's identity via the consumer market. As a consequence, freedom and individual fate have increasingly become privatized. And an increasingly privatized life feeds lack of interest in politics. Gill (2014) notes how neoliberal freedoms that revolve around macro-economic policy are part of a 'new constitutionalism' through things like the North American Free Trade Agreement and the Agreement on Trade-Related Aspects of Intellectual Property, wherein free trade trumps any social or environmental concerns. Neoliberal freedoms relate directly to capital accumulation and prevent collective publics from having any say in how they want labour to relate to production and production to relate to nature. Increasingly, then, freedoms of speech, media and assembly are orchestrated and exercised by private tech firms whose designers, engineers and legal teams set the terms of operation – i.e. how social media platforms moderate hate speech, how news algorithms are personalized and how surveillance is enabled.

To secure the privileges of being a 'free media at the heart of democratic life', social value for all rather than political or capital gain for the few must be at the core of news media practice. This will require a journalism that operates freely and without interference from vested interests that include state institutions and politicians, corporate pressures and fear of intimidation and persecution. But a democratic media operating for communicative freedoms is so much more than this. In the democratic way of life, institutions and structures (including those of our media and communications systems) are brought about by the subjects of the democratic process. They are the ones who correct and adjust the design and outcome by means of public deliberation. People assembled in the space of democratic media enable free cooperation in all major social spheres to overcome exclusion by constantly pointing out that the realization of freedom, equality and solidarity is not possible under the prevailing social and economic conditions. This forces a shift away from a focus on individual rights to the rights of all peoples and encourages us to think of communicative freedom among equals as central to progressive visions of *democratic media and communications systems that work for democracy*. This will also mean creating the conditions for a fairer, more equal society to exist for communicative justice to ensue.

Equality

Foregrounding communicative freedom among equals encourages us to view democracy as far more than free and equal participation in political will-formation. Rather, democracy understood as an entire way of life (Honneth, 2017) presages the importance of people's ability to participate equally at every nodal point in the mediation between differentiated peoples, the state and society. The social, political and economic equality of all people is an essential principle of this expanded view of democracy.

The rising inequality that we are now experiencing across the world is a clear indication that the various forms of representative democracy often heralded as the mark of civilized societies have not led to more economic redistribution and do not benefit the many. This has led economists around the world to argue for the reduction of inequality as a matter of global and national economic necessity. They point out that inequality is not inevitable; it is ideological and political and endures through what Piketty and Goldhammer

(2020, p. 51) describe as 'inequality regimes': justificatory mechanisms for the institutional structures of inequality – the legal system, the educational system, the fiscal system as well as our media and communications systems – entrench inequality in societies and vindicate inequality regimes.

Much of our capitalist media has long since peddled anti-equality discourse – 'the unworthy poor' (Golding and Middleton, 1982), anti-immigration (Berry, Garcia-Blanco and Moore, 2016), anti-Islam (Massoumi, Mills and Miller, 2017) and misogynistic discourses (Savigny, 2020) abound. These discourses may shift focus every now and again with a changing geopolitics but the locus has remained firmly on anti-equality agendas that blame individuals and turn structural problems into cultural or moral ones to justify neoliberal policies. Digital systems of information and communication organize and govern much of everyday life (often without us knowing it) and perpetuate racism, sexism, ableism and other intersectional forms of inequity. As Chapter 5 argues, the extent of inequalities now experienced across the world also reveals that, rather than being democratic, so-called liberal democratic states have extended the reach of capitalism and enabled wealth accumulation for the few. Inequality is linked directly to capitalist exploitation. Capitalism relies upon the expropriation of wealth and minerals from racialized peoples on stolen lands, which continues to the present day, with tech industries reliant on mining of rare metals and the dumping of their toxic waste in landfill sites most often located in the Global South.

Capitalism is also responsible for environmental breakdown that is highly unequal across income groups and regions. Chancel et al. (2022) estimate that the top 10 per cent (of income groups) of the global emitters are responsible for 40 per cent of the emissions and that since 2013 at least half of the inequality of carbon emissions is among classes within countries and the other half stems from inequality between countries. Capitalism relies upon social inequality and class power and is inherently anti-democratic. Capitalism extracts wealth from society and nature in the interests of private investors and creates debt that incapacitates states, communities, households and individuals with highly differentiated and heavily racialized and gendered consequences. States are then left with little capacity to deal with the societal problems capitalism has created. Neoliberal capitalism is de-democratizing and destroying the planet.

In order to stop the destruction of the planet, the world must become less unequal and more solidary. Evidence of the latter is emergent around the globe. Democracy is being reinvented by the popular egalitarian movements of recent years: the Occupy movement, the Indignados of Spain, the social protest movements of Chile, movements for algorithmic justice seeking equitable and accountable AI and many others are practising direct, participatory, non-hierarchical democracy that is very far from the cynical forms of liberal democracy we have become used to. Around the world we can see movements for affordable social housing, food security, universal basic income, a four-day working week, campaigns to unionize workers in media and tech sectors, as well as struggles for land rights, data ownership and public services. These movements are reconnecting the concept of democracy to struggles for equal participation and recognition, dignity and emancipatory social transformation. We must shift our understanding of democracy from political parties, elections and representative institutions to being something that is necessarily disruptive and contestatory, always in flux and located in people and publics. Today, we need this *egalitarian imagination* to be able to shape our futures in the face of devastating climate change, to prioritize the well-being of the many and their environment above the power of the few and their private interest.

Inequality is systemic and structural. Systemic and structural change in our media and tech worlds means moving towards *communicative egalitarianism* – a rejection of the concentrated power of ownership over media and data in favour of a people's media and communications infrastructure built on principles of socio-economic parity and social justice, the creation of a media commons that confronts inequalities and exclusions and seeks out transformational shifts in power relations across our institutionalized social order. Media and tech need to be conceived as shared public information and communications resources necessary for a healthy functioning democracy – resources that are co-owned and co-governed by the users and workers.

Public good

This book has been at pains to argue that democracy has been eviscerated of meaning but also that it is vitally important to hold onto the original expansive sense of the term. Democracy is not just about government, although governments may like to think that it is. Democracy as the power of anyone to influence decisions that impact on their own lives becomes another name for politics itself. Democracy is a project rather than an idealized form and as a project it asserts the perpetual struggle against the privatization of public life (Ross in Agamben et al., 2011) and enduringly seeks out the public good.

In the realm of corporate news production, commercialism has devoured communication for the public good. Market dominance and private gain are entangled with a neoliberal political elite intent on feathering their own nests at all costs – each support the other with fear and favour; each are on a mission to de-public everything, to valorize markets and to maximize shareholder returns. Private interest is driving our communicative frameworks and informational provision. The combination of a concentrated legacy media and oligopolistic digital giants is a toxic form of capitalism that chokes publicness. So we need public media more than ever. But in order to recast and reclaim democratic media for the public good we need to conceive of it anew by rooting it in social justice and justificatory processes and outcomes. Social justice is fundamentally a public issue and is at the heart of what democracy can be.

Seen from this perspective, if we assume that public media should function for democracy and operate for the public good, then our concern should be both with the content they provide and the extent to which they are democratically accountable to the publics they serve and justified in their approach. The logical consequence of this is that *peoples' media* function to support the communities they serve through justificatory frameworks that provide a means of gaining redress against exploitations of power. A people's media is necessarily different from private media and offers an alternative value system to capitalism.

Trust

Elite capture of our media and communications systems goes hand in hand with the capture of so-called democratic governments by global oligopolistic corporations that are mostly unaccountable to anyone bar their shareholders. Streeck (2017) notes how global financial markets now control elected governments at the same time as corporate capital persistently refuses and evades meaningful taxation, rendering them outside of public control. Our global corporate media and tech systems exemplify this relationship. One of the consequences is that the exercise of political power is starved of informed debate, accountability and legitimation leading to greater exposure to deal-making, corruption, spinning and indifference to facts, critique and truth and the subsequent demise of trust. This undermines public knowledge-making and demeans the political process and value of democracy as both concept and practice. While legislation that seeks to make media and tech industries more accountable can increase confidence in these industries, and this may lead to intermittent periods of increased trust, these periods will only ever be transient, because capitalism resents and resists public/governmental power.

The issue of trust and its relationship to capitalism can be illustrated through content moderators on Facebook. These essential workers review content submitted by Facebook's 2.8 billion users to its newsfeeds, assess each piece of flagged content and decide whether it is allowed to remain on the platform. Content moderators are employed mostly in the Philippines, India, Ireland, Poland, Germany and Kenya. Some are directly employed by Facebook, but most are outsourced and receive worse pay and mental health support than directly employed colleagues. Outsourcing companies often force moderators to sign gagging clauses to prevent them from speaking about their experiences. In Kenya, *TIME* magazine revealed that some moderators work for less than $2 per hour (Perrigo, 2023). Content moderators routinely look at extremely distressing content, and without them Facebook would collapse overnight. In other words, our trust in these platforms relies on the exploitation of workers, while the companies dodge their responsibilities as employers and use their wealth and power to block regulation and dodge taxes. Mechanisms of trust built on exploitation will always be prone to failure.

Media and tech that work with people and for people, that refuse the influence of vested interests and are wholly accountable and meaningfully democratic for everyone are beginning to emerge around the world – there is hope in these seeds of change.

Hope

In his article 'Hope in Common' David Graeber (2008, p. 1) assures us that '[h]opelessness is not natural. It needs to be produced'; that rulers make it their mission to ensure that alternatives and social movements are not perceived to be flourishing, and that despair renders change a fantasy. If hope changes nothing, if it is reduced to insignificant daydreams that simply help us to get through the day – what Berlant (2010) calls cruel optimism – then hope itself is rendered hopeless. In other words, hopelessness is an ideologically induced condition. Throughout this book I have tried to articulate the extent to which our media and tech systems peddle ideologies of hopelessness and the hopelessness of change in their endeavours to cling on to capitalist forms of (re)production. As capitalism depends on inequality, so hope is differentially established according to how marginalized you are. Conditions for hoping are themselves subject to the same conditions for democracy outlined in this book. In other words, hope too has a politics.

In her essay on paranoid and reparative reading, Sedgwick (2003) takes issue with the tendency of many progressive and critical academics to engage in paranoid readings, which persistently seek to uncover the socially damaging structure, effects, or unjust motivations underpinning even the most seemingly benign actions. If everything is wrong, then where does hope lie? If yesterday and tomorrow are just like today, corrupted by politics' relentless faults, then investing energy in pursuit of a transformative politics seems pointless. Similarly, Hage (2009) writes that critique, understood partly as the explication of the sustainability of capitalism and the suggestion of alternative means of organizing life, once centred on the transformative energies of hope. But with the rise of fascism in the mid twentieth century the hope that had fuelled critique crumbled as crisis was increasingly seen as another means for ensuring the reproduction of capitalist economy and society wherein belief in transformational change and in the revolutionary subject were abandoned.

Sedgwick suggests that a reparative approach offers something different:

> Hope, often a fracturing, even a traumatic thing to experience, is among the energies by which the reparatively positioned reader tries to organize the fragments and part-objects she encounters or creates. Because the reader has room to realize that the future may be different from the present, it is also possible for her to entertain such profoundly painful, profoundly relieving, ethically crucial possibilities as that the past, in turn, could have happened differently from how it actually did. (Sedgwick, 2003, p. 146)

In other words, a reparative mindset recognizes the horrors of racial oppression, imperialism and indigenous dispossession and puts their redress and reparation at the heart of reimagining a society without hierarchy, exploitation and expropriation. Solutions big enough to meet the challenges are only possible through transformative social action aimed at 'changing how we think, communicate, organize and act' (Bennett, 2020, p. 4). Lawrence and Laybourn-Langton

(2021) convincingly argue that to be successful, decarbonization must be part of a political strategy connecting reparative support for the Global South, democratic economic ownership and a new public commons. Several policy areas emerge from this, rooted in the need to holistically rethink (1) finance, (2) ownership models, (3) work, and (4) a commons for the twenty-first century. First is the importance of definancialization, including advocacy of green investment in the real economy, mission-driven public banks, green fiscal and monetary reform and challenging the asset-management industry. Second is promoting democratic economic ownership models, limiting shareholder influence and rewiring the extractive compulsions of the corporation. Third is the need to separate work and income, to decommodify the economy, decarbonize our use of time and expand low-carbon work such as care. The fourth is the call for a twenty-first-century commons: the sharing of resources and services stewarded for the public good, from digital infrastructures and media systems to mobility and land use.

In the field of media and communications, Pickard identifies three basic options to address the power of information and communication systems that he says are causing profound harm across the globe: (1) break up (anti-monopoly approach), (2) regulate, or (3) create non-commercial, public alternatives. While his preference is clearly for the third option as a means of creating and maintaining public media in every community that are collectively owned, cooperatively governed and universally guaranteed, such an approach does not fully deal with the multifaceted aspects of democratic crisis that the chapters in this book point towards, aspects that I have tried to argue above are inherent to capitalism and therefore must be addressed if we are to transform it. Capitalism reaches beyond political economic factors – it creates a type of society. This is no more apparent than in our capitalist media and tech worlds. Capitalism is a form of economic production but it also creates forms of social reproduction that are deeply unequal, discriminatory and exploitative and dependent on the expropriation of nature. Democratic media for democracy must deal with these injustices too. It is perfectly possible to break up monopolies, regulate media and tech industries and create non-commercial, public alternatives and still be in a democratic crisis marked by unfreedoms and social injustices.

Hence, we must avoid the democratic delusions of hope that make do with calls for improved public service media, delusions that put our faith in the small pockets of cooperative media and settle for a slightly expanded independent media sector where we find isolated examples of emergent forms of democratic media that we allow ourselves to imagine might just escape the sticky tentacles of capitalism and its mechanisms of exploitation and expropriation. We can point to disparate examples of workers unionizing in the tech sector and successful legal battles bravely tackling the worst abuses of tech giants. But the vast inequalities and hierarchies of private media and tech enterprise that shape the way we live and think and that reproduce and extend capital accumulation will remain largely the same.

Hope lies elsewhere. Hope fires up in the attempt to deliberately do what capitalism wishes to erase – the nurturing and care of one another, the repair and replenishment of nature and democratic self-rule for all.

Hope lies in the attempt to deliberately replace what capitalism seeks to preserve – private property and wealth accumulation – with public use and public good based on co-obligation, co-decision-making and co-governance.

To make hope possible, we must envision alternatives and then understand the obstacles and possibilities of transformation.

Creating a transformative media commons for social and communicative justice

Any theory of communication is a theory of community. A media commons speaks to the sharing of resources and services stewarded for the collective good rather than for private gain in a manner that is necessarily different from commercial media and offers an alternative value system to capitalism. A media commons must then take into account the multiple inequalities that prevent different people from communing equally and find ways of redressing those injustices.

A commons does not common alone. The acts of media commoning will reflect and support collective struggles as they seek conjointly to progress just systems. A media commons for social and communicative justice is thus engaged in understanding, exposing and challenging historical and systemic injustices (in the media and tech industries as elsewhere) that ideologically, institutionally and operationally reproduce the harms of capitalism, heteropatriarchy and settler colonialism. Media commoning sees social and communicative justice as a process that can enhance collective lives among heterogeneous publics.

Behind every emancipatory theory is an implicit theory of justice – a conception of what conditions would have to be met before the institutions of society could be just. I have tried to put forward a radical democratic egalitarian understanding of social and communicative justice such that all people would have equal access to the material and social means to live flourishing lives and be equally empowered to contribute to the collective control of the conditions and decisions which affect the common good. Of course, it is relatively easy to lay claim to principles, but how to put these into practice is far harder. The book has offered many examples of and insights into what such a democratic imaginary could be in our media and communications landscapes. Drawing on these examples, below I offer a broad brush-stroke summary of some of the conditions of possibility for a democratic media for just and transformative change to be enacted. These should be read as no more than navigational aids that may help steer a path towards and open up the conversation about what a transformational media commons might look like. As they have been written to apply to any media or tech organization at any level they are necessarily non-specific.

Conditions of possibility for a transformative media commons

Economic conditions

- Not for private profit, with the principle that any profit that is generated is fed back into social justice initiatives to redress marginalization and to counter oppression.
- Local digital and media community wealth-building strategies would underpin how data and media content are generated and used and how media and tech infrastructures are developed and owned, with the overarching goal of seeking to retain and grow value for communities rather than for global corporations. This may include sharing resources of space or systems of knowledge production for non-commercial, social justice ends.
- Sustainable public funding (through, for example, forms of hypothecated taxation of tech giants) should be directed to data, platforms and media that are decentralized and democratically owned and run, based on collective social ownership models that eschew private interest whether financial or political – e.g. the media/platform cooperative model.

Political conditions

- Meaningful democratic governance and control by workers, users and communities for collective self-determination.
- Actual accountability to the people that media and digital platforms serve through effective forms of regulation (within and beyond the nation state) to combat power inequalities between media organizations and users, data givers and data profiteers.
- Trade union recognition for workplace accountability and worker's rights and representation.
- Proactive legislation for media and tech plurality for the common good (not for market efficiency).
- Support and work with collective struggles for social justice and emancipatory social transformation.

Social conditions

- A media commons cannot be bestowed upon any given community but must be produced and sustained by it.
- Committed to communicative egalitarianism (not just universalism) through equal and participatory relationships in design, content production, data infrastructures and representation.
- Premised on addressing social and communicative injustices (which will include holding power to account but also growing the power of marginalized and minoritized groups) and providing redress for historical and contemporary injustices.
- Equal distribution of social value produced from media and tech to address communicative inequities through collective processes.

Ecological conditions

- Media and tech economies must be embedded in nature, social relationships and fairness, ending dependence on technologies that seek to endlessly reproduce, exploit and control nature for profit to become more concerned with egalitarian relationships across human and non-human life.
- Practices of decarbonization must result in reparative equity and social ownership for the collective good with reparative support for the Global South.

Conclusion: For hope

Capitalist media and tech industries have decided for us what their priorities should be, who gains from their forms of production, who should be represented and in what ways, how we communicate and with whom, and how we share information. All of these decisions should be made by collective, democratic decision-making processes that are inclusive and fully participatory. Hope lies in the holistic rearticulation of our media and tech industries across economic, political, social and ecological realms. Seen through the conceptual framings of power, participation, equality, freedom, pubic good, trust and hope, a transformational media commons is not some loose, cuddly concept, but rather a political construct that forms a new institutional power structure dependent on collective self-government, a construct that goes beyond the purely administrative domain to the institutions and rules people create together. As Dardot and Laval (2019) argue, the politics of the commons is rooted in the political tradition of a democracy to come that engenders new institutions, new projects, new collective relations and new practices based on justificatory frameworks. A truly just society must be commons-based. Information and knowledge production should be a common good instead of a commodity. AI and data should be held in common instead of controlled by capital. There should be common control of the conditions of communication, a people's media and tech run by and for communities and people for a transformational and just democracy. Therein lies hope.

NOTES

1 Civil Society Futures was a two-year independent inquiry funded by eight major foundations and conducted by a consortium made up of Forum for the Future; Goldsmiths, University of London; Citizens UK; and openDemocracy. Focusing on nine local areas around England, it looked at the current landscape and future prospects of civil society within a broad methodology of participatory action research. A follow-on British Academy-funded project (Policing the Political in UK Civil Society) involved archival desk research summarizing the existing literature on restrictions on political activity and collating and analysing documents produced by the main regulatory and funding bodies. Alongside this, interviews were conducted with twelve small CSOs involved in a range of work that pertains to 'political' activity, covering areas including disability, race and ethnicity, sexuality, gender, religion, climate change, the environment and poverty. The author of this book was the principal investigator for each project. Dr Tom Greenwood and Dr Deborah Grayson were researchers on the main research project, and Dr Deborah Grayson was the lead researcher for the British Academy project.
2 Ofcom is the communications regulator in the UK. It regulates the TV, radio and video-on-demand sectors, fixed-line telecoms, mobiles, postal services and the airwaves over which wireless devices operate.
3 Twenty Cabinet ministers met senior Murdoch executives 130 times in the first fourteen months of office. See the full list on the Number 10 website: http://www.number10.gov.uk/transparency/who-ministers-are-meeting/.
4 The GRA is often confused with, but is entirely different from, the Equality Act 2010, which allows for the protected characteristic of 'gender reassignment', meaning that any trans person – regardless of what stage of transition they may be in – is protected from discrimination. The Human Rights Act 1998 incorporated into domestic UK law the fundamental rights and freedoms set out in the European Convention on Human Rights which everyone in the UK is currently entitled to.

Some of the most notable rights in protecting LGBTQIA+ rights are Article 8, the right to respect for private and family life, and Article 14, the prohibition of discrimination. Article 8 encompasses matters of autonomy and self-determination, including the freedom to choose your own sexual/gender identity, your own personal relationships and the freedom to choose how you look and dress. Article 14 protects people from discrimination when exercising their other Convention rights.

5 Gender-critical beliefs refer to the view that someone's sex – whether they are male or female – is biological and immutable and cannot be conflated with their gender identity (whether they identify as a man or a woman). People who express gender-critical beliefs are often seen as transphobic or accused of being TERFs (trans-exclusionary radical feminists).

6 In June 2023 Andrew Tate was charged in Romania with rape, human trafficking and forming an organized crime group to sexually exploit women – allegations he denies.

7 Conviviality names a praxis of living together well and has been revived through the concept of convivialism in 'the Second Convivialist Manifesto' (2020), where the principle of common humanity and equal human dignity are seen as essential components of conviviality.

8 Newsmax was also sued by Dominion, retracted its claims of voting machine election fraud and settled for an undisclosed amount in 2021. It gave an official apology for broadcasting the story without substantiating evidence.

9 See discussion of the Reuters Institute Digital News Reports in Chapter 7 and in particular the criticisms that have been made of the research into trust.

10 This section builds on the work of the 'The BBC and Beyond Project' project, funded by the Joseph Rowntree Charitable Trust, which ran from 2021 to 2024 as part of the work of the Media Reform Coalition (MRC). This book's author was the co-project director with Dr Deborah Grayson, who was also the project co-ordinator to whom I owe enormous gratitude for their incredible hard work, insight and for bringing many of the ideas in this section to fruition in developing and coordinating the BBC and Beyond campaign. The project held a series of online public events around the UK focusing on a wide range of topics, including international coverage of Covid, lessons from community media, and public media and anti-racism. These events connected with around 30,000 people, and are all available to watch on the MRC YouTube channel. The project benefited from multiple forms of engagement, ranging from comments on social media and written submissions to public talks and debates. We also conducted interviews with people working at the BBC and Channel 4, and spoke to dozens of organizations and individuals about their visions of a media system fit for the future. Based on this broad range of discursive interactions we wrote a *Manifesto for a People's Media* (Media Reform Coalition, 2021).

11 It wasn't always like this. From 1972 to 2004 the BBC ran a Community Programme Unit designed to help members of the public create programmes to be broadcast nationally. It began with a series of ten programmes called *Open Door* for BBC2. This evolved into *Open Space*, which by the end of the 1980s was receiving up to twenty proposals a week from the public for programmes. The programmes were known for bringing under-represented or misrepresented groups or perspectives to the fore. When portable video equipment became available, the CPU broadcast a series of video diaries that later became *Video Nation* (Carpentier, 2003). It was closed due to budget cuts.
12 The inquiry was funded by eight major foundations and conducted by a consortium made up of Forum for the Future; Goldsmiths, University of London; Citizens UK; and openDemocracy. I led a team of researchers over a period of two years investigating the current landscape and future prospects of civil society within a broad methodology of participatory action research. The nine local sites were selected to cover a mix of geography (because we know place matters), politics (because council activity, local infrastructure and support is important) and socio-economic factors (because poverty and inequality are persistently relevant to civil society activity) (Civil Society Futures, 2018).
13 This section draws on and builds upon an earlier piece co-authored with Des Freedman (Fenton and Freedman, 2017). I am indebted to Des for his far superior intelligence.

REFERENCES

Abernathy, Penelope Muse (2016) *The rise of a new media baron and the emerging threat of news deserts*. Chapel Hill: University of North Carolina Press, 2016.

Acemoglu, D. (2021) *Harms of AI*. Cambridge, MA: National Bureau of Economic Research.

Agamben, G. et al. (eds.) (2011) *Democracy in what state?* New York: Columbia University Press.

Agência Pública (2021) *Agência Pública, a primeira agência de jornalismo investigativo do Brasil, Agência Pública*. Available at: https://apublica.org/ (accessed: 17 August 2023).

Agência Pública (2024) 'Who we are'. Available at: https://apublica.org/about-us/ (accessed: 9 July 2024).

Agrawal, A., Gans, J. S. and Goldfarb, A. (2023) 'Do we want less automation?', *Science*, 381(6654), pp. 155–8.

Andrejevic, M. (2013a) *Infoglut: how too much information is changing the way we think and know*. London: Routledge & CRC Press.

Andrejevic, M. (2013b) 'Public service media utilities: rethinking search engines and social networking as public goods', *Media International Australia*, 146(1), pp. 123–32.

Angwin, J. et al. (2016) 'Machine bias: there's software used across the country to predict future criminals. And it's biased against Blacks', ProPublica [Preprint]. Available at: https://www.propublica.org/article/machine-bias-risk-assessments-in-criminal-sentencing (accessed: 9 August 2022).

Angwin, J., Varner, M. and Tobin, A. (2017) *Facebook enabled advertisers to reach 'Jew haters'*. ProPublica. Available at: https://www.propublica.org/article/facebook-enabled-advertisers-to-reach-jew-haters (accessed: 10 June 2022).

Anheier, H. and Kendall, J. (2000) 'Trust and voluntary organisations: three theoretical approaches', LSE Research Online Documents on Economics [Preprint]. Available at: https://www.semanticscholar.org/paper/Trust-and-voluntary-organisations%3A-three-approaches-Anheier-Kendall/36342050b48ec2361aa03fb0464d7409faac0a6a (accessed: 16 August 2023).

Anspach, N. M. (2021) 'Trumping the equality norm? Presidential tweets and revealed racial attitudes', *New Media & Society*, 23(9), pp. 2691–707.

REFERENCES

Aouragh, Miriyam (2011) 'The Arab Spring. The Egyptian experience: sense and nonsense of the internet revolution', *International Journal of Communication*, 5, p. 15.

Arendt, H. (1970) *On violence*. New York: Harcourt.

Arguedes, A. R. et al. (2023) *News for the powerful and privileged: how misrepresentation and underrepresentation of disadvantaged communities undermine their trust in news*. Oxford: Reuters Institute. Available at: https://reutersinstitute.politics.ox.ac.uk/news-powerful-and-privileged-how-misrepresentation-and-underrepresentation-disadvantaged (accessed: 16 August 2023).

Armstrong, S. (2018) *The new poverty*. London: Verso.

Arnstein, S. R. (1969) 'A ladder of citizen participation', *Journal of the American Institute of Planners*, 35(4), pp. 216–24.

Arrighi, G. (2010) *The long twentieth century: money, power, and the origins of our times*. London and New York: Verso.

Baker, C. E. (1994) *Advertising and a democratic press*. Princeton: Princeton University Press.

Baker, C. E. (2006) *Media concentration and democracy: why ownership matters*. Cambridge: Cambridge University Press.

Balibar, É. (2004) 'Is a philosophy of human civic rights possible? New reflections on equaliberty', *South Atlantic Quarterly*, 103(2–3), pp. 311–22.

Balibar, É. (2014) *Equaliberty: political essays*. Durham, NC: Duke University Press.

Banet-Weiser, S. and Bratich, J. (2019) 'Pick-up artists to incels: con(fidence) games, networked misogyny, and the failure of neoliberalism', *International Journal of Communication*, 13, pp. 5003–27.

Banet-Weiser, S. and Higgins, K. C. (2023) *Believability: sexual violence, media, and the politics of doubt*. Cambridge and Hoboken, NJ: Polity.

Barcelona en Comú (2019) *Fearless cities – a guide to the global municipalist movement*. London: New Internationalist Publications.

Barnett, C. (2017) *The priority of injustice: locating democracy in critical theory*. Athens, GA: University of Georgia Press.

Barnett, S. (2012) 'Public interest: the public decides', *British Journalism Review*, 23(2), pp. 15–23.

Barnett, S. (2021) *Public broadcasting: does the UK's regulator have the public interest at heart? The conversation*. Available at: http://theconversation.com/public-broadcasting-does-the-uks-regulator-have-the-public-interest-at-heart-159717 (accessed: 15 August 2023).

Barwise, P. and York, P. (2020) *The war against the BBC: how an unprecedented combination of hostile forces is destroying Britain's greatest cultural institution . . . and why you should care*. London: Penguin.

Bauman, Z. (2003) *Liquid love: on the frailty of human bonds*. Cambridge and Malden, MA: Polity.

BBC (2019) *BBC annual plan 2019/20*. Available at: https://downloads.bbc.co.uk/aboutthebbc/reports/annualplan/annualplan_2019-20.pdf (accessed: 15 August 2023).

BBC (2020) *Guidance: individual use of social media*. Available at: https://www.bbc.co.uk/editorialguidelines/guidance/individual-use-of-social-media/bbc.com/editorialguidelines/guidance/individual-use-of-social-media/ (accessed: 15 August 2023).

BBC (2021) *Record number of kids turn to the BBC for education and entertainment.* Available at: https://www.bbc.co.uk/mediacentre/2021/bbc.com/mediacentre/2021/record-numbers-of-kids-turn-to-the-bbc-for-education-and-entertainment/ (accessed: 15 August 2023).

BBC (2023a) *BBC Group annual report and accounts 2022/23.* Available at: https://assets.publishing.service.gov.uk/government/uploads/system/uploads/attachment_data/file/1169710/BBC_annual_report_and_accounts_2022_to_2023.pdf (accessed: 15 August 2023).

BBC (2023b) *Editorial guidelines.* Available at: https://www.bbc.com/editorialguidelines/bbc.com/editorialguidelines/guidelines/ (accessed: 15 August 2023).

BBC (2023c) *Section 4: impartiality – guidelines.* Available at: https://www.bbc.com/editorialguidelines/guidelines/impartiality/bbc.com/editorialguidelines/guidelines/impartiality/guidelines/ (accessed: 15 August 2023).

BBC (2024) *Guidance on personal use of social media.* Available at: https://www.bbc.co.uk/editorialguidelines/documents/guidance-personal-use-of-social-media.pdf (accessed: 18 April 2024).

Benjamin, R. (2019) *Race after technology: abolitionist tools for the new Jim code.* Medford, MA: Polity.

Bennett, W. L. (2020) *Communicating the future: solutions for environment, economy and democracy.* Medford, MA: Polity Press.

Bennett, W. L. and Livingston, S. (2018) 'The disinformation order: disruptive communication and the decline of democratic institutions', *European Journal of Communication*, 33(2), pp. 122–39.

Benson, R. (2010) 'Comparative news media systems: new directions in research', in S. Allan (ed.), *The Routledge Companion to News and Journalism.* London: Routledge, pp. 614–27.

Bergström, A., Strömbäck, J. and Arkhede, S. (2019) 'Towards rising inequalities in newspaper and television news consumption? A longitudinal analysis, 2000–2016', *European Journal of Communication*, 34(2), pp. 175–89.

Berlant, L. (2010) 'Cruel optimism', in M. Gregg and G. J. Seigworth (eds.), *The affect theory reader.* Durham, NC: Duke University Press, pp. 93–118.

Bernholz, L., Landemore, H. and Reich, R. (eds.) (2020) *Digital technology and democratic theory.* Chicago: University of Chicago Press.

Berry, M. (2013) *Hard evidence: how biased is the BBC? The conversation.* Available at: http://theconversation.com/hard-evidence-how-biased-is-the-bbc-17028 (accessed: 15 August 2023).

Berry, M. (2016) 'No alternative to austerity: how BBC broadcast news reported the deficit debate, media', *Culture & Society*, 38(6), pp. 844–63.

Berry, M. (2019) *The media, the public and the great financial crisis.* Basingstoke: Palgrave Macmillan.

Berry, M., Garcia-Blanco, I. and Moore, K. (2016) 'Press coverage of the refugee and migrant crisis in the EU: a content analysis of five European countries'. Geneva: United Nations High Commissioner for Refugees. Available at: www.unhcr.org/56bb369c9.html (accessed: 9 August 2022).

Bhattacharyya, G. (2018) *Rethinking racial capitalism: questions of reproduction and survival.* London and New York: Rowman & Littlefield International.

Birkinbine, B. J. (2018) 'Commons praxis: towards a critical political economy of the digital commons', *tripleC*, 16(1), pp. 290–305.

Bloch, E. (1995) *The principle of hope.* Vol. 1. Edited by N. Plaice. Cambridge, MA: MIT Press.

REFERENCES

Bødker, H. and Morris, H. E. (eds.) (2022) *Climate change and journalism: negotiating rifts of time*. London and New York: Routledge, Taylor & Francis Group.

Boltanski, L. (2011) *On critique: a sociology of emancipation*. Cambridge and Malden, MA: Polity.

Bolukbasi, T. et al. (2016) 'Man is to computer programmer as woman is to homemaker? Debiasing word embeddings'. Available at: https://doi.org/10.48550/ARXIV.1607.06520 (accessed: 16 August 2023).

Borkin, S. (2019) *Platform co-operatives: solving the capital conundrum*. London: Nesta.

Boyle, K. (2019) *#MeToo, Weinstein and feminism*. Cham: Springer International Publishing.

Bradley, J., Gebrekidan, S. and McCann, A. (2020) 'Waste, negligence and cronyism: inside Britain's pandemic spending', *New York Times*, 17 December. Available at: https://www.nytimes.com/interactive/2020/12/17/world/europe/britain-covid-contracts.html (accessed: 17 August 2023).

Braidotti, R. (2017) 'Posthuman critical theory', *Journal of Posthuman Studies*, 1(1), pp. 9–25.

Bratich, J. (2020) 'Civil society must be defended: misinformation, moral panics, and wars of restoration', *Communication, Culture and Critique*, 13(3), pp. 311–32.

Brenan, M. (2022) *Americans' trust in media remains near record low*. Gallup.com. Available at: https://news.gallup.com/poll/403166/americans-trust-media-remains-near-record-low.aspx (accessed: 16 August 2023).

Brevini, B. (2021) *Is AI good for the planet?* Cambridge and Medford, MA: Polity.

Brevini, B. (2023) 'Making Big Tech pay for news: the Australian media bargaining code will not solve the crisis in journalism'. Available at: https://www.mediareform.org.uk/blog/making-big-tech-pay-for-news-the-australian-media-bargaining-code-will-not-solve-the-crisis-in-journalism (accessed: 4 August 2023).

Brevini, B. and Lewis, J. (eds.) (2018) *Climate change and the media*. New York: Peter Lang US.

Broumas, A. (2017) 'Social democratic and critical theories of the intellectual commons: a critical analysis'. *tripleC: communication, capitalism & critique*, 15(1), pp. 100–126.

Brown, B. (2020) *How many tweets on Trump Twitter archive*. Available at: www.thetrumparchive.com (accessed: 5 October 2023).

Brown, W. (2005) *Edgework: critical essays on knowledge and power*. Princeton: Princeton University Press.

Brown, W. (2015) *Undoing the demos: neoliberalism's stealth revolution*. New York: Zone.

Brown, W. (2019) *In the ruins of neoliberalism: the rise of antidemocratic politics in the West*. New York: Columbia University Press.

Bruns, A. (2019) 'Filter bubble', *Internet Policy Review*, 8(4). Available at: https://policyreview.info/concepts/filter-bubble (accessed: 16 August 2023).

Buolamwini, J. and Gebru, T. (2018) 'Gender shades: intersectional accuracy disparities in commercial gender classification', in *Proceedings of the 1st Conference on Fairness, Accountability and Transparency. Conference on Fairness, Accountability and Transparency*, PMLR, pp. 77–91. Available at: https://proceedings.mlr.press/v81/buolamwini18a.html (accessed: 10 June 2022).

Bureau Local (2022) 'A manifesto for a people's newsroom'. Available at: https://drive.google.com/file/d/1LW009i1Fbp0GQqBDemuJZjbcRlpefetW/view (accessed: 26 August 2022).

Cadwalladr, C. and Graham-Harrison, E. (2018) 'Revealed: 50 million Facebook profiles harvested for Cambridge Analytica in major data breach', *Guardian* [Preprint]. Available at: www.theguardian.com/news/2018/mar/17/cambridge-analytica-facebook-influence-us-election (accessed: 9 August 2022).

CAF (2017) *Do as I say, not as I do: UK policy and the global closing space for civil society: a 2017 update*. London: Charities Aid Foundation.

Cairncross, F. (2019) 'The Cairncross Review: a sustainable future for journalism'. HMSO. Available at: https://assets.publishing.service.gov.uk/government/uploads/system/uploads/attachment_data/file/779882/021919_DCMS_Cairncross_Review_.pdf (accessed: 5 May 2022).

Cammaerts, B. (2022) 'The abnormalisation of social justice: The "anti-woke culture war" discourse in the UK', *Discourse & Society*, 33(6), pp. 730–43.

Carpentier, N. (2003) 'The BBC's *Video Nation* as a participatory media practice: signifying everyday life, cultural diversity and participation in an online community', *International Journal of Cultural Studies*, 6(4), pp. 425–47.

Carpentier, N. (2016) 'Beyond the ladder of participation: an analytical toolkit for the critical analysis of participatory media processes', *Javnost – The Public*, 23(1), pp. 70–88.

Carpentier, N. and Dahlgren, P. (2013) 'The social relevance of participatory theory', *Comunicazioni sociali*, 3 [Preprint]. Available at: https://doi.org/10.1400/219089 (accessed: 31 March 2022).

Carter, N. (2018) *Dynamic security threats and the British Army*. Available at: https://www.gov.uk/government/speeches/dynamic-security-threats-and-the-british-army-chief-of-the-general-staff-general-sir-nicholas-carter-kcb-cbe-dso-adc-gen (accessed: 23 August 2023).

Castilla, E. J. and Benard, S. (2010) 'The paradox of meritocracy in organizations', *Administrative Science Quarterly*, 55(4), pp. 543–676.

Castoriadis, C. (1980) 'Socialism and autonomous society', *Telos*, 43, pp. 91–105.

Cathcart, B. (2012) *Everybody's hacked off: why we don't have the press we deserve and what to do about it*. London: Penguin.

Centre for Media Pluralism and Media Freedom et al. (2023) *Monitoring media pluralism in the digital era: application of the media pluralism monitor in the European Union, Albania, Montenegro, the Republic of North Macedonia, Serbia and Turkey in the year 2022*. European University Institute.

Chakravartty, P. and Silva, D. F. (2012) 'Accumulation, dispossession, and debt: the racial logic of global capitalism – an introduction', *American Quarterly*, 64(3), pp. 361–85.

Chalk, S. (2020) *VLV research shows a 30% decline in BBC public funding since 2010*. Voice of the Listener and Viewer. Available at: https://www.vlv.org.uk/news/vlv-research-shows-a-30-decline-in-bbc-public-funding-since-2010/ (accessed: 15 August 2023).

Chambers, D. and Steiner, L. (2010) 'The changing status of women journalists', in S. Allan (ed.), *The Routledge Companion to News and Journalism*. London: Routledge, pp. 49–60.

Chan, T. W. and Goldthorpe, J. H. (2007) 'Social status and newspaper readership', *American Journal of Sociology*, 112(4), pp. 1095–134.

REFERENCES

Chancel, L. et al. (2022) *World inequality report 2022*. World Inequality Lab. Available at: https://wir2022.wid.world/www-site/uploads/2022/03/0098-21_WIL_RIM_RAPPORT_A4.pdf (accessed: 9 August 2022).

Chancel, L., Bothe, P. and Voituriez, T. (2023) *Climate inequality report 2023. Fair taxes for a sustainable future in the Global South*. World Inequality Database. Available at: https://wid.world/news-article/climate-inequality-report-2023-fair-taxes-for-a-sustainable-future-in-the-global-south/ (accessed: 30 August 2023).

Chang, H.-J. (2008) *Bad Samaritans: the myth of free trade and the secret history of capitalism*. Reprint edn. New York, London, Oxford, New Delhi and Sydney: Bloomsbury.

Chui, M., Manyika, J. and Miremadi, M. (2016) 'Four fundamentals of workplace automation'. *McKinsey Digital*. Available at: https://www.mckinsey.com/capabilities/mckinsey-digital/our-insights/four-fundamentals-of-workplace-automation (accessed: 16 August 2023).

Chun, W. H. K. (2019) 'Queerying homophily', in C. Apprich, W. H. K. Chun and H. Steyerl (eds.), *Pattern discrimination*. Minneapolis: University of Minnesota and Meson Press, pp. 59–99.

Chun, W. H. K. and Barnett, A. (2021) *Discriminating data: correlation, neighborhoods, and the new politics of recognition*. Cambridge, MA: The MIT Press.

CICOPA (2019) *Uruguayan media cooperatives are in astonishingly good health*. CICOPA. Available at: https://www.cicopa.coop/news/uruguayan-media-cooperatives-are-in-astonishingly-good-health/ (accessed: 22 August 2023).

Civil Society Futures (2018) 'Civil society in England: its current state and future possibilities'. Available at: https://civilsocietyfutures.org/wp-content/uploads/sites/6/2018/11/Civil-Society-Futures__Civil-Society-in-England__small-1.pdf (accessed: 23 August 2023).

Clyne, R. and Savur, S. (2023) *Home truths: cultural and institutional problems at the Home Office*. London: Institute for Government. Available at: https://www.instituteforgovernment.org.uk/sites/default/files/2023-05/cultural-and-institutional-problems-home-office_0.pdf (accessed: 15 August 2023).

Coeckelbergh, M. (2022) *The political philosophy of AI: an introduction*. Cambridge: Polity.

Cohen, J. and Fung, A. (2021) 'Democracy and the digital public sphere', in L. Bernholz (ed.), *Digital technology and democratic theory*. Chicago: University of Chicago Press, pp. 23–61.

Cohen, S. (2011) *Folk devils and moral panics: the creation of the mods and rockers*. Abingdon and New York: Routledge.

Coleman, S. (2012) 'It's time for the public to reclaim to the public interest', *Television & New Media*, 13(1), pp. 7–11.

Commission on the Future of Localism (2018) *People power: findings from the Commission on the Future of Localism*. Available at: https://cles.org.uk/news/people-power-findings-from-the-commission-on-the-future-of-localism/ (accessed: 23 August 2023).

Coote, A. and Percy, A. (2020) *The case for universal basic services*. Cambridge and Medford, MA: Polity.

Cottle, S. (2023) 'Reporting civilizational collapse research notes from a world-in-crisis', *Global Media and Communication*, 19(2). Available at: https://doi.org/10.1177/17427665231186934 (accessed: 2 August 2023).

Cranberg, G., Bezanson, R. P. and Soloski, J. (2001) *Taking stock: journalism and the publicly traded newspaper company*. Ames, IA: Iowa State University Press.
Creech, B. (2020) 'Fake news and the discursive construction of technology companies' social power', *Media, Culture & Society*, 42(6), pp. 952–68.
Crouch, C. (2004) *Post-democracy*. Cambridge: Polity.
Crouch, C. (2011) *The strange non-death of neo-liberalism*. Cambridge: Polity.
Cudworth, E. and Hobden, S. (2018) *The emancipatory project of posthumanism*. London: Routledge.
Curran, J. et al. (2009) 'Media system, public knowledge and democracy: a comparative study', *European Journal of Communication*, 24(1), pp. 5–26.
Curran, J., Fenton, N. and Freedman, D. (2012) *Misunderstanding the internet*. London: Routledge.
Curran, J., Gaber, I. and Petley, J. (2019) *Culture wars: the media and the British left*. 2nd edn. London and New York: Routledge, Taylor & Francis Group.
Curran, J. and Seaton, J. (2010) *Power without responsibility: the press, broadcasting and the internet in Britain*. 7th edn. London and New York: Routledge.
Dahl, R. A. (1970) *After the revolution: authority in a good society*. New Haven, CT: Yale University Press.
Dahlgren, P. (2009) *Media and political engagement: citizens, communication, and democracy*. Cambridge and New York: Cambridge University Press.
Dahlgren, P. (2018) 'Media, knowledge and trust: the deepening epistemic crisis of democracy', *Javnost – The Public*, 25(1–2), pp. 20–27.
Danewid, I. (2019) 'The fire this time: Grenfell, racial capitalism and the urbanisation of empire', *European Journal of International Relations*, 26(1), pp. 289–313.
Dardot, P. and Laval, C. (2019) *Common: on revolution in the 21st century*. Translated by M. MacLellan. London, New York, Oxford, New Delhi and Syndey: Bloomsbury Academic.
Das, S. (2022) 'Inside the violent, mysogynistic world of TikTok's new star, Andrew Tate', *Observer*, 6 August. Available at: https://www.theguardian.com/technology/2022/aug/06/andrew-tate-violent-misogynistic-world-of-tiktok-new-star (accessed: 10 August 2022).
Davies, N. (2008) *Flat earth news*. London: Chatto & Windus.
Davies, W. (2016) 'Opinion: the age of post-truth politics', *New York Times*, 24 August. Available at: https://www.nytimes.com/2016/08/24/opinion/campaign-stops/the-age-of-post-truth-politics.html (accessed: 16 August 2023).
Davies, W. (2020) 'Who am I prepared to kill?', *London Review of Books*, 30 July. Available at: https://www.lrb.co.uk/the-paper/v42/n15/william-davies/who-am-i-prepared-to-kill (accessed: 5 October 2023).
Davies, W. and Gane, N. (2021) 'Post-neoliberalism? An introduction', *Theory, Culture & Society*, 38(6), pp. 3–28.
Davis, A. (2002) *Public relations democracy: public relations, politics and the mass media in britain*. Manchester: Manchester University Press.
Davis, A., Fenton, N., Freedman, D. and Khiabany, G. (2020) *Media, democracy and social change: putting politics back into political communications*. Los Angeles, London, New Delhi, Singapore, Washington, DC, and Melbourne: Sage.
Dean, J. (2009) *Democracy and other neoliberal fantasies: communicative capitalism and left politics*. Durham, NC and London: Duke University Press.

REFERENCES

Dean, M. (2013) *Democracy under attack: how the media distorts policy and politics*. 2nd edn. Bristol: Policy Press.

Della Ratta, D. (2020) 'Digital socialism beyond the digital social: confronting communicative capitalism with ethics of care', *tripleC: Communication, Capitalism & Critique*, 18(1), pp. 101–15. Available at: https://doi.org/10.31269/triplec.v18i1.1145 (accessed: 4 August 2022).

DeLong, D. (2012) 'Media ethics: Leveson's support for the Conscience Clause is a significant gain', *Ceasefire Magazine*, 2 December. Available at: https://ceasefiremagazine.co.uk/media-ethics-levesons-support-conscience-clause-significant-gain/ (accessed: 15 August 2023).

Department for Culture, Media and Sport (ed.) (2016) *A BBC for the future: a broadcaster of distinction*. London: HMSO.

DfE (2021) *Widening participation in higher education*. London: HMSO. Available at: https://explore-education-statistics.service.gov.uk/find-statistics/widening-participation-in-higher-education (accessed: 9 August 2022).

Diamond, L. J. (2015) 'Facing up to the democratic recession', *Journal of Democracy*, 26(1), pp. 141–55.

Dixon, T. L. (2017) *A dangerous distortion of our families: representations of families, by race, in news and opinion media*. Color of Change. Available at: https://colorofchange.org/wp-content/uploads/2019/05/COC-FS-Families-Representation-Report_Full_121217.pdf.

Dorling, D. (2014) *Inequality and the 1%*. London: Verso.

Douglas, O. (2019) 'Backstories / Black stories: Black journalists, ingos and the racial politics of representing Sub-Saharan Africa in mainstream UK news media'. Available at: https://doi.org/10.25602/GOLD.00026352 (accessed: 20 January 2023).

Dowling, E. and Harvie, D. (2014) 'Harnessing the social: state, crisis and (big) society', *Sociology*, 48(5), pp. 869–86.

Du Bois, W. E. B. (1903) *The souls of Black folk*. Chicago: A. C. McClurg and Co.

Dunn, J. (2000) *The cunning of unreason: making sense of politics*. New York: Basic Books.

Durand, C. (2020) *Technoféodalisme*. Paris: Zones.

Dussel, E. D. (2008) *Twenty theses on politics*. Durham, NC: Duke University Press.

Dutta, T. et al. (2016) 'Global demand for rare earth resources and strategies for green mining', *Environmental Research*, 150, pp. 182–90.

Dyer-Witherford, N., Kjøsen, A. M. and Steinhoff, J. (2019) *Inhuman power: artificial intelligence and the future of capitalism*. London: Pluto Press.

Edelman (2018) *2018 Edelman Trust Barometer*, Edelman. Available at: https://www.edelman.com/trust/2018-trust-barometer (accessed: 16 August 2023).

Edelman (2023) *2023 Edelman Trust Barometer*, Edelman. Available at: https://www.edelman.com/trust/2023/trust-barometer (accessed: 16 August 2023).

Edelson, L. et al. (2021) 'Far right news sources on Facebook more engaging', *Cybersecurity for Democracy*, 4 March. Available at: https://medium.com/cybersecurity-for-democracy/far-right-news-sources-on-facebook-more-engaging-e04a01efae90 (accessed: 16 August 2023).

Edwards, M. (2014) *Civil society*. 3rd edn. Cambridge: Polity.

Electoral Commission (2018) 'Digital campaigning – increasing transparency for voters'. Available at: https://www.electoralcommission.org.uk/who-we

-are-and-what-we-do/changing-electoral-law/transparent-digital-campaigning/report-digital-campaigning-increasing-transparency-voters (accessed: 21 August 2023).

Estrada, M. S. and Lehuedé, S. (2022) 'Towards a terrestrial internet: re-imagining digital networks from the ground up', *Tapuya: Latin American Science, Technology and Society*, 5(1), 2139913.

European Broadcasting Union (2021) *Trust in media 2021*. Available at: https://rm.coe.int/ebu-mis-trust-in-media-2021/1680a83792 (accessed: 16 August 2023).

FactCheckNI (2022) 'Does the UK have more food banks than McDonald's?', *FactCheckNI*, 24 October. Available at: https://factcheckni.org/articles/does-the-uk-have-more-food-banks-than-mcdonalds-%EF%BF%BC%EF%BF%BC/ (accessed: 21 August 2023).

Fang, L. (2021) 'Documents reveal pharma plot to stop generic Covid-19 vaccine waiver', *The Intercept*, 14 May. Available at: https://theintercept.com/2021/05/14/covid-vaccine-waiver-generic-phrma-lobby/ (accessed: 17 August 2023).

Farkas, J. (2023) *This is not real news: discursive struggles over fake news, journalism, and democracy*. Malmö University. Available at: https://doi.org/10.24834/isbn.9789178773169 (accessed: 17 August 2023).

Farkas, J. and Schou, J. (2019) *Post-truth, fake news and democracy: mapping the politics of falsehood*. Abingdon and New York: Routledge.

Fenton, N. (2010) 'NGOs, new media and the mainstream news: news from everywhere', in N. Fenton (ed.) *New media, old news: journalism and democracy in the digital age*. London: Sage, pp. 153–69.

Fenton, N. (2012) 'Telling tales: press, politics, power, and the public interest', *Television & New Media*, 13(1), pp. 3–6.

Fenton, N. (2016) *Digital, political, radical*. Cambridge: Polity Press.

Fenton, N. (2018) 'Regulation is freedom: phone hacking, press regulation and the Leveson Inquiry – the story so far', *Communications Law*, 23(3), pp. 1746–7616.

Fenton, N. (2020) 'Covid-19 and the ownership and control of the media', *Culture Matters*. Available at: https://www.culturematters.org.uk/index.php/culture/tv/itemlist/user/899-nataliefenton (accessed: 15 August 2023).

Fenton, N. and Freedman, D. (2014) 'The politics and possibilities of media reform', in T. Miller (ed.), *Routledge Companion to Popular Culture*. London: Routledge, pp. 458–70.

Fenton, N. and Freedman, D. (2017) 'Fake democracy, bad news', in L. Panitch and G. Albo (eds.), *Rethinking democracy*. London: The Merlin Press, pp. 130–49.

Fenton, N. and Titley, G. (2015) 'Mourning and longing: media studies learning to let go of liberal democracy', *European Journal of Communication*, 30(5), pp. 1–17.

Finlayson, A. (2021) 'Neoliberalism, the alt-right and the intellectual dark web', *Theory, Culture & Society*, 38(6), pp. 167–90.

Fisher, D. R. and Nasrin, S. (2021) 'Climate activism and its effects', *WIREs Climate Change*, 12(1). Available at: https://doi.org/10.1002/wcc.683 (accessed: 4 May 2022).

Fisher, K. E. and Karlova, N. A. (2013) 'A social diffusion model of misinformation and disinformation for understanding human information behaviour', *Information Research*, 18(1). Available at: https://informationr.net/ir/18-1/paper573.html (accessed: 16 August 2023).

REFERENCES

Fisher, M. (2009) *Capitalist realism: is there no alternative?* Winchester and Washington, DC: Zero Books.

Fishman, M. (1990) *Manufacturing the news.* 2nd edn. Austin: University of Texas Press.

Fitzpatrick, S. et al. (2020) **Destitution in the UK 2020.** York: Joseph Rowntree Foundation.

Fleck, A. (2022) *Infographic: The world's biggest R&D spenders*, Statista Daily Data. Available at: https://www.statista.com/chart/27214/companies-that-spent-the-most-on-research-and-development-in-2020 (accessed: 15 August 2023).

Ford, B. (2023) 'IBM to pause hiring for jobs that AI could do', Bloomberg.com, 1 May. Available at: https://www.bloomberg.com/news/articles/2023-05-01/ibm-to-pause-hiring-for-back-office-jobs-that-ai-could-kill (accessed: 16 August 2023).

Forst, R. (2001) 'Towards a critical theory of transnational justice', *Metaphilosophy*, 32(1–2), pp. 160–79.

Forst, R. (2002) *Contexts of justice: political philosophy beyond liberalism and communitarianism.* Translated by J. M. Farrell. Berkeley, CA: University of California Press.

Forst, R. (2011) *The right to justification: elements of a constructivist theory of justice.* New York: Columbia University Press.

Forst, R. (2013) *Justification and critique: towards a critical theory of politics.* Cambridge and Oxford: Polity.

Forst, R. (2019a) 'The justification of progress and the progress of justification', in *Justification and emancipation. The critical theory of Rainer Forst.* University Park, PA: Pennsylvania State University Press, pp. 17–37.

Forst, R. (2019b) 'Two bad halves don't make a whole: on the crisis of democracy', *Constellations*, 26(3), pp. 378–83.

Foster, J. B. (2022) *Capitalism in the Anthropocene: ecological ruin or ecological revolution.* New York: Monthly Review Press.

Foucault, M. (2010) *The birth of biopolitics: lectures at the Collège de France, 1978–79.* Edited by M. Senellart. Basingstoke: Palgrave Macmillan.

Fraser, N. (1990) 'Rethinking the public sphere: a contribution to the critique of actually existing democracy', *Social Text*, 25/26, p. 56.

Fraser, N. (1995) 'From redistribution to recognition? Dilemmas of justice in a "post-socialist" age', *New Left Review*, 1(212). Available at: https://newleftreview.org/issues/i212/articles/nancy-fraser-from-redistribution-to-recognition-dilemmas-of-justice-in-a-post-socialist-age (accessed: 24 January 2023).

Fraser, N. (2019) *The old is dying and the new cannot be born.* London: Verso.

Fraser, N. (2022) *Cannibal capitalism: how our system is devouring democracy, care, and the planet – and what we can do about it.* London and New York: Verso.

Fraser, N. and Honneth, A. (2003) *Redistribution or recognition? A political-philosophical exchange.* London and New York: Verso.

Friedman, M., Friedman, R. D. and Appelbaum, B. (1962) *Capitalism and freedom.* Chicago and London: The University of Chicago Press.

Furlong, A., Aarup, S. and Horti, S. (2022) 'Who killed the COVID vaccine waiver?', *Politico*, 9 November. Available at: https://www.politico.eu/article/covid-vaccine-poor-countries-waiver-killed/ (accessed: 17 August 2023).

Gallego, A. and Kurer, T. (2022) 'Automation, digitalization, and artificial intelligence in the workplace: implications for political behavior', *Annual Review of Political Science*, 25(1), pp. 463–84. Available at: https://doi.org/10.1146/annurev-polisci-051120-104535 (accessed: 2 August 2023).

Gangadharan, S. P. (2013) 'Toward a deliberative standard: rethinking participation in policymaking: toward a deliberative standard', *Communication, Culture & Critique*, 6(1), pp. 1–19.

Gangadharan, S. P. (2017) 'The downside of digital inclusion: expectations and experiences of privacy and surveillance among marginal Internet users', *New Media & Society*, 19(4), pp. 597–615. Available at: https://doi.org/10.1177/1461444815614053 (accessed: 2 August 2023).

Gendered Intelligence (2020) 'Briefing on the Gender Recognition Act 2004'. Available at: https://www.canva.com/design/DAD_nb9z3pI/4BiKX34Xq_HA4ofF7H7I0g/view?website#4:trans-people-continue-to-exist-and-to-thrive-in-all-parts-of-uk-society.-it-is-common-sense-that-where-barriers-to-societal-inclusion-are-removed-people-are-more-able-to-prosper-across-all-levels-meaning-better-outcomes-from-education-to-employment.-however-anti-trans-attacks-and-hate-crimes-have-jumped-exponentially-in-recent-years.-from-2015-2018-there-was-a-92-increase-in-the-number-of-reported-anti-trans-hate-crime-incidents (accessed: 24 January 2023).

Georgiou, M. and Titley, G. (2022) 'Publicness and commoning: pandemic intersections and collective visions at times of crisis', *International Journal of Cultural Studies*, 25(3–4), pp. 331–48.

Gerbaudo, P. (2017) *The mask and the flag: populism, citizenism and global protest*. New York: Oxford University Press.

Gethin, A., Martínez-Toledano, C. and Piketty, T. (2021) 'How politics became a contest dominated by two kinds of elite', *Guardian*, 5 August. Available at: https://www.theguardian.com/commentisfree/2021/aug/05/around-the-world-the-disadvantaged-have-been-left-behind-by-politicians-of-all-hues (accessed: 29 August 2023).

Geuss, R. (2008) *Philosophy and real politics*. Princeton: Princeton University Press.

Ghoshal, P. (2023) 'The environmental impact of digitalisation: what's your take on sustainable technology?', 21 April. Available at: https://www.fdmgroup.com/blog/environmental-impact-of-digitalisation/ (accessed: 2 August 2023).

Giansiracusa, N. (2021) *How algorithms create and prevent fake news: exploring the impacts of social media, deepfakes, GPT-3, and more*. Berkeley, CA: Apress.

Gibson-Graham, J. K. (2006) *A postcapitalist politics*. Minneapolis, MN: University of Minnesota Press.

Gilbert, J. (2013) 'What kind of thing is "neoliberalism"?', *New Formations*, 80/81, pp. 7–22.

Gilbert, J. (2014) *Common ground: democracy and collectivity in an age of individualism*. Cambridge: Polity.

Gilbert, J. and Williams, A. (2022) *Hegemony now: how big tech and Wall Street won the world (and how we win it back)*. New York: Verso.

Gill, S. (2014) 'Market civilization, new constitutionalism and world order', in A. C. Cutler and S. Gill (eds.), *New constitutionalism and world order*. Cambridge: Cambridge University Press, pp. 29–44.

Global Disinformation Index (2019) *The quarter billion dollar question: how is disinformation gaming ad tech?* Global Disinformation Index. Available at: https://www.disinformationindex.org/ (accessed: 16 August 2023).

REFERENCES

Golding, P. (2017) 'Citizen detriment: communications, inequality, and social order', *International Journal of Communication*, 11, pp. 4305–23.

Golding, P. and Middleton, S. (1982) *Images of welfare: press and public attitudes to poverty*. Oxford: M. Robertson.

González-Bailón, S. and Lelkes, Y. (2023) 'Do social media undermine social cohesion? A critical review', *Social Issues and Policy Review*, 17(1), pp. 155–80.

Goodier, M. (2023) 'Hate crimes against transgender people hit record high in England and Wales', *Guardian*, 5 October. Available at: https://www.theguardian.com/society/2023/oct/05/record-rise-hate-crimes-transgender-people-reported-england-and-wales (accessed: 3 January 2024).

Graeber, D. (2008) 'Hope in common', The Anarchist Library [Preprint]. Available at: https://theanarchistlibrary.org/library/david-graeber-hope-in-common (accessed: 8 August 2023).

Graeber, D. (2014) *The democracy project: a history, a crisis, a movement*. London: Penguin.

Graham, M. and Dittus, M. (2022) *Geographies of digital exclusion: data and inequality*. London: Pluto Press.

Grayson, D. (2021) *Manifesto for a people's media: building a media commons*. London: Media Reform Coalition.

Grayson, D. (2022) 'Building a vision for a people's BBC', *IPPR Progressive Review*, pp. 69–77. Available at: https://doi.org/10.1111/newe.12291 (accessed: 15 August 2023).

Greater Govanhill (2023) *Greater Govanhill Community Magazine*. Available at: https://www.greatergovanhill.com (accessed: 17 August 2023).

Greenberg, J. (2022) 'Most Republicans still falsely believe Trump's stolen election claims. Here are some reasons why', *Poynter*, 16 June. Available at: https://www.poynter.org/fact-checking/2022/70-percent-republicans-falsely-believe-stolen-election-trump/ (accessed: 31 July 2023).

Gringras, R. (2018) *Elevating quality journalism on the open web*. Google. Available at: https://blog.google/outreach-initiatives/google-news-initiative/elevating-quality-journalism/ (accessed: 16 August 2023).

Gringras, R. (2019) *A look at how news at Google works*. Google. Available at: https://blog.google/products/news/look-how-news-google-works/ (accessed: 16 August 2023).

Gulyas, A. (2020) *Mapping local news provision and reach in England*. Centre for Research on Communities and Cultures, Canterbury Christ Church University. Available at: https://storymaps.arcgis.com/stories/837bd6fbe374480f86f41a9bbc34bc23 (accessed: 5 May 2022).

Habermas, J. (1989) *The structural transformation of the public sphere: an inquiry into a category of bourgeois society*. Cambridge: Polity.

Habermas, J. (1996) 'Civil society and the political public sphere', in Jürgen Habermas (ed.), *Between facts and norms: contributions to a discourse theory of law and democracy*. Cambridge: Polity Press in association with Blackwell Publishers, pp. 329–87.

Hacker, J. S. and Pierson, P. (2010) *Winner-take-all politics: how Washington made the rich richer – and turned its back on the middle class*. New York: Simon & Schuster.

Hage, G. (2009) *Waiting*. Carlton: Melbourne University Publishing.

Hahnel, R. (2005) *Economic justice and democracy: from competition to cooperation*. London: Routledge.

Hameleers, M., Brosius, A. and de Vreese, C. H. (2022) 'Whom to trust? Media exposure patterns of citizens with perceptions of misinformation and disinformation related to the news media', *European Journal of Communication*, 37(3), pp. 237–68.

Hao, K. (2021) 'How Facebook got addicted to spreading misinformation', *MIT Technology Review*. Available at: https://www.technologyreview.com/2021/03/11/1020600/facebook-responsible-ai-misinformation/ (accessed: 16 August 2023).

Hardin, R. (2006) *Trust*. Cambridge: Polity.

Hardt, M. and Negri, A. (2009) *Commonwealth*. Cambridge, MA: Belknap Press of Harvard University Press.

Harris, S. et al. (2021) *Collision of crises: racism, policing, and the COVID-19 pandemic*. Runnymede Trust. Available at: https://www.runnymedetrust.org//publications/collision-of-crises-racism-policing-and-the-covid-19-pandemic (accessed: 23 August 2023).

Harrison, E. (2022) 'Molly-Mae Hague criticised for "gross" and "tone deaf" comments on wealth inequality', *Independent*, 7 January. Available at: https://www.independent.co.uk/arts-entertainment/tv/news/molly-mae-hague-criticised-poverty-b1987817.html (accessed: 16 April 2024).

Harvey, D. (2011) 'The future of the commons', *Radical History Review*, 109, pp. 101–7.

Hesmondhalgh, D. (2013) *The cultural industries*. 3rd edn. London: Sage.

Hess, C. (2008) 'Mapping the new commons'. Available at: https://doi.org/10.2139/ssrn.1356835 (accessed: 9 August 2022).

Hess, C. and Ostrom, E. (2007) *Understanding knowledge as a commons: from theory to practice*. Cambridge: MIT Press.

High Pay Centre (2022) 'FTSE 100 CEOs paid in less than 4 days what a typical UK worker is paid in a year'. Available at: https://highpaycentre.org/ftse-100-ceos-paid-in-less-than-4-days-what-a-typical-uk-worker-is-paid-in-a-year/ (accessed: 10 August 2022).

Hills, J., Cunliffe, J., Obolenskaya, P. and Karagiannaki, E. (2015) *Falling behind, getting ahead: the changing structure of inequality in the UK*. London: Centre for Analysis of Social Exclusion.

Hind, D. and Mills, T. (2019) *Entering the secret castle: a small step towards democratic public media?*, openDemocracy. Available at: https://www.opendemocracy.net/en/opendemocracyuk/entering-secret-castle-small-step-towards-democratic-public-media/ (accessed: 15 August 2023).

HM Government (2018) *A connected society. A strategy for tackling loneliness.* Available at: https://assets.publishing.service.gov.uk/government/uploads/system/uploads/attachment_data/file/936725/6.4882_DCMS_Loneliness_Strategy_web_Update_V2.pdf (accessed: 23 August 2023).

Home Office (2020) *Police powers and procedures, England and Wales, year ending 31 March 2020, second edition*. Available at: https://www.gov.uk/government/statistics/police-powers-and-procedures-england-and-wales-year-ending-31-march-2020 (accessed: 23 August 2023).

Honneth, A. (2004) 'Recognition and justice: outline of a plural theory of justice', *Acta sociologica*, 47(4), pp. 351–64.

Honneth, A. (2017) *The idea of socialism: towards a renewal*. Cambridge and Malden, MA: Polity Press.

Hope Not Hate (2022) *Fear and hope 2022*. Available at: https://hopenothate.org

REFERENCES

.uk/wp-content/uploads/2022/08/Fear-HOPE-2022-FINAL-1.pdf (accessed: 24 January 2023).

House of Commons (2022) *Elections Act 2022*. Available at: https://bills.parliament.uk/bills/3020 (accessed: 23 August 2023).

House of Commons Library (2018) *All Party Parliamentary Group on Inclusive Growth*. Available at: https://www.inclusivegrowth.co.uk/house-commons-library-research/ (accessed: 9 August 2022).

House of Lords Select Committee on Communications (2008) *The ownership of the news report*. Vol. 1. London, The Stationery Office Ltd. Available at: http://www.publications.parliament.uk/pa/ld200708/ldselect/ldcomuni/122/122i.pdf (accessed: 20 January 2023).

Huber, M. T. (2022) *Climate change as class war: building socialism on a warming planet*. London and New York: Verso.

Human Rights Watch (2021) 'Covid-19 triggers wave of free speech abuse', *Human Rights Watch*, 11 February. Available at: https://www.hrw.org/news/2021/02/11/covid-19-triggers-wave-free-speech-abuse (accessed: 17 August 2023).

Hume, T. (2024) 'Andrew Tate channels culled by YouTube after revelations about get rich quick "cult"', *Vice*, 18 January. Available at: https://www.vice.com/en/article/n7emvg/andrew-tate-channels-culled-by-youtube-after-revelations-about-get-rich-quick-cult (accessed: 31 January 2024).

IHRC (2019) *The shrinking political space for CSOs in the UK*. London: Islamic Human Rights Commission.

Inceoglu, Y. et al. (2022) *Monitoring media pluralism in the digital era: application of the Media Pluralism Monitor in the European Union, Albania, Montenegro, the Republic of North Macedonia, Serbia and Turkey in the year 2021. Country report: Turkey*. European University Institute.

Information Commissioner's Office (2018) *Investigation into the use of data analytics in political campaigns: a report to parliament*. London: ICO.

Inglehart, R. and Norris, P. (2016) 'Trump, Brexit, and the rise of populism: economic have-nots and cultural backlash', *Harvard Working Paper* [Preprint], HKS Faculty Research Working Paper Series RWP16-026. Available at: https://www.hks.harvard.edu/publications/trump-brexit-and-rise-populism-economic-have-nots-and-cultural-backlash (accessed: 19 April 2024).

Intercepted (2021) 'Big Pharma's deadly Covid-19 vaccine monopoly', *The Intercept*, 12 May. Available at: https://theintercept.com/2021/05/12/intercepted-covid-vaccine-intellectual-property-waiver/ (accessed: 17 August 2023).

IPCC (2023) *Climate change 2022 – impacts, adaptation and vulnerability: Working Group II contribution to the sixth assessment report of the Intergovernmental Panel on Climate Change*. Cambridge: Cambridge University Press. Available at: https://doi.org/10.1017/9781009325844 (accessed: 9 August 2022).

IPPR (2018) *Prosperity and justice: a plan for the new economy*. London: Polity.

ITU (2020) *ICT price trends 2020: measuring digital development*. Geneva: International Telecommunication Union.

ITU (2023) *Digital inclusion of all*. Available at: https://www.itu.int:443/en/mediacentre/backgrounders/Pages/digital-inclusion-of-all.aspx (accessed: 4 December 2023).

Jackson, S. J. et al. (2020) *#Hashtagactivism: networks of race and gender justice*. Cambridge, MA: The MIT Press.

Jensen, T. (2014) 'Welfare commonsense, poverty porn and doxosophy', *Sociological Research Online*, 19(3), pp. 277–83.
Jessop, B. (2002) *The future of the capitalist state*. Cambridge: Polity.
Johnson, M. and Suliman, S. (2020) *PROTEST: analysing current trends*. London: Routledge.
Joyce, R. (2014) *Child poverty in Britain: recent trends and future propsects*. Institute for Fiscal Studies. Available at: https://ifs.org.uk/uploads/publications/wps/WP201507.pdf (accessed: 9 August 2022).
Kantrowitz, A. (2017) *Google allowed advertisers to target people searching racist phrases*. BuzzFeed News. Available at: https://www.buzzfeednews.com/article/alexkantrowitz/google-allowed-advertisers-to-target-jewish-parasite-black (accessed: 10 June 2022).
Kavada, A. and Poell, T. (2021) 'From counterpublics to contentious publicness: tracing the temporal, spatial, and material articulations of popular protest through social media', *Communication Theory*, 31(2), pp. 190–208.
Kavanagh, T. (2011) 'Trevor Kavanagh's speech to the Leveson inquiry: full text', *Guardian*, 6 October. Available at: https://www.theguardian.com/media/2011/oct/06/trevor-kavanagh-leveson-inquiry-speech (accessed: 20 January 2023).
Kaye, J. et al. (2015) 'Dynamic consent: a patient interface for twenty-first century research networks', *European Journal of Human Genetics*, 23, pp. 141–6.
Kelly, M. and Howard, T. (2019) *The making of a democratic economy: building prosperity for the many not just the few*. San Francisco: Berrett-Koehler Publishers.
Kergueno, R. (2021) *Deep pockets, open doors: big tech lobbying in Brussels*. Transparency International. Available at: https://transparency.eu/wp-content/uploads/2021/02/Deep_pockets_open_doors_report.pdf (accessed: 15 August 2023).
Khisa, M. and Rwengabo, S. (2023) 'Militarism and the politics of Covid-19 response in Uganda', *Armed Forces & Society*, 17 April. Available at: https://doi.org/10.1177/0095327X231162848 (accessed: 17 August 2023).
Kiai, M. (2017) *Report of the Special Rapporteur on the Rights to Freedom of Peaceful Assembly and of Association on his follow-up mission to United Kingdom of Great Britain and Northern Ireland: note by the Secretariat*. UN Human Rights Council. Available at: https://digitallibrary.un.org/record/1298881 (accessed: 23 August 2023).
Kidd, D. (2019) 'Extra-activism: counter-mapping and data justice', *Information, Communication & Society*, 22(7), pp. 954–70.
Kidd, D. (2020) 'Standing rock and the Indigenous commons', *Popular Communication*, 18(3), pp. 233–47.
Kiel, P. et al. (2022) *America's highest earners and their taxes revealed*. ProPublica. Available at: https://projects.propublica.org/americas-highest-incomes-and-taxes-revealed/ (accessed: 9 June 2022).
Kim, J. W. et al. (2021) 'The distorting prism of social media: how self-selection and exposure to incivility fuel online comment toxicity', *Journal of Communication*, 71(6), pp. 922–46.
King, D., Paechter, C. and Ridgway, M. (2020) *Gender Recognition Act: analysis of consultation responses*. London: Dandy Booksellers Ltd.
Klein, N. (2020) 'How big tech plans to profit from the pandemic', *Guardian*, 13 May. Available at: https://www.theguardian.com/news/2020/may/13/naomi

REFERENCES

-klein-how-big-tech-plans-to-profit-from-coronavirus-pandemic (accessed: 17 August 2023).

Kompridis, N. (2005) 'Disclosing possibility: the past and future of critical theory', *International Journal of Philosophical Studies*, 13(3), pp. 325–51.

Kostelka, F. and Blais, A. (2021) 'The generational and institutional sources of the global decline in voter turnout', *World Politics*, 73(4), pp. 629–67.

Krämer, B. (2018) 'Populism, media, and the form of society', *Communication Theory*, 28(4), pp. 444–65.

Krzyżanowski, M. (2020) 'Discursive shifts and the normalisation of racism: imaginaries of immigration, moral panics and the discourse of contemporary right-wing populism', *Social Semiotics*, 30(4), pp. 503–27.

Ksiazek, T. B., Malthouse, E. C. and Webster, J. G. (2010) 'News-seekers and avoiders: exploring patterns of total news consumption across media and the relationship to civic participation', *Journal of Broadcasting & Electronic Media*, 54(4), pp. 551–68.

Kübler, D. and Goodman, C. (2019) 'Newspaper markets and municipal politics: how audience and congruence increase turnout in local elections', *Journal of Elections, Public Opinion and Parties*, 29(1), pp. 1–20.

Kundnani, H. (2020) *The future of democracy in Europe: technology and the evolution of representation*. Available at: https://www.chathamhouse.org/sites/default/files/CHHJ7131-Democracy-Technology-RP-INTS-200228.pdf (accessed: 5 April 2022).

Latour, B. (2004) 'Why has critique run out of steam? From matters of fact to matters of concern', *Critical Inquiry*, 30 (Winter), pp. 225–48.

Lawrence, M. (2019) 'Building a digital commonwealth', *openDemocracy*, 13 March. Available at: https://www.opendemocracy.net/en/oureconomy/building-digital-commonwealth/ (accessed: 22 August 2023).

Lawrence, M. and Laybourn-Langton, L. (2019) *The digital commonwealth*. London: IPPR.

Lawrence, M. and Laybourn-Langton, L. (2021) *Planet on fire: a manifesto for the age of environmental breakdown*. London and New York: Verso.

Lazzarato, M. and Jordan, J. D. (2012) *The making of the indebted man: an essay on the neoliberal condition*. Los Angeles: Semiotext(e).

Lee, F. L. F. and Chan, J. M. (2018) *Media and protest logics in the digital era: the Umbrella Movement in Hong Kong*. New York: Oxford University Press.

Leichnitz, J. (2023) 'The rise of far-right extremism', *CCPA monitor*. Canadian Centre for Policy Alternatives.

Leiserowitz, A. et al. (2018) *Climate change in the American mind: December 2018*. New Haven, CT: Yale University and George Mason University.

Levitsky, S. and Ziblatt, D. (2018) *How democracies die*. New York: Crown.

Lim, G. (2020) *Securitize/counter-securitize*. Data and Society. Available at: https://datasociety.net/library/securitize-counter-securitize/ (accessed: 17 August 2023).

Lindell, J. (2020) 'Battle of the classes: news consumption inequalities and symbolic boundary work', *Critical Studies in Media Communication*, 37(5), pp. 480–96.

Lipsitz, G. (2019) 'The white possessive and whiteness studies', *Kalfou*, 6(1). Available at: https://doi.org/10.15367/kf.v6i1.229 (accessed: 5 October 2023).

Littler, J. (2017) *Against meritocracy: culture, power and myths of mobility*. London and New York: Routledge/Taylor & Francis Group.

Luhmann, N. (2018) *Trust and power*. London: John Wiley & Sons.
Macdonald, T. and Hymas, L. (2019) *How broadcast TV networks covered climate change in 2018*. Media Matters for America. Available at: https://www.mediamatters.org/donald-trump/how-broadcast-tv-networks-covered-climate-change-2018 (accessed: 2 August 2023).
Macpherson, C. B. (2006) *The real world of democracy*. Toronto: Anansi.
Maitlis, E. (2022) 'McTaggart Lecture', *Broadcast* [Preprint]. Available at: https://www.broadcastnow.co.uk/broadcasters/emily-maitlis-mactaggart-lecture-in-full/5173772.article (accessed: 27 July 2023).
Mansell, R. (2002) 'From digital divides to digital entitlements in knowledge societies', *Current Sociology*, 50(3), pp. 407–26.
Martin, M. (2022) 'Elon Musk calls himself a free speech absolutist. What could Twitter look like under his leadership?' NPR, 8 October. Available at: https://www.npr.org/2022/10/08/1127689351/elon-musk-calls-himself-a-free-speech-absolutist-what-could-twitter-look-like-un (accessed: 9 July 2024).
Martinson, J. (2023) 'Fox News and Rupert Murdoch have been humiliated, but they won't change their ways', *Guardian*, 19 April. Available at: https://www.theguardian.com/commentisfree/2023/apr/19/fox-news-rupert-murdoch-defamation-settlement-electoral-fraud (accessed: 31 July 2023).
Mason, R. (2020) 'Dominic Cummings thinktank called for "end of BBC in current form"', *Guardian*, 21 January. Available at: https://www.theguardian.com/politics/2020/jan/21/dominic-cummings-thinktank-called-for-end-of-bbc-in-current-form (accessed: 15 August 2023).
Massoumi, N., Mills, T. and Miller, D. (2017) *What is Islamophobia? Racism, social movements and the state*. London: Pluto.
Maxwell, R. and Miller, T. (2012) *Greening the media*. Oxford: Oxford University Press.
McAfee, A. and Brynjolfsson, E. (2016) 'Human work in the robotic future: policy for the age of automation', *Foreign Affairs*, 95(4), pp. 139–50.
McAllister, L. et al. (2021) 'Balance as bias, resolute on the retreat? Updates and analyses of newspaper coverage in the United States, United Kingdom, New Zealand, Australia and Canada over the past 15 years', *Environmental Research Letters*, 16(9), 094008. Available at: https://doi.org/10.1088/1748-9326/ac14eb (accessed: 2 August 2023).
McCarthy, C. (2015) *Submission to DCMS BBC Charter Review Consultation, Co-operative Party*. Available at: https://party.coop/2015/10/08/submission-to-dcms-bbc-charter-review-consultation/ (accessed: 15 August 2023).
McChesney, R. (2012) 'This isn't what democracy looks like', *Monthly Review*, 64(6). Available at: https://monthlyreview.org/2012/11/01/this-isnt-what-democracy-looks-like/ (accessed: 9 August 2022).
McChesney, R. W. (2003) 'Theses on media deregulation', *Media, Culture & Society*, 25(1), pp. 125–33.
McCoy, S. K. and Major, B. (2007) 'Priming meritocracy and the psychological justification of inequality', *Journal of Experimental Social Psychology*, 43(3), pp. 341–51.
McGee, P. (2022) 'Meta and Alphabet lose dominance over US digital ads market', *Financial Times*, 23 December. Available at: https://www.ft.com/content/4ff64604-a421-422c-9239-0ca8e5133042 (accessed: 21 August 2023).
Meade, A. (2019) 'News Corp tabloid the Herald Sun offers journalists cash bonuses for clicks', *Guardian*, 24 June. Available at: https://www.theguardian

REFERENCES

.com/media/2019/jun/24/news-corp-tabloid-the-herald-sun-offers-journalists-cash-bonuses-for-clicks (accessed: 24 August 2023).

Media Reform Coalition (2017) 'Mapping changes in local news'. Available at: https://www.mediareform.org.uk/wp-content/uploads/2015/11/Mapping-changes-in-local-news-2015-2017-interactive.pdf (accessed: 5 May 2022).

Media Reform Coalition (2021) *Manifesto for a people's media: creating a media commons*. Available at: https://issuu.com/mediareformuk/docs/manifesto-peoples-media (accessed: 15 August 2023).

Melamed, J. (2015) 'Racial capitalism', *Critical Ethnic Studies*, 1(1), pp. 76–85.

Mendoza, G. (2022) 'The weaponization of "trust"', *RAPPLER*, 16 June. Available at: https://www.rappler.com/voices/thought-leaders/weaponization-trust-news-organizations/ (accessed: 16 August 2023).

Mentan, T. (2010) *The state in Africa: an analysis of impacts of historical trajectories of global capitalist expansion and domination in the continent*. Mankon: Langaa Rpcig.

Metz, C. (2023) '"The godfather of A.I." leaves Google and warns of danger ahead', *New York Times*, 1 May. Available at: https://www.nytimes.com/2023/05/01/technology/ai-google-chatbot-engineer-quits-hinton.html (accessed: 16 August 2023).

Milan, S., Treré, E. and Masiero, S. (eds.) (2021) *COVID-19 from the margins: pandemic invisibilities, policies and resistance in the datafied society*. Amsterdam: Institute of Network Cultures.

Milanović, B. (2012) *The haves and the have-nots: a brief and idiosyncratic history of global inequality*. New York: Basic Books.

Mills, T. (2016) *The BBC: Myth of a public service*. London: Verso.

Milner, Y. and Traub, A. (2021) *Data capitalism and algorithmic racism*. New York: Demos. Available at: https://www.demos.org/sites/default/files/2021-05/Demos_%20D4BL_Data_Capitalism_Algorithmic_Racism.pdf (accessed: 9 August 2022).

Mirrlees, T. (2021) 'Socialists on social media platforms: communicating within and against digital capitalism', *Socialist Register*, 57, pp. 112–36.

Misztal, B. A. (1996) *Trust in modern societies: the search for the bases of social order*. Cambridge and Malden, MA: Polity Press and Blackwell Publishers, Inc.

Mitchell, S. et al. (2021) 'Algorithmic fairness: choices, assumptions, and definitions', *Annual Review of Statistics and Its Application*, 8(1), pp. 141–63.

Mohan, J. and Breeze, B. (2016) *The logic of charity: great expectations in hard times*. Basingstoke and New York: Palgrave Macmillan.

Monahan, T. (2008) 'Crime in an insecure world', *Contemporary Sociology: A Journal of Reviews*, 37(5), pp. 468–9.

Monsees, L. (2023) 'Information disorder, fake news and the future of democracy', *Globalizations*, 20(1), pp. 153–68.

Moore, J. W. (2015) *Capitalism in the web of life: ecology and the accumulation of capital*. New York: Verso.

Moore, M. and Tambini, D. (eds.) (2018) *Digital dominance: the power of Google, Amazon, Facebook, and Apple*. New York: Oxford University Press.

Morozov, E. (2020) 'Digital socialism: reimagining social democracy for the 21st century', *Eurozine*, 21 February. Available at https://www.eurozine.com/digital-socialism/ (accessed: 19 April 2024).

Morozov, E. (2022) 'Critique of techno-feudal reason', *New Left Review*, 133/134, pp. 89–126.

Morwoski, P. (2020) 'How neoliberalism will exploit the coronavirus crisis', *Tribune*, 18 May. Available at: https://tribunemag.co.uk/2020/05/how-neoliberalism-will-exploit-the-coronavirus-crisis (accessed: 17 August 2023).

Moss, G. (2018) 'Media, capabilities, and justification', *Media, Culture & Society*, 40(1), pp. 94–109.

Mouffe, C. (2009) *The democratic paradox*. Repr. London and New York: Verso.

Muhlmann, G. (2010) *Journalism for democracy*. Cambridge and Malden, MA: Polity.

Muldoon, J. (2022) *Platform socialism: how to reclaim our digital future from big tech*. London: Pluto Press.

Murdock, G. (2018) 'Reclaiming digital space: from commercial enclosure to the broadcast commons' in G. F. Lowe, H. V. den Bulck and K. Donders (eds.), *Public service media in the networked society*. Sweden: Nordicom, pp. 43–59.

Murray, K. (2020) *Impact of COVID-19 on BAME community and voluntary organizations*. The Ubele Initiative. Available at: https://static1.squarespace.com/static/58f9e5924402434120513l4a/t/5eaab6e972a49d5a320cf3af/1588246258540/REPORT+Impact+of+COVID-19+on+the+BAME+Community+and+voluntary+sector%2C+30+April+2020.pdf (accessed: 23 August 2023).

Nacu-Schmidt, A. et al. (2023) 'Media and climate change observatory special issue 2022: a review of media coverage of climate change and global warming in 2022'. Available at: https://doi.org/10.25810/VTAZ-SN25 (accessed: 2 August 2023).

National Audit Office (2020) *Investigation into government procurement during the COVID-19 pandemic*. National Audit Office (NAO) press release. London: NAO. Available at: https://www.nao.org.uk/press-releases/government-procurement-during-the-covid-19-pandemic/ (accessed: 17 August 2023).

Neo, R. (2022) 'When would a state crack down on fake news? Explaining variation in the governance of fake news in Asia-Pacific', *Political Studies Review*, 20(3), pp. 390–409.

Newman, N. (2020) *Reuters Institute digital news report 2020*. Oxford: Reuters Institute. Available at: https://reutersinstitute.politics.ox.ac.uk/sites/default/files/2020-06/DNR_2020_FINAL.pdf (accessed: 15 August 2023).

Newman, N. (2021) *Reuters Institute digital news report 2021*. Oxford: Reuters Institute. Available at: https://reutersinstitute.politics.ox.ac.uk/sites/default/files/2021-06/Digital_News_Report_2021_FINAL.pdf (accessed: 17 April 2024).

Newman, N. (2022) *Digital News Report 2022*. Oxford: Reuters Institute for the Study of Journalism. Available at: https://reutersinstitute.politics.ox.ac.uk/digital-news-report/2022 (accessed: 16 August 2023).

Newman, N. (2023) *Digital News Report 2023*. Oxford: Reuters Institute for the Study of Journalism. Available at: https://reutersinstitute.politics.ox.ac.uk/sites/default/files/2023-06/Digital_News_Report_2023.pdf (accessed: 16 April 2024).

Noam, E. M. (2016) *Who owns the world's media? Media concentration and ownership around the world*. Oxford: Oxford University Press.

Noble, S. U. (2018) *Algorithms of oppression: how search engines reinforce racism*. New York: New York University Press.

REFERENCES

Nolan, R. (2021) '"We are all in this together!" Covid-19 and the lie of solidarity', *Irish Journal of Sociology*, 29(1), pp. 102–6.

Nussbaum, M. C. (2011) *Creating capabilities: the human development approach*. Cambridge, MA: Harvard University Press.

OECD (2021) *An updated OECD framework on drivers of trust in public institutions to meet current and future challenges*. OECD Working Papers on Public Governance 48. Available at: https://doi.org/10.1787/b6c5478c-en (accessed: 4 May 2022).

Ofcom (2020) *Small Screen: Big Debate Consultation: the future of public service media*. Ofcom. Available at: https://www.smallscreenbigdebate.co.uk/__data/assets/pdf_file/0032/208769/consultation-future-of-public-service-media.pdf (accessed: 15 August 2023).

Ofcom (2021) *Five-year Review: diversity and equal opportunities in UK broadcasting*. London: Ofcom. Available at: https://www.ofcom.org.uk/__data/assets/pdf_file/0029/225992/dib-five-years-2021.pdf (accessed: 9 August 2022).

Ofcom (2022a) *Media plurality and online news*. Available at: https://www.ofcom.org.uk/__data/assets/pdf_file/0030/247548/discussion-media-plurality.pdf (accessed: 31 July 2023).

Ofcom (2022b) *News consumption in the UK: 2022*. London: Ofcom. Available at: www.ofcom.org.uk/research-and-data/tv-radio-and-on-demand/news-media/news-consumption (accessed: 15 August 2023).

Ofcom (2022c) *Online nation: 2022 report*. Ofcom. Available at: https://www.ofcom.org.uk/__data/assets/pdf_file/0023/238361/online-nation-2022-report.pdf (accessed: 9 June 2022).

Ohlsson, J., Lindell, J. and Arkhede, S. (2017) 'A matter of cultural distinction: news consumption in the online media landscape', *European Journal of Communication*, 32(2), pp. 116–30.

O'Neil, C. (2016) *Weapons of math destruction: how big data increases inequality and threatens democracy*. London: Allen Lane.

Ostrom, E. (1990) *Governing the commons. The evolution of institutions for collective action*. Cambridge: Cambridge University Press.

Otto, M. (2023) *Global Digital advertising revenues: a look at the big three, visible alpha*. Available at: https://visiblealpha.com/blog/global-digital-advertising-revenues-a-look-at-the-big-three-alphabet-googl-meta-platforms-meta-amazon-com-amzn/ (accessed: 21 August 2023).

Oxfam (2019) *Public good or private wealth?* London: Oxfam GB.

Oxfam (2021) *Responding with equality: the case for combating extreme inequality to tackle crises, strengthen democracy and foster a fairer future in the wake of the coronavirus pandemic*. Oxford: Oxfam GB.

Oxfam (2022) *Pandemic creates new billionaire every 30 hours — now a million people could fall into extreme poverty at same rate in 2022*. Oxfam International. Available at: https://www.oxfam.org/en/press-releases/pandemic-creates-new-billionaire-every-30-hours-now-million-people-could-fall (accessed: 15 February 2024).

Painter, J. (2013) *Climate change in the media: reporting risk and uncertainty*. London: Published by I. B. Tauris & Co. in association with the Reuters Institute for the Study of Journalism, University of Oxford.

Panel on the Independence of the Voluntary Sector (2016) *An independent mission: the voluntary sector in 2015*. London: The Baring Foundation. Available at: http://www.civilexchange.org.uk/wp-content/uploads/2015/02

/Independence-Panel-Report_An-Independent-Mission-PR.pdf (accessed: 23 August 2023).

Papathanassopoulos, S. (2018) 'The Europeanization of the European media: the incremental cultivation of the EU media policy', in L. d'Haenens, H. Sousa and J. Trappel (eds.), *Comparative media policy, regulation and governance in Europe: Unpacking the policy cycle*. Bristol: Intellect Books, pp. 117–32.

Pariser, E. (2020) 'To mend a broken internet, create online parks'. Available at: https://www.wired.com/story/to-mend-a-broken-internet-create-online-parks/ (accessed: 9 August 2022).

Pateman, C. (1970) *Participation and democratic theory*. Cambridge: Cambridge University Press.

Pelizza, A., Milan, S. and Lausberg, Y. (2021) 'The dilemma of undocumented migrants invisible to Covid-19 counting', in S. Milan, E. Treré and S. Masiero (eds.), *COVID-19 from the margins. Pandemic invisibilities, policies and resistance in the datafied society*. Amsterdam: Institute of Network Cultures, pp. 70–78.

Perrigo, B. (2023) 'The $2 per hour workers who made ChatGPT safer', *Time*, 18 January. Available at: https://time.com/6247678/openai-chatgpt-kenya-workers/ (accessed: 10 August 2023).

Peuter, G. de and Dyer-Witheford, N. (2010) 'Commons and cooperatives', *Affinities: A Journal of Radical Theory, Culture, and Action*, 4(1), pp. 30–56.

Pew Research Centre (2019) *Many across the globe are dissatisfied with how democracy is working*. Available at: https://www.pewresearch.org/global/wp-content/uploads/sites/2/2019/04/Pew-Research-Center_Global-Views-of-Democracy-Report_2019-04-29_Updated-2019-04-30.pdf (accessed: 9 July 2024).

Pew Research Center (2021a) 'Mobile fact sheet'. Pew Research Center: Internet, Science & Tech, 7 April. Available at: https://www.pewresearch.org/internet/fact-sheet/mobile/ (accessed: 23 August 2023).

Pew Research Centre (2021b). 'Digital divide persists even as Americans with lower incomes make gains in tech adoption.' Available at: https://www.pewresearch.org/short-reads/2021/06/22/digital-divide-persists-even-as-americans-with-lower-incomes-make-gains-in-tech-adoption/ (accessed: 9 July 2024).

Phillips, A., Couldry, N. and Freedman, D. (2010) 'An ethical deficit? Accountability, norms, and the material conditions of contemporary journalism', in *New Media, Old News Journalism and Democracy in the Digital Age*. London: Sage, pp. 51–67.

Pickard, V. (2014) *Media democracy: the triumph of corporate libertarianism and the future of media reform*. New York: Cambridge University Press.

Pickard, V.W. (2020) *Democracy without journalism? Confronting the misinformation society*. New York: Oxford University Press.

Pickering, M. (2001) *Stereotyping: the politics of representation*. London: Red Globe Press.

Piketty, T. (2014) *Capital in the 21st century*. Cambridge, MA: Harvard University Press.

Piketty, T. and Goldhammer, A. (2020) *Capital and ideology*. Cambridge, MA and London: Harvard University Press.

Piketty, T. and Rendall, S. (2022) *A brief history of equality*. Cambridge, MA: The Belknap Press of Harvard University Press.

REFERENCES

PINF (2023) *Deserts, oases and drylands: mapping the UK's local news outlets.* Public Interest News Foundation. Available at: https://www.publicinterestnews.org.uk/_files/ugd/cde0e9_97c4fe55ab0c49a0a29f40937e71d216.pdf (accessed: 23 August 2023).

Platform Cooperativism Consortium (2019). Available at: https://platform.coop/about/vision-and-advantages/ (accessed: 22 August 2023).

Prainsack, B. (2019) 'Logged out: ownership, exclusion and public value in the digital data and information commons', *Big Data & Society*, 6(1). Available at: https://doi.org/10.1177/2053951719829773 (accessed: 19 April 2024).

Provost, C. and Kennard, M. (2023) *Silent coup: how corporations overthrew democracy*. London and New York: Bloomsbury Academic.

Puddington, A. and O'Toole, S. (eds.) (2020) *Freedom in the world. 2019: The Annual Survey of Political Rights and Civil Liberties*. Lanham, MD: Rowman & Littlefield.

Puttnam, Lord (2016) *An Inquiry into the future of public service television.* Final report. London: Goldsmiths, University of London. Available at: https://futureoftv.org.uk/wp-content/uploads/2016/06/FOTV-Report-Online-SP.pdf (accessed: 19 April 2024).

Pyle, E. and Evans, D. (2018) 'Loneliness – what characteristics and circumstances are associated with feeling lonely?', *Office for National Statistics*, pp. 1–19.

Quilter-Pinner, H. et al. (2021) 'Trust issues: dealing with distrust in politics'. IPPR. Available at: https://www.ippr.org/files/2021-12/trust-issues-dec-21.pdf (accessed: 4 May 2022).

Rancière, J. (1995) 'The uses of democracy', in *On the shores of politics*. London and New York: Verso, pp. 39–63.

Rancière, J. (2004) 'Introducing disagreement', *Angelaki*, 9(3), pp. 3–9.

Rancière, J. (2007) *Hatred of democracy*. London: Verso.

Rawls, J. (1999) *A theory of justice*. Rev. edn. Cambridge, MA: Belknap Press of Harvard University Press.

Rawls, J. (2001) *Justice as fairness: A restatement*. Cambridge, MA: Harvard University Press.

Raworth, K. (2017) *Doughnut economics: 7 ways to think like a 21st century economist*. Vermont: Chelsea Green Publishing.

Rebillard, F. and Sklower, J. (2022) *Monitoring media pluralism in the digital era: application of the Media Pluralism Monitor in the European Union, Albania, Montenegro, the Republic of North Macedonia, Serbia and Turkey in the year 2021. Country report: France*. European University Institute.

Redden, J. and Witschge, T. (2010) 'A new news order? Online news content examined', in N. Fenton (ed.), *New media, old news? Journalism and democracy in the digital age*. London: Sage, pp. 171–87.

Reeves, R. (2007) 'We love capitalism'. *New Statesman*. Available at: https://www.newstatesman.com/long-reads/2007/02/capitalism-work-ownership-real (accessed: 9 August 2022).

Reis, E. P. and Moore, M. (eds.) (2005) *Elite perceptions of poverty and inequality*. Cape Town, London and New York: David Philip and Zed Books.

Resolution Foundation (2022) *Lack of support for low-income families will see 1.3 million people pushed into absolute poverty next year*. Available at: https://www.resolutionfoundation.org/press-releases/33284/ (accessed: 9 August 2022).

Reuters (2017) *Reuters Institute digital news report*. Oxford: Reuters Institute for the Study of Journalism.

Reviglio, U. (2022) 'The untamed and discreet role of data brokers in surveillance capitalism: a transnational and interdisciplinary overview', *Internet Policy Review*, 11(3). Available at: https://doi.org/10.14763/2022.3.1670 (accessed: 31 January 2024).
Rhizomatica (2015) *About Rhizomatica*. Available at: https://www.rhizomatica.org/about/ (accessed: 17 August 2023).
Robinson, C. J. and Kelley, R. D. G. (2021) *Black Marxism: the making of the Black radical tradition*. Revised and updated 3rd edn. London: Penguin.
Robinson, W. I. (2022) *Global civil war: capitalism post-pandemic*. Oakland, CA: Kairos PM Press.
Rodney, W. (2018) *How Europe underdeveloped Africa*. London and New York: Verso.
Rosanvallon, P. (2008) *Counter-democracy: politics in an age of distrust*. Translated by A. Goldhammer. Cambridge: Cambridge University Press.
RSA (2016) 'Citizenship 4.0: an invitation to power change', *Medium*, 16 November. Available at: https://medium.com/@thersa/citizenship-4-0-an-invitation-to-power-change-910bf07d319c (accessed: 23 August 2023).
Runciman, D. (2018) *How democracy ends*. London: Profile.
Saar, M. (2010) 'Power and critique', *Journal of Power*, 3(1), pp. 7–20.
Sambrook, R. (2014) 'Journalism, sources, privacy and the law'. Available at: https://www.jomec.co.uk/blog/journalism-sources-privacy-and-the-law/ (accessed: 20 January 2023).
Sánchez, M. L. and Gómez, I. P. (2023) 'Indigenous communication in Latin America for social re-existence: communicative experiences in the Colombian Cauca', *Journal of Applied Communication Research*, 51(2), pp. 109–25.
Santos, B. and Mendes, J. (2020) *Demodiversity: toward post-abyssal democracies*. London: Routledge & CRC Press.
Savage, M. (2015) *Social class in the twenty-first century*. London: Penguin.
Savigny, H. (2020) *Cultural sexism: the politics of feminist rage in the #MeToo era*. Bristol: Bristol University Press.
Scahill, J. (2013) *Dirty wars: the world is a battlefield*. London: Serpent's Tail.
Schäfer, A. and Streeck, W. (2015) *Politics in the age of austerity*. Cambridge: Polity.
Scharenberg, A. (2020) 'Transeuropa: transnational activism in a changing Europe'. Ph.D. thesis, London: Goldsmiths, University of London.
Schlosberg, J. (2017) 'The media–technology–military industrial complex', *openDemocracy*, 27 January. Available at: https://www.opendemocracy.net/en/media-technology-military-industrial-complex/ (accessed: 16 August 2023).
Schmuecker, K. et al. (2022) *Going without: deepening poverty in the UK*. Joseph Rowntree Foundation. Available at: file:///Users/nataliefenton/Downloads/going_without_-_deepening_poverty_in_the_uk_0.pdf (accessed: 9 August 2022).
Scholz, T. and Schneider, N. (eds.) (2017) *Ours to hack and to own: the rise of platform cooperativism, a new vision for the future of work and a fairer internet*. New York: OR Books.
Schyns, C. (2023) *The lobbying ghost in the machine: big tech's covert defanging of Europe's AI Act*. Brussels: Corporate Europe Observatory. Available at: https://corporateeurope.org/sites/default/files/2023-03/The%20Lobbying%20Ghost%20in%20the%20Machine.pdf (accessed: 31 July 2023).

REFERENCES

Scott, M., Bunce, M. and Wright, K. (2019) 'Foundation funding and the boundaries of journalism', *Journalism Studies*, 20(14), pp. 2034–52.

Sedgwick, E. K. (2003) 'Paranoid reading and reparative reading; or, you're so paranoid, you probably think this essay is about you', in E. K. Sedgwick (ed.), *Touching Feeling: affect, pedagogy, performativity*. Durham, NC: Duke University Press, pp. 123–55.

Senate Environments and Communications References Committee (2021) *Report of the Inquiry into Media Diversity in Australia*. Parliament of Australia. Available at: https://apo.org.au/node/315537 (accessed: 21 August 2023).

Sentencing Council (2020) *Investigating the association between an offender's sex and ethnicity and the sentence imposed at the Crown Court for drug offences – sentencing*. Available at: https://www.sentencingcouncil.org.uk/publications/item/investigating-the-association-between-an-offenders-sex-and-ethnicity-and-the-sentence-imposed-at-the-crown-court-for-drug-offences/ (accessed: 23 August 2023).

Seymour, R. (2014) *Against austerity: class, ideology and socialist strategy*. London: Pluto.

Sheila McKechnie Foundation (2018) *The chilling reality: how the Lobbying Act is affecting charity and voluntary sector campaigning in the UK*. London: Sheila McKechnie Foundation. Available at: https://smk.org.uk/wp-content/uploads/2020/08/SMK_The_Chilling_Reality_Lobbying_Act_Research.pdf (accessed: 23 August 2023).

Shivji, I. G. (2020) 'Democracy and democratization in Africa: interrogating paradigms and practices', in B. Santos and J. Mendes (eds.), *Demodiversity: towards post-abyssal democracies*. London: Routledge.

Siapera, E. and Viejo-Otero, P. (2021) 'Governing hate: Facebook and digital racism', *Television & New Media*, 22(2), pp. 112–30.

Skeggs, B. and Wood, H. (eds.) (2012) *Reality television and class*. London and New York: Palgrave Macmillan on behalf of the British Film Institute.

Slocock, C. (2017) *A shared society? The independence of the voluntary sector in 2017*. Available at: http://www.civilexchange.org.uk/wp-content/uploads/2011/02/A-Shared-Society-2017final.pdf (accessed: 23 August 2023).

Sloss, D. (2022) *Tyrants on Twitter: protecting democracies from information warfare*. Stanford, CA: Stanford University Press.

Social Mobility Commission (2019) *State of the nation: social mobility in Great Britain 2018 to 2019*. Available at: https://www.gov.uk/government/publications/social-mobility-in-great-britain-state-of-the-nation-2018-to-2019 (accessed: 4 August 2022).

Soriano, C. R. and Tandoc, E. (2022) 'Scaffolding our notions of trust', *RAPPLER*, 11 March. Available at: https://www.rappler.com/technology/features/scaffolding-our-notions-of-trust-facts-first-philippines-study-research/ (accessed: 16 August 2023).

Spinoza, B. de (1996) *Ethics*. Translated by E. M. Curley. London: Penguin.

Statista (2023) *Global search engine desktop market share 2023*. Available at: https://www.statista.com/statistics/216573/worldwide-market-share-of-search-engines/ (accessed: 21 August 2023).

Stearns, J. (2022) 'Democracy Fund's new equitable journalism strategy', *Democracy Fund*, 3 October. Available at: https://democracyfund.org/idea/democracy-funds-new-equitable-journalism-strategy/ (accessed: 4 January 2024).

Steyerl, H. (2019) 'A sea of data: pattern recognition and corporate animism', in C. Apprich et al. (eds.), *Pattern discrimination*. Minneapolis: University of Minnesota and Meson Press, pp. 1–23.

Stiglitz, J. (2013) *The price of inequality*. London: Penguin.

Stonewall (2022) *Public attitudes towards trans people: a research briefing*. Available at: https://www.stonewall.org.uk/sites/default/files/polling_on_trans_people.pdf (accessed: 2 August 2023).

Streeck, W. (2011) 'The crises of democratic capitalism', *New Left Review*, 73. Available at: https://newleftreview.org/issues/ii71/articles/wolfgang-streeck-the-crises-of-democratic-capitalism (accessed: 9 August 2022).

Streeck, W. (2014) *Buying time: the delayed crisis of democratic capitalism*. Brooklyn, NY: Verso.

Streeck, W. (2017) *Buying time: the delayed crisis of democratic capitalism*. 2nd edn. London: Verso.

Sunstein, C. R. (2017) *#Republic: divided democracy in the age of social media*. Princeton: Princeton University Press.

Susskind, J. (2018) *Future politics: living together in a world transformed by tech*. Oxford and New York: Oxford University Press.

Sustainable Development Solutions Network (2021) *European Sustainable Development Report 2021*. Available at: https://s3.amazonaws.com/sustainable development.report/2021/Europe+Sustainable+Development+Report+2021.pdf (accessed: 9 August 2022).

Taiwo, O. O. (2022) *Elite capture: how the powerful took over identity politics (and everything else)*. London: Pluto Press.

TallBear, K. (2019) 'Caretaking relations, not American dreaming', *Kalfou*, 6(1). Available at: https://doi.org/10.15367/kf.v6i1.228 (accessed: 10 August 2023).

Tambini, D. (2017) 'Fake news: public policy responses'. Media Policy Project, London School of Economics and Political Science. Available at: https://core.ac.uk/download/pdf/80787497.pdf (accessed: 16 August 2023).

Tambini, D. (2021) *Media freedom*. Medford: Polity Press.

Tenove, C. (2020) 'Protecting democracy from disinformation: normative threats and policy responses', *The International Journal of Press/Politics*, 25(3), pp. 517–37.

Thane, P. (2018) *Divided Kingdom: a history of Britain, 1900 to the present*. Cambridge: Cambridge University Press.

The Policy Institute (2021) 'Public split on whether "woke" is compliment or insult, and unsure what "culture wars" means – despite huge surge in media coverage'. Available at: https://www.kcl.ac.uk/news/public-split-on-whether-woke-is-compliment-or-insult-and-unsure-what-culture-wars-means-despite-huge-surge-in-media-coverage (accessed: 25 January 2023).

The Sutton Trust (2019) 'Elitist Britain', 24 June. Available at https://www.suttontrust.com/our-research/elitist-britain-2019/ (accessed: 5 May 2022).

Therborn, G. (2020) *Inequality and the labyrinths of democracy*. London and New York: Verso.

Thorson, K., Xu, Y. and Edgerly, S. (2018) 'Political inequalities start at home: parents, children, and the socialization of civic infrastructure online', *Political Communication*, 35(2), pp. 178–95.

Ticktin, M. (2020) 'Building a feminist commons in the time of COVID-19', *Signs: Journal of Women in Culture and Society*. Available at: http://signsjournal.org/covid/ticktin/ (accessed: 5 October 2023).

REFERENCES

Tinson, A. et al. (2016) *Monitoring poverty and social exclusion*. York: Joseph Rowntree Foundation. Available at: https://www.jrf.org.uk/report/monitoring-poverty-and-social-exclusion-2016 (accessed: 9 August 2022).

Toynbee, P. and Walker, D. (2020) *The lost decade: 2010–2020, and what lies ahead for Britain*. London: Guardian Books.

Trans Media Watch (2011) *The British press and the transgender community*. Available at: https://transmediawatch.org/wp-content/uploads/2020/09/Publishable-Trans-Media-Watch-Submission.pdf (accessed: 2 August 2023).

Trappel, J. (2019) 'Inequality, (new) media and communications', in J. Trappel (ed.), *Digital media inequalities: policies against divides, distrust and discrimination*. Göteborg: Nordicom, pp. 9–30.

Trappel, J. and Meier, W. A. (2022) 'Soaring media ownership concentration: comparing the effects of digitalisation on media pluralism and diversity'. Available at: https://doi.org/10.48335/9789188855589-7 (accessed: 31 July 2023).

Trappel, J., Nieminen, H. and Nord, L. (eds.) (2011) *The media for democracy monitor: a cross national study of leading news media*. Göteborg: Nordicom.

Trappel, J. and Tomaz, T. (2021a) 'Democratic performance of news media: dimensions and indicators for comparative studies'. Available at: https://doi.org/10.48335/9789188855404-1 (accessed: 31 July 2023).

Trappel, J. and Tomaz, T. (2021b) 'The Media for Democracy Monitor 2021 (Vol. 1): How leading news media survive digital transformation', p. 520. Available at: https://doi.org/10.48335/9789188855404 (accessed: 31 July 2023).

Trappel, J. and Tomaz, T. (2022) 'Success and failure in news media performance: comparative analysis in the Media for Democracy Monitor 2021'. Available at: https://doi.org/10.48335/9789188855589 (accessed: 1 April 2022).

Tsipursky, G. (2017) 'Towards a post-lies future', *TheHumanist.com*, 77(2), pp. 12–15.

TUC (2018) 'Two million self-employed adults earn less than the minimum wage'. Available at: https://www.tuc.org.uk/news/two-million-self-employed-adults-earn-less-minimum-wage (accessed: 9 July 2024).

Tully, J. (2004) 'Approaches to recognition, power, and dialogue', *Political Theory*, 32(6), pp. 855–62.

Tully, M. (2022) 'Responses to misinformation: examining the Kenyan context', in H. Wasserman and D. Madrid-Morales (eds.), *Disinformation in the Global South*. New Jersey, US: Wiley, pp. 179–92.

Tyler, I. (2013) *Revolting subjects: social abjection and resistance in neoliberal Britain*. London: Zed Books.

UNESCO (2022a) *Journalism is a public good: world trends in freedom of expression and media development; global report 2021/2022*. UNESCO Digital Library. Available at: https://unesdoc.unesco.org/ark:/48223/pf0000380618.page=17 (accessed: 15 August 2023).

UNESCO (2022b) *World trends in freedom of expression and media development: 2021/2022 online report*. Available at: https://www.unesco.org/reports/world-media-trends/2021/en/journalism-public-good (accessed: 26 July 2023).

Varga (2020) 'No power grab in Hungary', *Politico*, 27 March. Available at: https://www.politico.eu/article/coronavirus-hungary-no-power-grab/ (accessed: 17 August 2023).

Varoufakis, Y. (2023) *Technofeudalism*. London: Penguin.

Vettese, T. and Pendergrass, D. (2022) *Half-earth socialism: a plan to save the future from extinction, climate change, and pandemics*. London and New York: Verso.

Vogl, J. (2022) *Capital and ressentiment: a brief theory of the present*. Translated by N. Solomon. Cambridge: Polity Press.

Vraga, E. K. and Bode, L. (2020) 'Defining misinformation and understanding its bounded nature: using expertise and evidence for describing misinformation', *Political Communication*, 37(1), pp. 136–44.

Waisbord, S. (2018) 'Truth is what happens to news', *Journalism Studies*, 19(13), pp. 1866–78.

Waldfogel, J. and Washbrook, E. (2010) *Low income and early cognitive development in the U.K.* London: The Sutton Trust.

Walton, A. (2021) 'The quiet disappearance of Britain's public libraries', *Tribune* [Preprint]. Available at: https://tribunemag.co.uk/2021/01/the-quiet-disappearance-of-britains-public-libraries (accessed: 5 October 2023).

Wang, Y. (2016) 'Network exec on "circus" of 2016 race: "It may not be good for America, but it's damn good for CBS"', *Washington Post*, 1 March. Available at: https://www.washingtonpost.com/news/morning-mix/wp/2016/03/01/network-exec-on-circus-of-2016-race-it-may-not-be-good-for-america-but-its-damn-good-for-cbs/ (accessed: 31 July 2023).

Wardle, C. (2017) 'Fake news. It's complicated', *First Draft*, 16, pp. 1–11. Available at: https://firstdraftnews.org/articles/fake-news-complicated/ (accessed: 17 August 2023).

Wardle, C. (2020) 'Understanding information disorder'. *First Draft*. Available at: https://firstdraftnews.org/long-form-article/understanding-information-disorder/ (accessed: 17 August 2023).

Warrell, H. (2011) 'Police chief testifies on Met public relations staffing', *Financial Times*, 20 July. Available at: https://www.ft.com/content/ef6997cc-b1e5-11e0-a06c-00144feabdc0 (accessed: 20 January 2023).

Warren, E. (2017) *This fight is our fight: the battle to save America's middle class*. New York: Metropolitan Books/Henry Holt and Company.

Waters, M. (2001) *Globalization*. 2nd edn. London and New York: Routledge.

Waterson, J. (2022) 'Hundreds of jobs to go as BBC announces World Service cutbacks', *Guardian*, 29 September. Available at: https://www.theguardian.com/media/2022/sep/29/hundreds-of-jobs-to-go-as-bbc-announces-world-service-cutbacks (accessed: 15 August 2023).

Watkins, L. (2021) 'Media influence matrix: United Kingdom'. CEU Democracy Institute and the Media Reform Coalition. Available at: https://cmds.ceu.edu/sites/cmcs.ceu.hu/files/attachment/basicpage/1923/mimukfinalreport_0.pdf (accessed: 5 May 2022).

Watson, A., Harrington, T. and Hind, G. (2020) *BBC licence fee settlement*. London: Enders Analysis. Available at: https://mcusercontent.com/e582e02c78012221c8698a563/files/59969c2e-1e85-4eaa-b2a4-e8a3fd1ecb28/BBC_Licence_Fee_settlement_Further_cuts_will_wound_the_sector_2020_114_.01.pdf (accessed: 15 August 2023).

Weber, M. (1994) *Weber: political writings*. Edited by P. Lassman. Translated by R. Speirs. Cambridge: Cambridge University Press.

WHO (2022) *World failing in 'our duty of care' to protect mental health and well-being of health and care workers, finds report on impact of COVID-19*. Available at: https://www.who.int/news/item/05-10-2022-world-failing-in

REFERENCES

--our-duty-of-care--to-protect-mental-health-and-wellbeing-of-health-and-care-workers--finds-report-on-impact-of-covid-19 (accessed: 17 August 2023).

'WHO (2024) WHO Covid-19 dashboard'. Available at: https://data.who.int/dashboards/covid19/deaths?n=o (accessed: 9 July 2024).

Wike, R., Silver, L. and Castillo, A. (2019) *Many across the globe are dissatisfied with how democracy is working*. Pew Research Centre. Available at: https://www.pewresearch.org/global/wp-content/uploads/sites/2/2019/04/Pew-Research-Center_Global-Views-of-Democracy-Report_2019-04-29_Updated-2019-04-30.pdf (accessed: 3 August 2022).

Wilkinson, R. and Pickett, K. (2009) *The spirit level: why equality is better for everyone*. London: Penguin.

Wilkinson, R. P. and Pickett, K. (2018) *The inner level: how more equal societies reduce stress, restore sanity and improve everyone's well-being*. London: Allen Lane.

Williams, R. (1961) *The long revolution*. London: Penguin.

Williams, R. (1963) *Culture and society 1780–1950*. Harmondsworth: Penguin in association with Chatto and Windus.

Williams, R. (1976) *Communications*. 3rd edn. Harmondsworth and New York: Penguin.

Williams, R. (1989) *Resouces of hope: culture, democracy, socialism*. London: Verso.

Williams, R. (2014) *Keywords: a vocabulary of culture and society*. London: Fourth Estate.

Williamson, M. (2016) *Celebrity: capitalism and the making of fame*. Cambridge and Malden, MA: Polity.

Wilson, A. (2021) 'Defunding the police as environmental justice', *Crown Family School of Social Work, Policy, and Practice*. Available at: https://crownschool.uchicago.edu/student-life/advocates-forum/defunding-police-environmental-justice (accessed: 10 August 2023).

Wood, E. M. (1995) *Democracy against capitalism: renewing historical materialism*. Cambridge: Cambridge University Press.

Wood, E. M. (2005) *Empire of capital*. London: Verso.

Wood, E. M. (2017) *The origin of capitalism: a longer view*. Reprint edition. London and New York: Verso.

Woodhouse, J. (2022) *TV licences for the over-75s*. London: House of Commons Library. Available at: https://researchbriefings.files.parliament.uk/documents/SN04955/SN04955.pdf (accessed: 15 August 2023).

Wren-Lewis, S. (2018) *The lies we were told: politics, economics, austerity and Brexit*. Available at: https://search.ebscohost.com/login.aspx?direct=true&scope=site&db=nlebk&db=nlabk&AN=1929047 (accessed: 31 January 2022).

Wright, E. O. (2019) *How to be an anticapitalist in the 21st century*. London: Verso.

Wright, S. (2021) 'Discourses of fake news', *Journal of Language and Politics*, 20(5), pp. 641–52.

YouGov (2021) 'What does "woke" mean to Britons?' Available at: https://yougov.co.uk/politics/articles/35904-what-does-woke-mean-britons (accessed: 9 July 2024).

Young, I. M. (2022) *Justice and the politics of difference*. Stanford, CA: Princeton University Press.

Zelizer, B. (2017) *What journalism could be*. London and New York: Polity.

Zucker, L. G. (1986) 'Production of trust: institutional sources of economic structure, 1840–1920', *Research in Organizational Behavior*, 8, pp. 53–111.

Zuckerman, E. (2020) 'The case for digital public infrastructure'. Available at: https://knightcolumbia.org/content/the-case-for-digital-public-infrastructure (accessed: 9 August 2022).

INDEX

15M protest movement 67

Abernathy, P. 60–1
accountability 22, 99, 153–5, 211
   justificatory mechanisms 137, 153
   press freedom and 81–4, 88
advertising revenue 80–1
affected interests, principle of 50
Agência Pública 188–9
agenda-setting 11, 33, 35, 71, 83, 88, 173, 174
agonistic theories of democracy 22–3
Alba Party 94
algorithms 46, 141, 158, 167, 174, 176, 177, 201
   algorithmic silencing 57
   discriminatory nature of 113, 114, 119
   racially encoded 113
Alibaba 33
Alphabet 4, 32
alt right 112–13
Amazon 4, 32, 33, 110
anarchism 29–30, 43
Andrejevic, M. 12, 127
Anheier, H. 167
anti-trust regulation 41, 199
apathy 12
Apple 110
Arab Spring 52
Arendt, Hannah 43
Arnstein, S. 48–50
artificial intelligence 80, 114, 162, 175–81, 196, 199, 204

AI-powered journalism 175, 176, 180
   attempts to regulate 142
   capitalist logic 176–7
   deepfake 175
   economic consequences of 176
   GPT 175
   job elimination and 176
   systemic inequalities, reproduction of 175
Assange, Julian 24
austerity politics 3–4, 13, 30, 33–4, 56
   neoliberal 57
Australia 25–6, 94, 199
authoritarian regimes 2, 13, 76, 77

Badiou, Alain 45
Balibar, É. 101
balkanization of public services 50
Banet-Weiser, S. 184–5
Barcelona Digital City Plan 67
Barcelona en Comú 67
Barnett, C. 6, 30
Bauman, Z. 192, 201
BBC 16, 69, 127, 132, 145–53, 159, 160
   accountability 152, 154
   acritical defence of 160
   audience share 146
   centralized management 154
   Community Programme Unit 215n 11
   complaints system 154

245

BBC (cont.)
  cost-cutting and resource-stripping 149–50
  defunding and privatization campaigns 149
  devolved structure proposal 69–70, 154
  diminishing trust in 146, 168
  diversity and inclusion strategy 155–6
  erosion of independence 69
  establishment coterie 132, 147
  exclusionary employment practices 156
  funding 145, 150–1, 158
  governmental influence and 132, 146–8, 151, 152, 159
  licence fee 149, 151
  market-based regulation 152–3
  People's BBC 69–70
  as a public good 145–50, 158
  staff use of social media 147
  standards of impartiality and accuracy 146, 147, 148
  suggestions of political bias 146, 147, 149
  technological innovation 151
  top-down statist model 152
Beirut 68
Benard, S. 102
Benefits Street 116
Bennett, W. L. 178, 207
Benson, R. 76
Berlant, L. 206
Berry, M. 34, 35, 117
Bertram, Theo 110
bias 11, 114, 146, 147, 149, 164, 165, 173
Biden, Joe 144
big data society 124–5
Big Pharma 182
binary choices, simplistic politics of 14
Birkinbine, B. J. 126
Black Lives Matter 52
Black radical politics 92
Blair, Tony 132
Blais, A. 50
Bloch, E. 190
Braidotti, R. 196
Brazil 188–9
Brexit 31, 34, 56, 148, 164, 170

The Bristol Cable 38–9
British Digital Corporation (BDC) 127–8
Brooks, Rebekah 87
Brown, W. 26–8, 43, 73, 100, 112
Buolamwini, J. 114
Bureau Local 128

Cambridge Analytica 31–3, 68
Cameron, David 85, 86
Cammaerts, B. 95
Canada 7, 63
Canan, Penelope 144
cancel culture 92
capitalism
  communicative capitalism 69, 169
  constant crisis 19
  contesting from within 191, 192
  counter-hegemonic project 19–20, 191, 192, 197–8, 199–200, 209
  data capitalism 113–14
  digital capitalism 181
  ecological dimensions 15, 194–6, 203
  exchange value over use value 16
  extractive relations 125, 194–5, 196, 203
  inherently anti-democratic 15, 16, 19, 197, 203
  liberty and 101
  media role in legitimating 33
  neoliberal 7, 12, 35, 171, 172, 203
  non-economic dimensions 194–5
  participation and 200
  politics of inequality 11, 15, 19, 101, 102, 112, 121, 203, 207
  post-war democratic capitalism 3
  racial capitalism 111, 112
  social injustices 191
  social reproduction 208
Carter, General Nicholas 53
Castilla, E. J. 102
Castoriadis, C. 101
celebrity, democratization of 119
celebrity influencers 169
Chancel, L. 203
Charity Commission 56, 93
ChatGPT 80
children
  educational disparity 120
  inequalities 120

Chile 67, 181, 204
Chun, W. H. K. 52, 114, 115
churnalism 80, 175
circular economy 67
Citizen Media Assemblies 154
citizens
  participation *see* participation
  recast as consumers 172
civil society 129, 185, 187
  algorithmic silencing of 57
  associational life 54–5
  depoliticization of 55–7
  as the 'good society' 55
  political participation and 54–5
  as public sphere 55
Civil Society Futures 169–70, 171, 187, 213n 1
Clegg, Nick 109–10
clickbait 2, 80, 81, 113, 160, 172, 173
climate action groups 52
climate catastrophe 2, 15, 19, 192–7
  causation 193
  media coverage of 193–4, 195
  role of capitalism in 194–6, 203
  tech industry contribution to 194
climate change denial 14, 26
Clinton, Hillary 179
Coeckelbergh, M. 199
Cohen, J. 64, 96
Colau, Ada 67
Cole, G. D. H. 42
colonialism 6, 7, 8, 18, 195
  colonial appropriation and exploitation 7, 8, 63, 101, 111, 112, 195
commodification of public knowledge 16
commoning 126, 198
  media commoning 127–8
  subversive commoning 126
commons 40–1, 67, 103, 130, 163, 186–7
  alternative to capitalism 125, 127, 187
  de-commodification of 130, 192
  digital commons 42, 123, 124, 125, 127
  generative commons 40–1, 125
  new public commons 163, 208
  politics of the commons 127, 212

see also media commons; public good
communicative capitalism 69, 169
communicative democracy 62, 201
communicative egalitarianism 122–8, 158, 204, 211
communicative freedoms 25, 96–7, 98, 99, 150, 202
  interdependence 150
communicative justice 17, 58, 100, 201, 210
communicative oppression 58–9
  geographic exclusion 59, 60
  informational exclusion 59, 61–2
  material exclusion 59–60
communism 29
conspiracy theorists 14
consumer rights 124
cooperativism 29, 37–41, 42, 198
  multi-stakeholder co-ops 38, 39–40
  platform cooperatives 38, 41, 67
  principles of 37
  worker co-ops 38, 40
Coote, A. 66
Corbyn, Jeremy 127
Cottle, S. 194
Coulson, Andy 85
Covid-19 pandemic 13–14, 34, 46, 56, 58, 60, 101, 103, 107, 179, 180–4
  business opportunism 13, 182–3
  digital connections, importance of 46, 56
  disinformation 26
  elite power projects 182, 183
  enhanced surveillance and control 181
  intensification of inequalities 181
  legitimation of authoritarianism 181
  media scrutiny 183–4
  neoliberal opportunism 181
  opportunistic media coverage 162
  public service media 146
  social and economic costs 181
  vaccine apartheid 13, 182
Creech, B. 178
Crouch, C. 2, 24, 25, 172
Cudworth, E. 196
cultural capital 62
cultural democracy 47
culture wars 46, 92–4, 160, 192
Cummings, Dominic 149

INDEX

Dahl, R. 50
Dahlgren, P. 24, 173
Danewid, I. 112
Dardot, P. 212
data capitalism 113–14
data collection and control 63
data injustices 113–15
data ownership 67
Data Protection Act 68
data sovereignty 17, 67
datafication 4, 115, 122
  of journalism 177
Davie, Tim 147
Davies, W. 14, 169
de Peuter, G. 40–1
Dean, J. 69
debt regimes, racialized 113
decarbonization 196–7, 208, 211
decision-making, participation in 8, 17, 19–20, 22, 40, 48, 54, 55, 63, 66
decolonizing practices of communication 186
deepfake 175
defamation law 77, 143, 144, 159
degrowth 197, 198
deliberative democracy 22, 23, 43, 51, 64–5, 68–9, 70, 134, 200
Deliveroo 41, 108
democracy
  agonistic democracy 22–3
  as collective self-rule 22
  communicative democracy 62, 201
  consent to being governed 30, 45
  crisis of 25, 191
  cultural democracy 47
  deliberative democracy 22, 23, 43, 51, 64–5, 68–9, 70, 134, 200
  demise of democratic values 4
  disconnect between citizens and political elites 12, 45
  emergent forms of 8, 9, 204
  as entire way of life 202
  fake democracy 172–3, 184
  free media as supposedly vital to 1–2, 5
  healthy 1, 100
  hollowing-out of 4, 8, 15, 27, 99, 171, 198
  horizontalist form of 48
  incompatibility with capitalism 15, 16, 19, 197, 203
  interrogating 6–10, 12
  justificatory democracy 98
  key concepts 8–9
  liberal *see* liberal democracy
  low-intensity democracies 7
  media–democracy relationship 10, 75, 84, 97–8
  neoliberal democracy 4, 5, 8, 9–10, 14, 27, 28, 35, 45, 84, 88
  power–democracy relations 21, 43, 198
  as project 204–5
  representative democracy 2, 12, 22, 24–5, 29, 45, 48, 65, 121–2, 133, 202, 204
  value and practice 18
democratic imaginaries 18–19, 68
  see also egalitarian imagination
democratic media 2, 18, 36–7, 44, 66, 202
  conditions of possibility for 210–11
  emergent forms of 208, 209
  for the public good 18, 36, 150, 156, 205
  see also media commons; public service media
democratic recession 13
democratic revolutions 129
democratic society 46, 64, 65, 66, 68, 98, 101, 128, 185, 200
democratic will formation 96
Diamond, L. 13
digital capitalism 181
digital commons 42, 123, 124, 125, 127
digital dictatorship 17
digital divide 47, 59
digital economy 41–2
digital exclusion 47, 59–60, 61, 62, 63
digital literacy 41, 62
disconnect between citizens and political elites 12, 45
distribution, politics of 89, 90, 91, 95, 122
distrust and disaffection 12, 35
  see also trust, loss of
Dittus, M. 59
diversity politics 102
diversity washing 40, 126–7

Dominion Voting Systems lawsuit 143–4
'Doughnut Economics' 196
Dowling, E. 116–17
Du Bois, W. E .B. 13
due impartiality, concept of 148
Dunn, J. 30
Durand, C. 4
Dussel, E. 29, 43, 90
Dyer-Witherford, N. 40–1, 176, 199
Dyke, Greg 147

e-politics 47
ecoactivism 197
economic inequality 47, 91–2, 100, 103–8, 121
   pay 120–1
   social impact 104
   structural causes of 192
   wealth disparity 33, 103–4, 105–6, 123
   see also poverty
educational equality 123
Edwards, M. 55
egalitarian imagination 9, 45–6, 103, 129–30, 192, 197, 204
Egypt 40
elections 22, 30, 45, 48
   decline of voter participation 50, 172
   digital campaigning 31–2, 48
   frameworks of constraint 57
   multi-elite party systems 104–5
   subverting of 53
Elections Act 2022 57
electoral democracy see representative democracy
elites
   access and advantage 105
   elite capture 65, 123, 173, 205
   executive elites 109
   inequality and 108–11
   institutional 108–9
   occupational 109
   political influence 105, 110
   revolving door of privilege 109–10
   taxation of 105–6
   wealth elite 109
equaliberty 101
equality 100–30, 202–4
   anti-equality discourse 112–13, 120, 203

centrality to democracy 101
   liberty and 100–1
   political equality 4, 100, 121
   see also inequality
Erdoğan, Recep Tayyip 141
ethnonationalism 102, 112
European Bank 3
European Convention of Human Rights 81
European Human Rights Act 82
European Union General Data Protection Regulation (GDPR) 124

Facebook (now Meta) 31, 33, 52, 109, 110, 114–15, 123, 167, 177
   advertisements 177
   algorithms 177
   content moderators 206
   patterns of discrimination 115
facial recognition systems 114
fake democracy 172–3, 184
'fake news' 53, 140, 162, 164, 173, 174, 177, 178, 180, 184
   ad revenue 177
   malinformation 179
   misinformation and disinformation 178
   polarizing and divisive 178
   political and economic phenomenon 180
   securitization of 178–9
   who gets to define 179, 185
far right 2, 73, 91–2, 112
   rise of 13, 112
Farkas, J. 172, 178–9
Finland 163
Finlayson, A. 112
Fisher, K. E. 178
Fisher, M. 190
Fishman, M. 175
Floyd, George 52
Forst, R. 6–7, 9, 134–7
fossil fuel industry 2
Foucault, Michel 158, 198
Fox News 143–4
Frankfurt School 23, 190
Fraser, N. 3, 19, 62, 89, 122–3, 134, 135, 191, 195
Free Press (NGO) 97
free trade 110, 201

INDEX

freedom 72–99, 201–2
  and agency 89
  neoliberal framings of 73, 97, 201
  political 72
  privatization of 201
  relationship to justice/injustice 89, 201
  relationship to power 89, 95, 201
  socially inscribed 90
  unsocial freedom 73, 94
freedom of association 72, 74
freedom of expression 72, 73, 74, 81, 95, 123, 141–2
freedom of the press 22, 27, 72–3, 74–7, 81–4, 95, 138, 143, 189
  and accountability 81–4, 88
  'commonsense understanding' of 84
  conflict with right to privacy 82, 87
  free-market argument 76, 88
  libertarian defence 86
  political-economic constraints 84
  public interest defence 82
French Revolution 129
Fung, A. 64, 96

Gangadharan, S. P. 62–3
Garcia-Blanco, I. 117
Gates, Bill 105
gender-critical beliefs 92, 214n 5
Gender Recognition Act (GRA) 74, 90–1, 94, 95, 213n 4
Gender Recognition Certificate (GRC) 90
Georgiou, M. 126
Germany 139
Gethin, A. 104
Geuss, R. 63
Giansiracusa, N. 177
Gibb, Nick 132
Gibb, Sir Robbie 132
gig economy 41, 108
Gilbert, J. 24, 118
Gill, S. 201
global financial crash (2007/8) 3, 33–5, 117
  media coverage of 33, 34
  social consequences 33–4
globalization 159
Goldhammer, A. 109, 115, 122, 202–3
Golding, P. 60, 115, 116
Gonzalez, M. 186

Google 24, 26, 32, 110, 113, 141, 142, 167, 173, 174, 176–7
  advertisements 176–7
  algorithms 174, 176
Gove, Michael 109, 148
GPT 175
Graber, D. 29, 30, 206
Graham, M. 59
Greater Govanhill 188
Greece 139, 163
green capitalism 195
green investment 208
Greenwald, Glenn 24
Gringras, Richard 174
Grossberg, Abby 143

Habermas, Jürgen 28, 134
Hacked Off 79
Hacker, J. S. 105
Hage, G. 207
Hague, Molly-Mae 118
Hancock, Matt 183
Harding, Verity 110
Hardt, M. 88
Harvie, D. 116–17
hermeneutics of suspicion 14
heteropatriarchy 18, 19, 40, 74, 125, 130, 186, 209
Higgins, K. C. 184–5
Hinton, Geoffrey 175–6
Hobden, S. 196
homophily 114, 115
Hong Kong 52
Honneth, A. 89–90, 134
hope, democratic 10, 190–1, 206–12
  democratic delusions of 208–9
  reparative mindset 207
Hope Not Hate 91–2
hopelessness 9, 206–7
Hungary 140–1, 180

Iceland 51
identity politics 91, 92, 94, 105, 114
immigration 73, 148
  asylum seekers 148
  media framing of 117
  scapegoating of immigrants 13, 73, 102, 117
imperialism 2, 63
Indignados 28–9, 204
individualism 90, 102, 172

INDEX

inequality 5, 8, 13, 15, 90, 99, 101–17, 155
  alt right view of 112–13
  anti-equality discourse 112–13, 120, 203
  babies and children 120
  capitalism and 11, 15, 19, 101, 102, 112, 121, 203, 207
  digital 47
  economic *see* economic inequality
  gender and 111
  growing 2
  inequality regimes 122, 203
  institutional structures of 122, 203
  meritocracy and 101–2, 117–21
  in news consumption 61–2
  and participatory exclusion 45, 53–4
  political choice 11, 106, 107, 122, 202
  and poverty 103–8, 115–17
  and the rise of elites 108–11
  social *see* social inequalities
  and social injustices 111–13
  systemic and structural 129, 130, 204
  see also racism
influencer culture 118–19, 169
infoglut 12, 16
informational exclusion 59, 61–2
infowar 178
injustice 89–90
  cultural dimensions 89
  economic dimensions 89
  injustice-centred theory of democracy 89–90
  structural 89
  see also social injustices
intellectual monopolization 4
Intergovernmental Panel on Climate Change (IPCC) 192, 193
International Cooperative Alliance (ICA) 37
International Monetary Fund 3
internet
  alternative telecommunications infrastructures 185–6
  global internet use 47
Italy 68

Jensen, T. 116
Johnson, Boris 24, 109, 132, 149, 184

journalism
  accountability 81–4, 99
  advertising revenue and 80–1
  AI-powered journalism 175, 176, 180
  churnalism 80, 175
  civic value 177
  community-based journalism 188–9
  datafication of 177
  diminishing independence 141, 142, 155
  ethical frameworks 82–3, 85, 99
  as a 'fourth estate' 72
  government regulation 65, 73, 77–8, 81, 84, 99
  job insecurity 40, 79, 83
  local 60–1
  loss of trust in 162, 163–6, 189
  media cooperatives 39–40
  neoliberal structure 84
  persecution of journalists 141
  political constraints 76, 77, 81
  professional codes of conduct 82
  socio-demographics of journalists 83–4, 110–11
  solidarity journalism 10
  speaking truth to power 43, 173
  structural field theory perspective 76
  tabloid journalism 86
  see also freedom of the press
justificatory frameworks 115, 122, 133, 136, 137, 151, 153, 155, 156, 158, 203, 205, 212

Karlova, N. 178
Kavannagh, Trevor 86
Kendall, J. 167
Kennard, M. 181, 184
Kidd, D. 63
Kjøsen, A. M. 176, 199
Kostelka, F. 50
Krishna, Arvind 176
Kundnani, H. 12

La Diaria 40
labour movement 10, 25, 40, 188
Laclau, E. 129
Latour, B. 14
Laval, C. 212
Lawrence, M. 42, 125, 196–7, 207–8

Laybourn-Langton, L. 42, 196–7, 207–8
Lebanon 68
Lebedev, Evgeny 86–7
Leveson Inquiry 78, 79, 85, 86, 87, 91
Levitsky, S. 12
libel law 77, 81, 98, 140, 144, 145
liberal democracy 2, 7, 8, 14, 21, 24, 25, 27, 28, 30, 43, 65, 121, 133, 179
  approach to power 29, 30
  discontent and disillusionment with 166, 170, 179, 180
  dominant hegemonic understandings of 14
  fissures and failures 25, 27, 28, 179
  in imperialist-capitalist countries 7
  see also representative democracy
liberal privatism 73, 88
libertarianism 112, 120, 121
libraries, closure of 16, 34
Lim, G. 178, 179
Lineker, Gary 147, 148
Lipsitz, G. 7
Littler, J. 102
Livingston, S. 178
lobbying 5, 56, 110, 142
Love Island 118, 121

Mada 40
Maitlis, Emily 132
Malaysia 179
malinformation 179
market justice 88
marketplace of ideas 86, 87
Martínez-Toledano, C. 104–5
Maude, Francis 132
May, Theresa 132
McChesney, R. 121, 134
media commons 17, 18, 103, 125–8, 129–30, 209
  building 150–60, 209–11
  communicative egalitarianism 122–8, 152
  intradependency 152, 153
  media commoning 127–8
  transformative media commons 204, 209–11
media deregulation 23, 74, 87, 88, 131, 139
media justice initiatives 97

media ownership
  alternative models of 18, 36, 99, 156
  concentration 5, 23, 26, 32–3, 78, 79, 98, 99, 123, 131, 138–40, 142, 158
  democratizing 42
  deregulation of restrictions 87, 139
  direct/indirect owner influence 78
  elite power complex, part of 88, 173, 205
  lack of transparency in 139
  new media barons 60–1
  political actors 78–9, 143, 145
  strategic agendas 142, 143
  white-dominant 97
Media Reform Coalition 61, 69, 70, 151, 154
Meier, W. A. 142, 158
Mendes, J. 7, 18–19
Mentan, T. 8
meritocracy 90, 101–2, 113, 115, 126
  mediating 117–21
Mermaids 93
Meta 24, 26, 31, 32, 142, 173, 199
MeToo movement 52
Mexico 185–6
Microsoft 110, 176
Middleton, S. 115, 116
Milanović, B. 121
Mills, T. 159
Milner, Y. 113–14, 124–5
misinformation and disinformation 53, 142, 178–9
misogyny 8, 26, 119
Moonves, Leslie 144
Moore, K. 117
moral panic 92
Morozov, E. 16
Morrison, Scott 94
Mouffe, C. 129
Movement for Black Lives 197
Muldoon, J. 41, 42, 70
municipalist movement 67–8
Murdoch, Rupert 25, 78, 79, 85, 87, 132, 143, 158
Murdock, G. 127
Musk, Elon 13, 94, 119

Negri, A. 88

neo-colonialism 28
neoliberalism 3, 4–5, 16, 17, 27, 102, 103, 112, 123, 158, 159, 171, 198
  capture of democracy 28, 171
  contradictions of 35
  Covid-19 pandemic and 181
  democratic vocabulary 27–8
  governmentality 27
  hollowing out of democratic values 5, 27
  interventionism 27
  neoliberal capitalism 7, 12, 35, 171, 172, 203
  neoliberal democracy 4, 5, 8, 9–10, 14, 27, 28, 35, 45, 84, 88
  neoliberal freedoms 73, 97, 201
  state–markets alignment 158
Netherlands 139
Neurath, Otto 42
The New Internationalist 39–40
Newman, Marie 93
News Corporation 25–6, 80
news media
  agenda-setting power 33, 35, 88, 173, 174
  business model 74, 76–7, 80–1, 86
  commercial pressure on legacy media 145
  decline in local newspapers 60–1
  free-market position 77, 82
  gatekeeper power 141
  illegal and unethical practices 23
  loss of trust in 163–6, 167, 170, 171, 189
  market competition 79–81
  marketization 81, 85, 86, 87–8
  media–political entanglement 26, 33, 35, 86–7, 98, 99, 131–3, 142, 159, 167, 172–3
  political citizenship, activating 81
  privatization and marketization of news 185
  public disengagement from mainstream media 163, 164
  as a public good 131, 137–8, 145–50, 157
  regulation 65, 73, 77–8, 82, 167
  revolving door between government and 109–10, 132
  self-regulation 82, 85

social value 75
tax privileges and subsidies 23
unrepresentative of marginalized groups 166, 185
see also freedom of the press; journalism
News of the World 85, 87
Noam, E. M. 139
Noble, S. U. 114
Non-/low-profit news 156–7
North American Free Trade Agreement 201
Nussbaum, M. C. 134

Obama, Barack 51
Oborne, Peter 83
Occupy movement 204
Ofcom 59, 111, 142, 146, 152, 154, 155–6, 174n 2
Online Safety Bill 65, 68
open government concept 51
oppression 58–9
  see also communicative oppression
Orbán, Viktor 140
Osborne, George 109
'owning the libs' 92–3
Oxfam 196

Pandora Papers 110
paranoia of delusion 6
Pariser, E. 127
participation 47–50, 200–1
  in capitalist societies 200
  cultural 47
  democratic 45–6
  egalitarian framing 200
  media and communications 46
  political *see* political participation
  power as central concept in 49
  socio-economic inequalities and 53–4
  technology-enabled 46
Pateman, C. 48
pay
  executive elites 109
  gender gap 111
  socio-economic factors 120–1
paywalls 157–8
Percy, A. 66
Pew Research Center 166
phone-hacking 23, 73, 78, 84, 85–9

INDEX

Pickard, V. 109, 208
Pickett, K. 53, 104
Pierson, P. 105
Piketty, T. 104–5, 108, 109, 111, 115, 122, 202–3
platforms
  advertising 113, 119
  capital accumulation strategies 177
  citizen engagement 46
  cooperatives 38, 41, 67
  democratizing 42
  information pollution 169
  news consumption through 163
  owners' strategic agendas 142
  social commons 123
  see also social media
pluralism in media markets 23, 24, 25, 26, 28, 38, 41, 81, 86, 99, 138, 139, 174
  anti-concentration frameworks 138–9
  'diversity washing' 40, 126–7
  private gain, prioritization of 141–2, 160
  proactive legislation 138, 150
  threats to 139
Podemos 51, 67
polarization of society 51
Police, Crime, Sentencing and Courts Act 2022 39, 57
policing
  discriminatory practices 58, 114
  predictive policing 58, 114
political campaigning 31–2
political equality 4, 100, 121
political freedom 72
political-industrial complex 179
political legitimacy 22, 45
political participation 45–71, 100
  affected interests and 50
  centrality of power to 49
  civil society and 54–5
  disengagement from 50–1, 53
  exclusion from 46–7, 50–1
  illusion of 48, 49
  multi-levelled 62
  news consumption and 60, 62
  partial/full 48, 70
  roadblocks to 49
  technology-aided 51, 52
  through social movements 52

Poor Law 108
popular sovereignty 21, 22
populism 13, 51, 112
  anti-media populism 164
Pörtner, Hans-Otto 193
post-democracy 2, 25, 172
post-truth 12, 169
poverty
  disability and 107
  ethnicity and 107
  inequality and 103–8, 115–17
  and political disenfranchisement 50, 107
  scapegoating 116–17
  stigmatization 116
poverty porn 116
Powell Jobs, Laurene 105–6
power 21–44, 100, 198–200
  ascendancy view of 29
  bottom-up power 22, 29, 30
  citizen power 48, 49
  concentrations of 105
  constitutive power 23, 30
  counter-hegemonic conceptualization of 198–200
  democratic power 29
  as domination 23
  institutionalized exercise of 48, 51
  liberal democratic approach to 29, 30
  obediential power 29
  political participation and 48, 49
  political power, dwindling legitimacy of 35
  power over / power to 23, 29, 30, 42, 43
  power–democracy relations 21, 43, 198
  redistribution of 35, 41, 44, 48
  relational 37, 43
  speaking truth to power 1, 38, 43, 173
  symbolic power 23, 109
  tokenism (pseudo power) 49
  top-down power 29–30
powerlessness 21, 29, 35–6
  addressing 29, 30, 36, 41, 42, 43, 66
  marginalized communities 37
Prainsack, B. 124
prefigurative politics 191

Press Complaints Commission 85
Preventing Violent Extremism agenda 56
Pring, George 144
ProPublica 52
protest politics 50, 204
  criminalization of protest 57
Provost, C. 181, 184
psyops 53
public good 36, 128, 133–8, 141, 198, 204–5
  both process and outcome 135
  conceptualizing 133–4
  defining 135, 137
  justificatory framework 136–7, 153
  multiple publics 135–6
  news media as 131, 137–8, 145–50, 157
  private-sector provision of 137–8, 158
  see also commons
public service media 5, 17, 49, 69, 99, 127, 145
  British Digital Corporation (BDC) 127–8
  citizen participation 49, 127
  commitment to technological innovation 151
  dilution of public mission to serve capital interests 16
  diversity and inclusion 155–6
  'fourth estate' 150
  funding 127, 145
  government pressures on 145, 146–8
  justificatory mechanisms 151–2, 153
  liberal acritical defence of 160
  part of media commons 152
  for the public good 136, 153, 160
  trust in 164–5
  underlying principles 69
  see also BBC
public sphere 25, 28, 43, 52–3
  civil society as 55
  counter public spheres 51
  fractured 52
  marketization of 167

racism 8, 58, 65, 97, 112
  algorithmic racism 113

environmental 197
institutional 102
racial capitalism 111, 112
radical democracy 64, 129
Rancière, J. 7, 21, 70
Rawls, J. 134
Raworth, K. 196
Reagan, Ronald 132
The Real World 119
reality television 101–2, 116, 117–18, 121
recognition, politics of 89, 90, 91, 95, 122, 134
Regulatory and Investigatory Powers Act 77
relationality 96, 187, 189
representative democracy 2, 12, 22, 24–5, 29, 45, 48, 65, 121–2, 133, 202, 204
Reuters Institute 146, 163–4, 165
Rhizomatica 185–6
Robinson, Tommy (Stephen Yaxley-Lennon) 120
Robinson, W. I. 182
Rochdale Pioneers 37
Rosanvallon, P. 9, 191
Ross, Douglas 94–5
Rudd, Kevin 25

Saar, M. 23
Santos, B. 7, 18–19
Savage, M. 109
Schlosberg, J. 173–4
Schou, J. 172
Scotland 94–5, 188
Sedgwick, E. K. 5–6, 207
Serbia 140
Sharp, Richard 132
Shivji, I. G. 6, 7
SLAPP lawsuits 144–5
Snowden, Edward 24
social contract 166
social democratic project 16
social inequalities 19, 54, 56, 100, 103, 105, 122, 126, 203
social injustices 1, 10, 11, 59, 95, 97, 103, 111–13, 191
social justice 29, 43, 58, 88, 98, 99, 100, 103, 113, 134, 135, 186, 205, 210
  see also communicative justice

INDEX

social media
 algorithms 119
 business model 74, 177
 capital accumulation strategies 177
 covert operations on 53
 echo chambers 52, 142, 169
 filter bubbles 52, 169
 news consumption through 163, 174–5
 polarized networks 115
 trolling and hate speech 62, 68, 74, 201
 weaponization of 53
social mobility 120, 121
social movements 48, 50, 51, 52, 64, 190
socialism 101
 participatory socialism 122
solidarity economies 8, 10, 37, 185
Soriano, C. R. 164
sound bite culture 2
Soviet Union, collapse of 7
Spain 28–9, 51, 67, 204
speaking truth to power 1, 43, 173
Spinoza, Baruch 23
Stanistreet, Michelle 83
status hierarchies 11
Steinhoff, J. 176, 199
Steyerl, H. 114–15
Stiglitz, J. 103–4
Stonewall 94
stop and search 58
Streeck, W. 3, 205
subprime mortgages 113
Sugar, Alan 148
Sunak, Rishi 132, 149
Sunflower Movement 51
surveillance practices 32, 58, 63, 77, 114, 158, 181, 201
 racialized 114
Susskind, J. 176
systemic change, need for 55, 192

Taiwan 51–2
Taiwo, O. O. 65
TallBear, K. 7
Tambini, D. 31, 79, 99, 178
Tandoc, E. 164
Tate, Andrew 119, 120, 214n 6
taxation 99, 105, 105–6, 110
 evasion 17, 110, 198, 205

progressive 122
 tax havens 110
Taylor, Breonna 52
Taylor Greene, Marjorie 93
tech giants 4, 17, 123, 172
 advanced capitalism 33
 anti-trust practices 17
 capital accumulation 4
 contribution to climate catastrophe 194
 ineffective self-regulation 94
 legislative attempts to rein in 198–9
 oligopolistic 4, 12, 24, 32–3, 99, 123, 158, 205
 tax evasion 17, 198
 technofeudalism 4
 see also media ownership
techno-solutionism 2
Telecomunicaciones Indigenas Comunitarias (TCC) 186
Thane, P. 108
Thatcher, Margaret 107, 115
Therborn, G. 104
Ticktin, M. 18
Titley, G. 126
Tomaz, T. 13
Toynbee, P. 33
trade unions 40, 129, 155, 211
Trans Media Watch 91
transformative media commons 210–11
 ecological conditions 211
 economic conditions 210
 political conditions 211
 social conditions 211
transgender rights 73, 74, 90–5
 anti-trans rhetoric 91, 92, 93, 94–5
Trappel, J. 13, 142, 158
Traub, A. 113–14, 124–5
Trump, Donald 12–13, 24, 31, 94, 132, 140, 143, 144, 164, 170, 180
Trump, Ivanka 132
trust 162–89, 205–6
 building trust networks 185–6, 189
 characteristic-based trust 167
 class divide 170–1
 concepts of 166–71
 in governance systems 168
 institutionally based trust 167

loss of 12, 51, 55, 146, 162, 163–6, 168, 170, 171, 189
process-based trust 167
in public service media 146
resocializing the political 187
severing of trust from confidence 167
trusted object and trusting subject 167
trustworthiness 168
see also 'fake news'
Turkey 141
twenty-four-hour television news 79–80
Twitter 13, 65, 93, 94, 119
Tyler, I. 116

Uber 41, 51, 108
Ukraine, war in 34, 107
Umbrella movement 52
'undeserving poor' 2, 90, 115–16, 203
United Kingdom (UK)
  austerity policies 33–4
  BBC see BBC
  Brexit 31, 34, 56, 148, 164, 170
  civil society agency 55–6
  Covid-19 pandemic 34, 183–4
  debates around asylum and migration 117
  decline in local newspapers 61
  deregulated newspaper industry 79
  digital exclusion 59–60
  digital political campaigning 31–2
  economic and social inequalities 101, 102, 106–8, 120
  ineffective press regulation 65, 73, 84, 85
  legislative frameworks of constraint and repression 57–8
  low-wage workforce 41
  media cooperatives 38–9
  media plurality 142
  mistrust of news media 164
  phone-hacking scandal 23, 73, 84, 85–9
  political alienation 53–4
  psyops 53
  public attitudes to welfare and poverty 115–17
  transgender rights 74, 90–1

United States (US)
  2020 presidential election 12–13, 143, 144, 177
  Capitol insurrection 12, 143
  decline in local newspapers 60–1
  economic inequality 104
  mistrust of news media 164
  moribund democracy 12
  racialized representations of the poor 117
  rise of the far-right 13
  settler-colonial mythology 7
universal basic service provision 66–7
universal capital endowment 122
Universal Declaration of Human Rights 7
universal free broadband 62, 66, 67
urban gentrification 112
Uruguay 40

Vogl, J. 177
voter fraud 57
Vučić, Aleksandr 140

Waisbord, S. 178
Walker, D. 33
Wardle, C. 179
wealth inequalities 33, 103–4, 105–6, 123
weapons of mass destruction 178
Weber, Max 23
welfare 66, 73, 107, 108, 115–16
  anti-welfare rhetoric 73, 90, 115–16
  rise of the welfare state 122
white supremacism 97, 112
WikiLeaks 24
Wikipedia 59
Wilkinson, R. P. 53, 104
Williams, A. 118
Williams, Raymond 1, 17, 160–1, 188
wokeism 92
  anti-wokeism 92, 120
Wood, E. M. 11, 15–16
workplace democracy 17, 40
World Bank 3
World Health Organization (WHO) 181
Wren-Lewis, S. 33, 34
Wright, E. O. 191

INDEX

X 173
xenophobia 8

yellow journalism 178
Young, I. M. 58–9, 62, 89
Yucel, James 149

Zapatistas 29
Ziblatt, D. 12
Zucker, L. G. 167
Zuckerberg, Mark 31
Zuckerman, E. 127